To Live & Die
On Zug Island

by Ryan Bartek

**Ask your local book store to carry Anomie Press.
Anomie Press is a D.I.Y. Publisher
www.AnomiePress.com // www.BigShinyPrison.com

"Just a thought – a man wishes to write a novel in which a character goes mad. While working on the book he himself goes mad by degrees, and finishes it in first person."

to the fallen

This manuscript is based on a true story;

spoken by a man who once, and finished by his Omega.

First Sentence: 9/12/2001

— — —

First Draft: 3/5/2004

— — —

Final Draft #111: 4/11/2019

* * *

:: all names have been changed to protect the guilty parties ::

– introduction –
Defrosting An Ice Age

Imagine a world that can scarcely be imagined –
the Old Detroit, at lowest decline, spanning the
Early 80's – May 2002.

Imagine the life of a strange teen; a young male
indoctrinated with Punk Rock logic & Heavy Metal
obsession – reading comic books in a Misfits
shirt, blasting KMFDM on his stereo &
mosh-pitting at Slayer concerts.

16 in 1997 – when Nine Inch Nails were at peak,
Clinton was still president & Marilyn Manson was
still The Antichrist.

Here, we have perhaps the last of the great
unknown autobiographies concerning a specific
mentality & specimen of American Youth.

Not only does this work uniquely capture such a
mindset in *Catcher In The Rye* fashion, but it
expresses commentary on the Detroit Underground:
from Outlaw Rave Parties to Extreme Metal gigs,
Punk Rock Chaos to The Occult.

"*To Live & Die On Zug Island*" transports you back to
the world before your SmartPhone – *no F-Book, M-
Space, Insta-G or dating apps*. Back in time, to the
age of 56k modems, rabbit-eared TV's, newspapers &
magazines with total monopoly on information.

Comprehend being this far in the dark – almost a
Stone Age of Technology by now – and thinking you
were living in "The Future?"

Yet here you were, the fresh crop of youth
supplanted in this rapidly collapsing non-screen
reality, this fabled "2000" of Science Fiction lore
– and it was moving so fast you'd be like an Old Man
within a decade, in the body of a 20 something.

The public schools of your generation had no chance to prepare any of your generation – because The Internet did not yet widely influence reality.

Contemplate being bred for a society from Kindergarten to Graduation yet finding it ceased to exist the very moment you were released from their public schools into the adult stream? They molded a citizen for a hopelessly sinking ship...

* * *

This tract began 9-12-2001 – a storytellers self therapy & personal diary to make sense of all that went horribly wrong & the great lessons of life.

The author who beget this work was 19 & hooked to The Beat Generation. He was raised on movies, comic books, folkloric myths, classic authors & WWF – and whatever punk & metal zines he could find.

At 18 he was a Delivery Driver for the Ford Motor Company, transporting semi-truck parts to the most war-zone like areas of Detroit, Monday through Friday, 8am-6pm, reading Kerouac obsessively.

As he read, he'd daydream his escape from Detroit, that one day he'd hit the road – and eventually write his own book. He desired to bring the soul-searching inertia of Kerouac's vision to his generation, or at least those who'd listen.

It wasn't until November 2003 when it came pouring out of him. Although he'd completed & DIY published a short story collection "The Silent Burning" – and had been getting aggressively published as a music journalist – he'd yet to embark upon "The Book."

Every writer sees "The Book" as a sort of Holy Grail – "at least once, for the sake of literature and my sanity, I will complete a true work of art."

R. Bartek was no different then many others. However, unlike so many whom never finalize a manuscript, it came exploding from him - up for days at a time, furiously typing & editing.

It was like a 2 month boxing match with his computer, pacing around chain-smoking & drinking endless black coffee in a manic volcano of genius.

He'd lost his job - *yes*. He'd lost his woman - *true*. But this freed him - and that the clock was ticking on depleting finances & he'd have to work again soon - this made him fly like lightning.

In 5 months, he'd a 350+ page First Draft - one that he continued to refine for years, awaiting The Right Moment. As he sat upon this work he called "*To Live & Die On Zug Island*," his short story collection "The Silent Burning" was published.

He began writing content for larger magazines & grew in reputation, as he could now travel doing so. He played in a number of bands, continued writing, and stayed busy. Yet every year, he would say "not yet." He'd pull out "*Zug Island*," the secret Ace up his sleeve, and give it a due refinement.

So here, for the first time available to the public, is the Crown Jewel of R. Bartek's literary canon - sitting quietly "on the shelf" just over 15 years. And now it's very much time to party.

Welcome kids, to one irate kid of Old Detroit.

It's a tale of comedy, madness, magick & one half-cracked character that is as well meaning as he is unintentionally (*and intentionally*) destructive.

It is a tale of anguish as much as hilarity - and a poignant tract on drug abuse & mental illness.

Completed 2004 & sitting "on the shelf" 15+ years, it's high time to party. And so, Dear World, here in it's complete form is the one & only:

"*To Live & Die on Zug Island.*"

Disclaimer: Confessions of a Gutter Saint

Motionless I stand before a vast audience of none – a theater of tragedy far removed from mankind's base conception of malicious irony. An impulsive, rotating cycle of loss & dismay has forged an iron cast - *organic, breeding...* Frenzied fits of stark hysteria bludgeon my psyche – *for all my paranoid delusions have come true...*

2 weeks ago, furiously typing away – *through the sweat, strain & fragmented digging* – stray bullet velocity propelled me into calm night. Compulsive nicotine fix habit eased starlit sky in radiant majesty, moon gibbous, clouds gently coasting as humble fog; *shadows solid, concrete...*

"God, if you're up there, if you can hear me – it's time to wash away the scum and the filth. Time to flush this all down the fuckin' toilet... All the good books have been written, all the great cinema filmed. All the songs have been sung & masterpiece accomplished. This race is at its end... God, if you're up there, I want my miracle – I want The Apocalypse. I triple fuckin' dog dare you – I'm callin' you out, Bitch Boy. If you got The Balls, then bring down The Hammer..."

(–6.66 hours later–)

"Wake up you lazy fuck – We're going to War!" Groggy confusion... half-glimpsed paintings of tugboats, cornflower blue wallpaper & checkered blankets: *"Um, you're getting a divorce?"*

My mom is out her mind, erratically pacing the hallway: *"No you lazy shit – it's fuckin' World War 3!"* She rampages incoherently, darting off to another quadrant of the 3-level historic home, pacing in circles.

I stumble out of bed, slobbing in a spavined haze. Bracing disjointedly, I shoulder the wall. I plop onto the king-size mattress in my folk's bedroom & rub my eyes – focus, focus on the TV… Pixilated images – *grainy horror, rampage, panic*… Exploding airliners like steel vultures, napalm gliding through concrete… *Arabic mugshots, Pentagon crumbling in flames*… September 11th, 2001; *my miracle, live via satellite*…

* * *

From my vantage point, God is not a sentient judgmental being but rather the physical universe itself. The physical universe is composed of infinite matter charging forward in a constant state of chaotic flux – all molecular structure revolving around a base core; the very nucleus of existence. This is only half of God; the other half is that which is revolving.

There is no omnipotence lifting the scales of justice over a golden throne, simply a mass which is dictated by the whole of its contents – from life-like essence to anti-matter.

Surely its essence is perpetuation. But what is *IT* – what are we – evolving into? No one can answer this because humanity cannot comprehend it…

As with many Celtic bloodlines, I've a strong "Sixth Sense." It's not something I'm apt to talk about in person, because I've no interest convincing anyone, nor do I wanna hear "homeboy's gone cuckoo."

This receptive trait I believe, is something that develops within someone more *in tune* with the mass energy, the universe, the unseen, the cold & lifeless even – then the average individual.

In the same way children have yet been blinded, perhaps as cats see at night. some people maintain this lifted veil unlike their more earth-minded counterparts.

So to whom this may concern, herein lies a reason of insanity: there's a distant, distorted radio in the back of my head picking up stray transmissions. It's a sprawling, integrated canyon of imagination...

But sometimes these snippets aren't artistic day-dreaming alone. Sometimes they seem to be the fragmented thoughts of others... I just know things I shouldn't and often answer questions before they ask the question.

Modern psychiatry would likely attribute this to my psychological orientation towards life; surely, I'll submit to that assessment. All of the weird shit happening to me all the time is just my artistic dreamscape amplifying things in a child-like way. *Cool.* Poltergeist aren't real. *Sweet.*

"You're just really smart & read body language like a champ & trust me Kiddo – you ain't no psychic type of any way/shape/form. Americans kiddo – well they're absolute dumb-bells & you're waaaaay over their heads. Professor X? More like surrounded by dumbfucks."

Anyway, it's just... I seem to know what people are thinking. Not all the time, not constantly – just in doses. This does not take shape in any conventional form of language. It is a language of *feeling* – of dominant emotional impression.

This just adds to the confusion 'cause I'm an introverted person & it's near impossible to feel empathize with anything outside the infantile world of my own creation. At least I'm honest.

The above articles can sometimes be accepted socially 'cause most have experienced something of what I've revealed. But the cut off is "The Paranormal Factor" – and it kills romance, quick.

I am a magnet for poltergeist activity. It's like I walk into a haunted house & *"excite"* it; whenever that internal radar goes "BLIP" I pick up one of those impressions.

But unlike the ones I get from the statistically living, these are not fun. These ones make me feel like my stomach is free-falling & they never make sense either, like a mentally retarded schizophrenic on LSD...

So... Am I a Whackadoo Prophet lauching a Cult? Nope, just a totally confused stoner. Let's be real here – I'm on par with Tommy Chong, not Jim Jones. I'm into the Magick & Alchemy jibber-jabber, but I ain't no corny Witch-Man with eye-liner.

I'm 20 years old, and I smoke blunts constantly. My life is exploring Wasteland Detroit like an astronaut, Gravity Bongs, riotous Extreme Metal gigs, massive underground rave parties, The Beat Generation, Raw Is War & Comic Books in general.

I'm more then an American – I'm a Detroit Male. I like Halloween & Horror movies, Heavy Metal & Punk Rock, Industrial/Goth & kitschy shit like Go-Karts & Put Put, cheesy Pro Wrestling & Weird Al.

But I'm not "nerdy," per se. I'm unstable & volatile with a nasty streak. I combat my own nature constantly, and never quite know the crazy thing I might do next. In 6 months, I'll finally be able to step foot in a bar...

So, theoretical observation – whatever you consider the human soul to be, the idea is the same in principle – all creatures are born with a life-force; a definitive essence to sustain the heart, spleen, kidneys, etc.

This life force is only a microcosmic splinter of the mass energy (*God*). When someone dies, the personality/intellect expires with the body while the life-force is recycled into the energy from which it came.

What a ghost is – what I assume, at least – is that sometimes a personality is so strong that it literally imprints itself upon the "soul." Sometimes the inner spirit is so titanic – *so earthbound* – it refuses death. When this happens a splinter of the personality remains attached to the life-force & somehow makes its way back to a familiar base or station in life.

Thus a lingering incoherent energy working on subconscious motor function floating around an office building, church, junkyard or creepy ass old house somehow manifesting a convergence of the material on occasion. And for some reason I pick up the blip...

If all that isn't enough, I still have to bring up the *"Jigsaw Premonitions"* thing. I have a tendency to dream splinters of my life before they occur. "Déjà vu," as they say – how some guy knew not to board a Flight X 'cause he dreamed the engine would catch on fire & create violent fireworks. How some lady knew not to drive a route to work 'cause she'd have been catapulted out the window during a 15 car pile-up. You know the bit.

What separates me from them is the sheer fact that whatever I do to avoid or change the outcome – *even if I don't do anything at all* – the outcome remains the same. It's as if I've already lived my life. It never pertains to anything of worldly importance though, just key moments.

I'll dream a jigsaw before the puzzle unites – like a glimpse of a full-rounded movie still that contains an image (*such as who/what I'm looking at*), smell, focus point, thought pattern, line of dialogue, emotion – a slab of distant reality intense & symbolic.

Just like this World Trade Center thing, you know, ringing so dramatically when I remembered finding stacks of drawings from my 5 year old self; pictures in sloppy crayon of Arabs in turbans crashing airplanes into identical buildings & the Islamic star crescent hovering in the full eclipse of the black & red sun...

By now I either have your full attention or you've labeled me a pathological liar. This book is not intended make you like me, nor has it been written to make you believe. Quite honestly, I could give a fuck less.

I am not an intellectual, philosopher, artist, poet, revolutionary, martyr or laureate – I am a mutant and a clown; an inartistic wretch of a human being that deserves a straight-jacket & swift kick in the pants.

I am a bastard in every sense of the word; a drug addled immoral pervert hooligan with nothing on his mind except the ego-maniacal pursuit of self-fulfillment.

The content of this literature is in fact violent, obscene, eccentric, paranoid, filthy & neurotic, created solely to entertain my self-serving cathartic shedding of skin & to test the limits of free speech.

If you're searching for genius, you've come to the wrong place. All you will find here is a 6th rate quasi-plagiarist imitation; a point blank take-no-prisoners manifesto of immeasurable pretentiousness.

This work is a shit-stain on the Bill of Rights, a puddle of vomit on a burning flag, a karate kick to the scrotum of Jesus Christ – an enormous middle finger swinging across the infinite reaches of the universe...

Until a month ago, rock bottom had become a way of life. When all roads led to dead end, I swallowed whatever pride I retained and moved back in with my parents. I secured a job as a landscaper, received a 1996 Sable, my anti-novel was nearing completion, and I was regularly getting laid...

For weeks I worked under harsh conditions to fund my first solo event as a rave promoter. It was all locked down – we were throwing the only *real party* in Detroit that Saturday & I was ready to bank.

The night of our party an unnamed mega-DJ wheels into town & makes a surprise free appearance elsewhere. When it was all said & done, after we hustled every damned cent we could, we'd had 10 very large, very angry *Los Vatos* wondering where their $600 paycheck was.

After narrowly escaping hospitalization or worse, I once again found myself in poverty – dreams trampled, stomach growling, half pack of smokes, quarter tank of gas. Cassum (*my partner in crime*) comes to learn the reason of his blackouts, blood spewing, nervous twitching & constant fatigue are due to an early onset Parkinson's disease...

According to a cat-scan he's destroyed 30% of the 10% brain that humans use & 40% of the rest. The sharp, stabbing pains in his head come from the serotonin oasis turned dust bowl & the blood spewing comes from the absence of any stomach lining whatsoever, dissolved from 5-10 pills of pure MDMA each day for the past 6 months...

I shy from human contact, focusing on my anti-novel. Eventually I call my bondage-bunny nymphomaniac candy-girl sidekick and as I go deep, deep, deep with explaining the amount of passion I feel for her – *of her warmth and loving kindness, how she tastes like Pez and all things skittles and rainbows* – she comes out with it: *"I've been snorting heroin everyday for the past 3 months – how do I know if I'm addicted?"*

Shattered, I ended the phone call & furiously began typing – the forever expanding vortex of my first book *"The Silent Burning,"* which for 3 years I continued to build upon gradually, incrementally; my magnum opus of short stories, poetry, dream narratives, social/political/religious essays, experimental prose, idealistic sentiment & self destructive psalms...

Amidst inspiration, I bugged out & ran into the night – and I told God if It had any balls to bring on the apocalypse. And, well... *Irony*.

Thus, I now type this insane fucking manuscript addressed to a vast audience of none in the basement of my parents house completely broke & disheveled reeking like gasoline...

So, back a bit – July 2000, a very disastrous time-frame...

The future of my current path would surely lead to prison if I didn't change my nefarious ways. Truth was, my friends were bad news. Not that I disliked them personally – *shit, I loved these dudes*. I just knew somehow I'd be in the wrong place at the wrong time.

Most everyone I ever knew who went to jail was just standing next to someone who did something foolish or sloppy.

Whether it be slung, or from the bad blood of some totally disconnected feud that had nothing to do with you whatsoever – Detroit was a place where someone else's "BEEF" would get you haplessly thrust into an ugly street fight, drive-by, molotov cocktail house attack or worse.

It was a place where real bullets did fly, even if they were simply paintball welts from cowards.

Most my friends were hot-heads itching for fist-fights or sloppily transporting their "secret stashes" in car rides without notifying anyone what they were riding with. Getting a ride to the gas station meant possibly getting pulled over by a cop car & searched.

The police in our hometown especially hated our group of people, legitimately, ever since middle school. From 7th grade all the way until graduation, we were the kids they constantly had to respond to.

We were the ones they put their sites on. We were the ones they'd stalk & cruise up on & try to shake info from about other "Bad Kids."

We were the ones the educational staff of our high schools convened to authorities about, because they honestly shared inter-departmental information back then, just as they likely do now.

It isn't clear if it's even legal for the cops to interfere with the school system and extract info like spies as to single out the troubled kids – their "Disenchanted Youth" list (*actual name!*).

The Police Department had created these Gang Units and paired a squad to each high school that would work like counselors to the actual public school staff. *Gestapo!*

These Gang Units worked in tandem with the military recruiters (and kept mutual tabs!) to make "Bad Kids" into "Good Kids" by brainwashing them to enlist as killers for The Pentagon. Is this not a prime example of the poisoned logic of the "American Hero Cop?"

They had to know who the problem kids were early on, and to know who the cop's "adult enemies" would be later in life, basically, by rendering a low-key spy army.

You claim me paranoid, perhaps, but this is well-documented & experienced. They kept tabs on us; hated us. And the piggies of Dearborn, Michigan viewed us as if a borderline gang...

Thus, I moved somewhere far from my woes & into my first apartment, focused on completing my debut book *"The Silent Burning."* On New Years Day 2001, I returned to West Dearborn, a rough draft in hand.

The result was a mess, further mutating as I attempted to streamline it – it was gaining momentum, producing a black radiance of its own. Personally, I fell into a kind of limbo, battling depression in that frozen Michigan climate of January-March, when you've long ago "tapped out" from Winter yet it just will not cease; when the grayness & darkness & endless snow has driven you cuckoo from frigid mental rot.

Lacking the income, I moved in with an old friend from high school & his brother – a joyless, cynical degenerate that spent all of his energy in malicious criticism towards art/music, clinging feebly to Velvet Underground elitism in that lame, indie rock way...

My writing, my art, even learning guitar scales & chords like anyone else – it somehow became the laughing stock of the childlike "intellectuals" inhabiting that grim reality.

Because what is a Hater but a Doubter who's been proven wrong? They didn't want me to ever prove them wrong – they wanted to promulgate. My perspective on life, my reasoning & idealism – all of it head-to-head with their dead-end 9 to 5 Warehouse Worker abyss.

Years before, they praised my "head in the clouds." Yet at 20, I was infuriating. And what was the real reason? They couldn't complete any screenplay they tried, couldn't never finish a short story.

As comic artists they produced a half-filled sketchbook of designs, some rough layouts – but they all gave up, like disgruntled old men once High School ended; they scoffed: "*kid shit.*" Not me.

After a back-stabbing eviction & another Rock Bottom run, by July 2001 my car died. I was left to The Streets or my folks'. I didn't have options – websites were still barely used for non-corporate rentals. No landlord would take me without credit. I had to go to community tack-boards at hardware stores, community colleges...

Well, here we are. September 2001. WWIII looms stark, as does rampant mutated airborne germ warfare or a ditty nuclear suitcase...

So Virtuous Reader, understand I am liberated & unrestrained; these words shall read as an epitaph on the Grand Sepulcher, brilliant & luminous, if only the archaeologists of the future are wise enough to decode them. *Any critic in the way gets bulldozed...*

* * *

Since the time of writing the forgoing war has been declared...

Immense waves of propaganda now flood the bandwidths of every news syndicate. Hysteria & speculation abound as the democratic nations push for a One World Government under guise of The U.N.

More guards, more guns, metal detectors, mace cans, prison cells, training camps, calamity... Homeland security, neatly bundled, like frantic & deadly hopscotch... Gears of war, goliaths of greed, behemoths of propaganda & industry pitted in imperialist rogue frenzy...

In the cutthroat human chess our politicians have waged since the atrocities of 9/11; Many have conformed to blind patriotism, boldly waving the flag in solidarity; *t-shirts, bumper stickers, sneakers, parasols, squid hustlers, demagogues & cranks...*

I remain on the sidelines, for I do not consider myself an American. No, I'm something else – *a human being.* I refuse to choose a side for each side is equally insane. An agnostic cannot declare allegiance to a thinly veiled religious crusade. God "speaks" to our president; *whispers military domination...*

The truly free man must never allow himself the dishonor of dying for a fool's errand. Martyrdom for idealism is noble, but to perish for the wild capitalism of The State is abomination.

These pauper pits of Detroit underbelly, this flesh-train of working class offspring spawned of workhorse fathers enlist, goaded by retribution – they march forward, mute & blind, as vanguards of a foreign earth...

Not because they believe in any of it – nor for college, training, or job security – but to slaughter Arabs in a racist, legal shooting gallery. In their perverted distortion of rage their bloodied axes grind bone & hope.

My world has died & I am somewhere between worlds, that long interval when bus riders anxiously check their watches, the snapshot of non-existence where everything crumbles in fear of the blank, unanswerable cesspool.

I am the fly & spider, spinning my belly-grumbling web midst this sad, ironic retread of endless human stupidity; I digest images, skyscrapers, sewer mains, tragic escalations as if by blindly searching for myself in all things, mutilating & ingesting all, some new form of man will unsheathe...

Every magnetic pull of the compass leads back to Square One. Yet this pivotal moment of my world, age 20, staring again into that horizon – no modest pull forward but a frantic leap. And it is this leap which will only herald more confusion in an isolated journey few can console...

You are about to read the lives of 100 men – no consistency save for a consistency of dueling opposites. In their freedom of shapelessness, thoughts liberate & confine... *Philosopher, assuredly – though tongue in cheek; Poet, certainly, but as a desideratum dermabrasion born posthumously into an antiquated age of mongrels.*

I am Jack of No Trades, yet Leviathan of them all...

ELEMENTARY STATUS REPORT

Grade: K – "*Ryan is a bright boy who is eager to learn. He has enjoyed his year in Kindergarten and should do well in the first grade. Ryan is an absolute joy to have in the classroom.*"

Grade: 1. Comments: "*I've enjoyed Ryan immensely. He is a deep thinker – he apparently enjoys school, works well with others, and offers much in discussion. He should enjoy Second Grade. His scores on IOWA were above average and more.*"

Grade: 2. Comments: "*Ryan had difficulty adjusting to the students in our school and was getting into many fights. By the second semester things had greatly improved. Regarding the above, Ryan is a very interesting, intelligent boy. He appears, however, at times to become so deeply involved with his own thoughts that he is completely oblivious to everything else around him. He is a very nice boy and is extremely interested in the world around him.*"

Grade: 3. Comments: "*Ryan is a very capable student and had made significant progress in accepting responsibility for completing his work on time. He was really motivated to develop independent research and reporting skills. Ryan continued to receive social worker services this year. I discussed with Mrs. Clemence:*

* * * * *

1. He frequently slams his head (on a locker, file cabinet, desk, etc.)

2. His writing is inappropriate and contains much violence – blood and guts (i.e. stabbing a sibling, etc.)

3. He has trouble getting along with his peers and gets into many fights.

4. Ryan responds well to positive reinforcement and praise."

Les Preludes

I was born into the fire April 4th, 1981, on the West Side of Dearborn, Michigan. Premature & 7 ounces, I was named after a TV Soap Opera & also St. Patrick, directly celebrating the man whom ended The Druids.

My momma was Irish/Scottish & my father Maltese/Hungarian – thus producing the mutant strain of primordial evolution that has developed into the fine mess of a nonperson which you are now reading the inane gibberish, memoirs & eccentricities thereof...

The bulk of my childhood is sketchy at best, because something happened to me I don't quite remember. My memories pick up about 8th Grade, when I was exiting a distorted fog – one might call it a schizophrenic break, or an extreme onset of bipolar depression gone horribly awry & introverted to where thoughts became senseless.

Something happened though, and I cannot recall it. There's a black hole of time – from 5th Grade to 8th Grade – where my mind collapsed on itself. Like the mouth of a river, the whole of my violent childhood led to an early nervous collapse.

Where other children easily transitioned with their evolving hormones, mine were like a grenade. That adolescent body-growing jump that scrambles all young men's minds – it came too fast.

But something else happened, something quite dark. I just don't know what it is. I remember fairly clearly, at least in disjointed chunks, up until I was 10. And then my Mom started to get weird.

I was an only child with a single mother. At one end, she was the most loving, caring parent you could ever ask for – but on the other, she was silently unhinged with a nasty side she restrained that slithered around her like some serpentine shadow. It was the kind of subdued temper you'd never think existed, but no one ever actually poked this rattlesnake. I was always waiting for this shy bookworm to go full Roddy Piper on someone for cutting in line at the grocery store.

As an only child, observing her closely, I knew early on that she wasn't "all there." She was a sober straight arrow though, with a quiet desk job & zero friends. No else caught how strange she really was.

The most vivid memories I can recall are the earliest – mom holding me closely, swayingin a rocking chair weeping in soft darkness, singing: *"You Are My Sunshine/My Only Sunshine"*…

Jumping through plate glass window imitating Lou Ferigno; watching Incredible Hulk on TV made me think I could smash through walls. I charged at the window, smashed it, and found myself dangling over a spike-shard in my underwear, hands nor feet touching the ground. My father freaked out & rushed me to the sink to wash off the blood – *miraculously, all of it was his*…

In 1985 they divorced. Lacking finances, we moved into my grandmother's home in East Dearborn, the largest Arab population outside the Middle East. The house was tiny; an oak front door & dirty white aluminum siding wrapping the auburn brick.

The mid-level was living room, kitchen, two bedrooms. The upstairs had a slanted ceiling covered with *Rocky Horror Picture Show* posters, courtesy of my uncle Craig.

The basement looked a dungeon from a Hammer film; a monstrous furnace jutting dozens of pipes through the ceiling like a dormant robot eager to retract its steel tentacles from subterranean foundations. Through its gridiron smile lava & brimstone crackled the night.

During this period I was in close contact with the few blood relatives I've ever known, since my father's side faded as quickly as he did.

My uncle Craig (*the youngest in his mid-20's*) was deemed my Godfather in true Catholic fashion. He looked like a young Travolta, black-belt trained and engrossed with the prospects of rock stardom.

My uncle Thomas is eldest; a big fellow with a shy, awkward way of socializing. He's the wacky, covertly depressed type that speaks to the kids in Donald Duck tones. He had kids – a girl & boy my age.

DD is second oldest. In the 50's she was a leather-jacket-beehive-switchblade-sister greaser teen. She's funny, 'though highly Archie Bunker & terrified of black people. She is the godmother of road rage…

My aunt Sylvia has a real infatuation with Mark Twain. In college she aimed for a librarian degree but dropped her pursuit when she met my uncle Glen, a die-hard Trekkie & mathematician.

They went on two dates before deciding to get married. They have two children who I spent much time with when aunt Sylvia would babysit.

My uncle Ray wasn't blood, but he married my Grandma's sister who's been long deceased. Ray was bound to a wheelchair, half paralyzed by a stroke, and would smoke two packs of Camels a day while eternally staring at reruns of the Lawrence Welk show.

Back in WWII Ray stormed the beaches of Normandy. He commanded a tank nicknamed "Buttercup" but didn't get far into French territory before he was captured.

Locked up in a Nazi concentration camp, it was two years before the Allies set him free. Ray went on to be a big shot at Ford Motor Co...

Ray had 2 kids, both boys. The youngest in his early 20's lived with him & was his caretaker. He was a cassette trader, exchanging heavy metal tapes with pen pals across the globe. He was deep into Iron Maiden.

No one in the family associates with the other brother, who proudly came out of the closet. The Catholic thing was heavy, and this made him a black sheep. Ray remained in denial for the rest of his life.

My mom was a very low self-confidence person – ultra-Catholic guilt-ridden masochistic mentality. And it hooked into an overall paralysis of the will. She was a Doubter and a Hater, as Rappers say, buying Gossip magazines to scorn the disreputable, immoral actions of movie stars & celebrities she would never meet, and whom simply did not care. Her hobby was scorning, moralizing & talking shit to a vacuum.

Now, don't get me wrong – she was all about Monty Python, Kids In The Hall, weird stuff in general. Like a death metal teenager, she read endlessly about UFO's & Serial Killers & Cryptids & The Paranormal.

She had a subscription to *Fortean Times Magazine* and watched more Professional Wrestling then most my friends in high school did. She thought *Beavis & Butthead* were hilarious, and *Ren & Stimpy* too.

This was the very human side of my mother that I connected with. However, she was venomous in disparaging ways. This red-haired Irish woman could flip the script & get "stone cold" as the mom from *Carrie*.

Like many American adults, she became bitter & defeatist – scorning & mocking things dogmatically, or predicting failure & uselessness everywhere. Her negativity was epic in its pessimism.

She graduated high school in '74; a bookwormy storehouse of information, she answers nearly every question on *Jeopardy*. I watch it night after night, staggeringly. No matter how much I scream at her to try out for the show, she won't budge. It's like having a winning lotto ticket that refuses to cash itself in. It is infuriating.

As a teen my mother was a hardcore Alice Cooper freak; a teen existence of Tolkien & Led Zeppelin. Mentally abused by a long line of losers, I've only been told fragmented memories & vague recollections, hints of childhood sexual molestation. She was with my father for 2 years before being married for 5, yet I know nothing of this period...

But whenever she snapped into Jesus & started talking God, she always went to this creepy, ice-cold place. You could tell, deep inside her, there was all kinds of bizarre & freakish religious ideas.

She'd sadistically talk Angels destroying Sodom & Gomorrah, how all sinners & would be wiped out, how AIDS was God's bidding...

4 year old, in East Dearborn 1985 – my only friend was this slow kid with a funny eye that sometimes lived next door. We used to play this board game called *"Fantasy Forest"* a lot. I had a Rottweiler named Sultan, and Mr. Nobody, a voice that came from the ventilation system.

It was actually my Uncle Craig, who'd ask all sorts of questions because I never told my mom anything because she was never around. If I ever did tell her anything, I just got yelled at or got some sort of talk that I didn't want to have. Mr. Nobody was aware of this & earned my trust as a supernatural confidant.

One time I told Mr. Nobody that my mommy was bad & he lied about keeping everything secret. This hurt her terribly & for Xmas she bought me a light up Gumby doll. I thought she was just trying to steal Bunny, this stuffed animal I loved, and I flipped out full throttle.

The family, for the first time, saw the violence in me – shouting at them, threatening them, screaming at them like a demon. They were shocked & had no idea what to do. This innocent kid turned absolute devil child, threatening them. I told her I hated her & ran in my room to protect my rabbit. She bawled in tears & everyone looked down on me in shame.

Afterwards I refused to look at Gumby. felt extreme guilt for emotional attachment to my Bunny. Soon all I saw in the clouds were shapes of Bunny & Gumby...

It was the beginning cycle of guilt & distrust between my mother & also outsiders who told me I could tell them anything and it would be OK, hence my overbearing apprehension towards therapists...

Then there was grandma – my best friend. I'd sit on her bed all day playing Rummy, Old Maid, Go Fish, and she'd just talk talk talk.

She'd tell me how our family was special with sixth sense stuff & all about ghosts & how they weren't here to hurt us but were watching 'cause they were curious, kind of like angels, and how she knew I was really special 'cause she sensed these things in me.

And then when the sun went down I'd hug her & retire to my room adjacent to hers, listening to her scream all night through the thin walls; my family freaking out trying to stabilize her as I'd jam the pillow over my head to drown it out...

See, grandma was being eaten alive by cancer – she had emphysema. Her flesh was turning brown, and she'd cough rivers of blood. She was pumped full of so many drugs they would bead through the pores of her skin, intermingled with reddish brown blood...

I was locked in a room with this until 1987, watching her decay like a still-life projection of fruit. Just watching, waiting, not feeling much anything because I knew this would happen to everyone around me – my mother, my uncles, aunts, dog, goldfish...

I saw my first ghost was when I was 5 years old. I woke in the middle of the night and found this misty, vaporous thing staring at me, just hovering over the foot of my bed. It had black eyes, like a skull; I froze.

It just kind of floated towards the door, turned into a bright, white ball & zipped through the keyhole. It was what they call an "Orb." Next morning, I hid a knife under my pillow. My family found what I was doing, and Grandma told me it was just grandpa, curious like all the rest...

My grandpa is the reason my family is so fucked up. When he was a child his mom, dad & brother traveled to Michigan from the Canadian French Quarter in search of a higher life quality.

They stopped for gas and the family went inside as Great Grandpa fueled the tank. When they came back out he was gone, abandoning them on the outskirts of Detroit – never to be heard from again.

My Grandpa's mom died early on, and he was forced to raise his brother alone. My Great Uncle grew up to be a member of "The Big Four" – these hardcore, above-the-law Charles Bronson types legendary in the history of the Detroit Police Department. They were handpicked and dispatched by the mayor as his rough n' tumble vigilante goon squad...

My Grandpa fought in WWII as well as my Uncle Ray, where he witnessed an abundance of horror freeing death camps. Fighting Rommel in Africa he supposedly met a cannibal tribe. He asked them what human flesh tasted like – the translator told him *"salty pork."*

He was a writer & artist –, a one time a student of Norman Rockwell. My grandma was an artist too, hammering out primitive, tortured, charcoal expressions. They had a creative existence together as they struggled through poverty.

After 5 kids he started acting funny, unable to hold a job, pounding whiskey all night in his rocking chair writing poetry for hours on end…

Grandpa slowly drifted into madness. No one knew what was wrong with him. He just kept drinking and hearing voices, writing manically because he knew in his gut that he was going down.

No one would ever publish his work though, poets seldom reap such financial rewards. His stuff was strange too, and saturated with obscure Gaelic terms, the ancient Celtic language that he spoke fluently.

The deeper he went into his dark trance, the more he drank. And the more he drank, the more he went into violent episodes, beating the kids. He broke my uncle Thomas' arm once, threw him across the room. It came to the point where the headaches would thrust him into beating his head against the wall to try and shut it off…

By time of discovery, the brain tumor was the size of a grapefruit, which had been crushing his brain against the lining of his skull. The doctors who operated on it were amazed he was still alive.

Little was known about cancer in those days, and even though they removed it as a perceived success, he soon died. Grandpa left behind a trunk full of unpublished literature.

Brilliant work might I add – somewhere between Robert Frost, Walt Whitman and the Beat Generation although he hadn't the slightest clue who any of those guys were…

After an experimental drug from Canada failed to have any effect, grandma buckled under in a dreary yellow and white painted hospital room. My mom and Thomas were crying, blurry in my mind.

Grandma was in her last 10 minutes of life, and mustered the strength to give me on last smile. This sickly deathbed smile, blackened gums, bleeding teeth...

I looked in her distanced blue eyes and was led into the hallway where I sat alone, this cold and impersonal gray corridor. Fluorescent lights flickering on and off, waiting for her to die.

When I heard my family sobbing I knew it was all over. When they took my hand to lead me out, I didn't cry or feel anything but a static, removed observance.

I don't remember the aftermath, only the wake, wearing these uncomfortable dress shoes that painfully dug into my heels. My cousins were too young to have any real comprehension of death. She looked like wax in her coffin; static unemotional observance.

I was still in that hallway, just waiting, like I have been my entire life, never really having left that hospital. But that smile she gave me – that isolated, supreme cold – that cancer-grin... *I wanted to put that smile on everyone's face...*

During the ride home from the wake I sat in the backseat removed from everything, talking to the other me in my head. That second train of thought which developed out of fear and distrust of real communication. An internal Mr. Nobody mixed with the mold of a twin brother...

My school in East D was called Woodworth Elementary, the same my aunts & uncles attended. It was a creepy, massive building constructed in the early 1900's that went kindergarten through graduation.

It was predominantly Arabic but race and culture had no effect because we were all so young. I was well liked, well behaved, one of the leaders of my class and if I were to have stayed there, I probably would have ended up one of the most popular kids in that school.

During recess we played "*Smash The Roach.*" Myself and a dozen Arab boys would run through the halls stomping roaches, sometimes in the bathrooms, the classrooms. I was king when I splattered 8 in two minutes.

We also played this game where we would huddle inside a bathroom stall, whip out our dongs and battle our piss streams like lazar blasts. Fucking Yemenis, they just don't make any sense...

My best two friends at Woodworth were a fat kid & a skinny weirdo named Sal. We were all about Ghostbusters. I told them about the time I woke up and pissed a little, butcher knife and all.

From then on we'd try to hunt & fight invisible enemies like Winston & Egon. We had ghost-busting guns with sliding, transparent picture discs that would spin around in front of a flashlight, projecting a villainous ghoul onto the wall with all sorts of lazar explosion noises.

I used to like the fat kid until I spent the night at his house. All he did was eat soggy leftover sandwiches and listen to Beach Boys vinyl's. The next morning he picked up a piece of shit from the cat box and started chewing on it like it was a Tootsie Roll...

Sal was genuinely terrified about the ghost stuff. I spent the night at his house a week before I moved to West Dearborn. When we woke up there was this green ectoplasm jelly dripping down the wall that looked exactly like the jizz Slimer would leave after zipping through a solid object. Sal was petrified, demanding to know why I put it there.

I kept demanding to know why he was trying to scare me. We were deadlocked in creepiness and he refused to budge on his position. Years later I brought it up to him in high school & he looked like he was about to cry, dead serious that I was still messing with him...

Grandma willed the house to Uncle Craig and we moved into my mom's boyfriend's house. It was deep in the ghetto, near Mound & 6 Mile. He looked like a young George Kennedy, mustache an untrimmed bush.

That was Ed, owner of a foul-mouthed parrot named Artie that he inherited from a WWII vet that won it in a poker game in Morocco. It would constantly holler "*ANSWER THE FUCKING PHONE!!*"

Eddie had a childish air about him; he always wore jeans & plain colored t-shirts; face a permanent five-o-clock shadow. One of my earliest memories of him was sitting in the Argyle St. basement, playing with toys. He snuck behind the stairs with a creepy "*Hey kid? You want your Easter eggs or what?*"

I jerked my head to find a shadowy figure, half drunk & lurking upon me in a full-body pink bunny suit with a cigar between his yellow teeth. My mom was laughing hysterically as he dragged me up the stairs like a Cro-Magnon returning his fresh kill to a mountain cave...

His house was a deteriorating shamble; interior decorated with musty old furniture, olive green carpeting, chipping paint and peeling wallpaper; ashtrays brimming with Kool cigarette butts, empty Budweiser long-neck bottles, 60's style radiation TV set in the living room and iron bars on the windows to secure the house from the riots of yesteryear.

My Mother worked as a secretary at the Police Station while he worked at the Gibraltar World Trade center as a piano salesman. Eddie worked mechanic odds & ends gigs.

He was tied into this skuzzy Detroit bar with a biker clientele. I used to hang & eat burgers there all day, play darts & pool whilst chatting it up with middle-aged alcoholics. The bar soon got raided cause coke smuggling out the basement; the owner was sent away for 20 years...

The LOCALS

Where I live is East Dearborn; *"Little Lebanon"* as it's called, where 2 out of every 3 adults are Arabic, and 4 out of 5 children as well.

The feds are everywhere – raiding homes, cruising in unmarked vans, surveying the area like bloodthirsty hawks for a quaint mouse dinner. They make it sound as if this terrorism fiasco materialized from Jupiter...

We "Locals" are enjoying the whole thing, delighted that all our *"paranoid delusions"* have come true. My first order of business on 9-11 was to grab my katana & zoom to Ricky's – the preordained checkpoint in event random apocalypse. The strategy, as concluded, was to utilize our homes as fortresses sharing food, resources, weapons, explosives...

All that's resulted is 6 kids smoking dope in a disorganized living room, watching replays of the World Trade Center's controlled demolition on one screen & playing *WWF No Mercy* on the other.

I interrupt Cassum from a cell phone to ask what the next step should be. *"Eat Pills,"* he replies. *"Yes, but what about the police?"* Ricky butts in while fumbling with a ten-strip: *"Fuck 'em, we'll kill them too."* Harsh words from a 15 year old.

One of Johnny's buddies busts through the front door ecstatic, *"Hey, you guys hear? There's an army of A-RABS marching down Michigan Ave!"* This is bunk 'cause I just came from that direction – merely panic-stricken honkies filling their gas tanks instinctively.

Nez bolts in next, breaking my concentration. *"Bartek! Wondered when you were finally gonna show up."* He gives me the handshake (*the cool one with the multi-tasking hand movements complete with the climactic side-snap*) and I ask him where Teeth is, our faithful compatriot whose speedy reactions are slug-like at best. *"Probably still at home,"* Nez replies, and we abruptly take our leave…

Instead of heading directly to Teeth's we cruise the streets; it is a veritable ghost town. Usually there are a hundred Arabs at the park this time of the day cooking swarmas on the public barbecues we regularly urinate on. Instead its dead silent, not one bubbling hygeeli…

The skies are clear blue yet there's an electricity comparable to the moments preceding thunderstorm. *"This is fucking creepy,"* Nez blurts. *"You know, I always thought you were crazy when you'd go off about this bin Laden guy."* He trails off and I reply: *"I was hoping that too."*

We park and observe something that redefines the situation. We've spotted our first Arab family packing all of their essentials into an SUV. Across the street a 5-year-old girl stares at us through the windowpane. The mother quickly grabs her & slams the curtains shut; The SUV barrels out & speeds into obscurity. *No terrorists – only the terrorized...*

There are things you need to know about the state of Dearborn and all of these unsavory characters that compose the "East Side Crew."

In Dearborn, just like everywhere, cliques have developed within the youth; small infrastructures of tightly knit units. The difference here is that every clique is like a gang fighting for territory. Maybe it's just that we're all mean spirited fuckers from factory rat homesteads…

Or maybe this is a result of us all growing up on Pro Wrestling. Detroit always ate that shit up, and *WrestleMania 3* was in our backyards. Everyone had an older brother or cousin who went to it & it became a child-wide playground topic, like secretaries at water coolers. The weird, cartoonish logic of WWF carnival had a profound sense on many.

Metro Detroit was a place where people always flaunted their perceived roughness, like a badge of honor. We were a city of self-perceived, working class Anti-Heroes, and every Metro Detroiter played into it helplessly, graciously. We were a redneck society at heart, built on boxing, hockey & Rock N' Roll.

The "Extreme Attitude" of the 1990's – all the *Beavis & Butthead* non-political correctness & post-Nirvana dark realism – this notion was exaggerated & amplified, because that was our reputation in the world.

Detroit was the hardcore city filled with violent lunatics, and Detroit was not only exemplary of this "90's Attitude," but helped define key notions about what that meant for USA Culture. Basically, most in America referred to Detroit's people like: *"those psychos over there."*

Every typical male age 10-40 loved Black Sabbath. And we were also where Punk Rock originated, as did the holiday "Devil's Night." The late 90's were exemplified for so many young Detroit-area men by a potpourri Pantera & Stone Cold Steve Austin, Ford Trucks & Carhart.

The comic book underground was thriving – we had Caliber Comics & plenty of indies. We also had tons of people playing heavy metal, rock & punk, even if the best of them we rarely heard.

Regardless, a great metal show would be packed, and the mosh pits were unequaled to the rest of the USA. People were reenacting riots, basically – and all male teens were hooked ECW in it's prime.

One thing they never mention which really set Detroit apart from anywhere else, not just in the 1980's but the whole general tone of what we as a larger community considered entertainment, or "normal" – the moment Saturday & Sunday morning cartoons ended for kids, they were basically headlined by WWF Pro Wrestling for 1 hour.

And then afterwards, on every channel, 2 movies played back-to-back like a grindhouse – one Horror, one Sci-Horror-Action. Literally, TV programming for us children & young adults in Detroit was 1 hour of *Hulkamania*-era WWF, an old-school Monster Movie of rubber suit variety, a John Carpenter film 75% of the time...

The endless "hardcore-ness" of Detroiters is, of course, partially our comedic way to deal with the larger system of misery pervading all.

Of course we're hardcore – we get put through the ringer. We're all broke, no one has health care, the cops get paid more money if they write more tickets, there is no sustainable economy anymore – all commerce & goods sold simply accommodate the actions of people searching for jobs.

The tragedy is that, like all Americans, they rail against the things which will help them. You can look a man straight in the eye who had a heart attack & was cursed with a $10,000 medical bill which he has been bankrupted by but he was still absolutely, unequivocally defend it & ideologically declare that any kind of government healthcare is communism, and that it's all *his fault* that he has this invoice, because he didn't work hard enough for college to get a degree where a job with insurance would've taken care of him. And it does not matter if he now starves in the streets, he simply will not take Food Stamps either because Workin' Man's Pride & he ain't no god-damn commie...

Well, insofar as Dearborn is concerned (*and Detroit at large*), The long-eclipsed foundations of economic vitality were directly rooted in Henry Ford – Hitler drinking buddy, wage-slaver & world-class vulture of the highest order.

It was this mans disregard for the ecosystem which cultivated the toxicity in which we were raised, the prevailing risk of cancer 1000 fold worse then any other area in the USA.

Just as the Mississippi fueled the development of the South, the Rouge River provided Dearborn with its lifeblood – *a dead stream of toxic waste, raw sewage, mutated animals & discolored vegetation.*

At its peak of contamination in the late 70's a simple gulp held enough impurity to kill a man within hours. The mouth roots from the Steel Mills in South Dearborn bordering Southwest Detroit (*a.k.a. Del Ray*).

Del Ray is the visual clone of *Bladerunner;* grim factories shoot gigantic flames from filthy industrial stacks, dumping vile, murderous waste into the Detroit River. *Archipelagos of pink grass and toxic death...*

Although a few families exist on the outskirts – the majority Black or Hispanic – Del Ray is a vast a no-man's land of abandoned homes; a dead fishing village once sustaining the burgeoning origins of Dearborns' essence. The aluminum siding of every half-rotted house is corroded from the yellow steam & cancerous ash of the local smokestack canopies.

The Del Ray core denizens are crackheads & squatters living by candlelight, meth-labs or chop shops, safe-houses for automatic weapons/mob vendettas. Crazies prowl streets of broken glass & rusted nails – for 3 miles all payphones are cut or gutted...

Zug Island is the core of Del Ray, at the mouth of the Rouge River, where the steel corporations decided to build a massive refinery slightly off shore. It is a monument of disease – steel tentacles jutting into brown waters; the mechanized harlot flames eternal infernal...

In the murky depths of my subconscious all dreams larvae in interconnected amalgam. All deep-slumber reveries take place within this infinite Detroit composite, comprised of all I've witnessed. Except that it is mutated & transfixed, in every dream living the life of another denizen within the barbaric, light-less city. Sometimes a prisoner, sometimes a carpenter, dockworker, alley-lurker, private eye or chef...

At the core of the dreamscape Zug Island appears as living organism; the blackened heart excreting black rivers, foul stench. *Diminutive humanoids take shelter in its cancerous womb, craving sadism & maliciousness. Zug puppeteers lecherous strings of an abysmal vector...*

Dearborn is split into four distinguishable quadrants, all matters of the compass – East, West, North & South...

North & West Dearborn is where all the whites evacuated after the Arabs poured in during the 40's and the race riots of the 60's chased everyone from Detroit proper.

Dearborn' Mayor Hubbard decided, as a preventative measure, to ban blacks from owning property in the city. With Ford's influence intervening, Hubbard embraced the Middle Eastern community with open arms – wage slaves for the assembly line & a racial checkmate barrier...

West & North Dearborn are tragically Midwestern with a mean redneck bite. Upper-middle class to the perpetually impoverished, this is the paint-by-numbers grid of boomer sprawl. No big fantasies – just stark weather, cold beer, red meat & the 401k...

North & West Dearborn are cut off from East & South by a huge stretch of undeveloped land the Ford Estate owns. The ride linking it is Ford Road, of course, a 50 mph quick-shot between the territories. There is civilization yes, but mainly corporate sub-division centers and hidden condos. A few miles parallel is Michigan Avenue, the other quick shot, yet fully civilized. You see, block by block, the schism into Arab territory.

Our little slice of the pie (East Dearborn) is along the Ford Road stretch, where East Dearborn officially starts immediately past Greenfield Road. This neighborhood is essentially a long strip boxed in by West Detroit and South Dearborn, both areas dominated by Arabs.

One block is all it takes to cross from East Dearborn into West Detroit, and immediately the discrepancy is visible. In a heartbeat it mutates from run-down, "historic home" suburb into g-thug land ripe with boarded homes & pot-hole blacktop...

It's far friendlier then South Dearborn though, where every business sign has that indecipherable Middle Eastern cursive language. South Dearborn borders Southwest Detroit (*the outskirt territory 7 miles from Zug Island*), especially filled with Yemenis, Syrians, Afghani's, Palestinians & Egyptians...

Our area is cleaner, mainly a Lebanese concentration, although plenty of black-dressed Saudi Arabian ninja-like women and the occasional light-blue bee-hive burka. Business signs are a mix of Arabic & English writing, a factory rat neighborhood built in the early 20th century.

It feels old, and in the hidden contours lay stationary steel-lugging trains engulfed by rust & gang graffiti – *brown bricks & barb-wire; corroding cars & weed-sprouting concrete...*

South of Dearborn running all the way to Ohio is "Downriver" – pure hill-jack confederate flag hootenanny... Northwest of Dearborn is sprawl grid bourgeoisie as well, same as the general suburbs North of Detroit...

The East Side of Detroit (*not to be confused with our East Side*) is at the other end of the map, where places like Grosse Pointe & Eastpointe are located. It might as well be another planet, because A) there is no public transportation and B) to get there one must brace the 50 mile stretch of I-94 (the straight-shot artery spanning the breadth of the city).

I-94 is a doom-ridden death trap, because if you break down on that shoulder anything could happen. Few tow trucks even want to respond to a call, and the cops won't show for hours, if they even do appear.

On I-94, in nearly every deep-Detroit environment, you're absolutely fucked for dozens of miles – the only other way to East Detroit is by going over the city via 8 mile, through the North, and that's just a massive pain in the ass. So most just swallow their fears and take the straight-shot, making sure to keep that concealed weapon in the glove box.

For this reason there is a standing feud between West & East Detroiters – it's like an entirely different city. The blacks are ridiculous about it, tough-guy & gun slinging as it comes. They don't even need to be in a gang for fights to break out of bullets to fly – the territories themselves are local-bred cultural feudalism.

North of Detroit is the only place a man such as myself is safe – the duel communities of Ferndale & Royal Oak. Part college town, part punk rock haven, the hot-bed of the Metro queer community. It's fairly much the only place where pigs won't harass you for funny colored hair…

Now Detroit itself, that war-zone metropolis… No matter how many television specials you've witnessed or books you've read – nothing can truly prepare you for sights like "*The Jefferson Street Vortex*," "*The Teeter Totter People*," "*The Mt. Elliot Doll Tree*."

Then there are the 1000+ gangsta territories, the countless no-man's-land quadrants: *Del Ray, Blackstone, Cass Corridor, Dragoon Drive, Harpo's Helltown, Packard Pen, Deep East, the East Gratiot Black Castle Route, Grand River, The Mt. Elliot Stretch…*

It's a sad situation. Add in the completely bi-polar weather driving everyone up the wall, the outlandish racism & obvious class warfare, the paranoia & violence that has everyone at each other's throats – loser sports teams, right wing morning radio, dull media, the fact that all but 5% of the population are two-faced, selfish, greed-driven, lazy, negative, self-righteous, easily led & addicted uncreative individuals that cannot produce but a minute shred of positive energy...

You know everything that is shitty about Kid Rock – all that gibberish about Hockeytown, flashy clothing, Hollywood posing, blatant hypocrisy, underlying racism & overt homophobia? That's the Detroit mentality to a tee with a slice of Ted Nugent male supremacy & Marshall Mathers' loudmouthed, ego-driven cockiness...

So where do I stand among this animosity? I'm kind of like a nomadic, unifying ambassador of sorts. The genesis was an embryo of Cassum, Vic and myself; the spring of 1994, the trail end of 8th grade...

Pushed too far, humiliated & degraded, we made a pact to forever have each other's backs no matter the circumstances. United we were a tight nucleus; by high school our numbers around 20. By sophomore year we'd exploded to triple digits and that's when the "Prozac Nation" began.

We were a dystopian sect living life between the contours. When our nucleus grew outside our territory, when our subversion meshed with other tribes of outcasts created from near-identical situations, that's when the ambassador role came into its own.

This haphazard meshing, however, ultimately leveled the foundations. 7 years later we stand at the shattered, drug-addled trail end of it all. Just Cassum & myself, the last two of "The Old World," with the current world a conglomeration of randoms...

Of course the World Trade Center is not the cause of our rapidly disintegrating reality. No – it's the collapse of the Detroit Rave Scene.

The Underground was the key factor in holding "The Family" together. Unfortunately it has plummeted on all fronts due to legal troubles, drug overdoses, suicides, deaths, internecine infighting...

The Detroit Rave scene is not, as one would assume, obnoxious trendy kids in phat pants with candy bracelets. Here it is more sinister – a monstrously deviant, hard-assed version of other rave environments. Parties are less hoppin'-boppin' fun then they are literal LSD stalags & mobster-run MDMA camps...

It's actually the hoppin-boppin brain-dead trend-kids that fucked it up for everyone. Dopey little 14 year old kids see *Groove* and have their moms drop them off at a defunct auto warehouse in the ghetto naïvely assuming that these are secure, legal events.

Then poor little Susie gets shot, or overdoses, or paddy-wagon; 16 year old Georgie gets pulled over with 3 pills & faces 75 years in prison (*yes, 25 years per pill*), thereby snitching out the entire kitchen sink, thereby creating a chain effect of stool pigeons and insider informants devouring themselves whole.

Thus a bottomless whirlwind cultivating a far-reaching maelstrom of heat. The news media clamp on, the churches forewarn, the politicians rage. One by one the production companies go down, bodies slammed behind bars; futures ended, lives destroyed...

Cassum is intent on following the abyss to its forlorn climax, and his production company MKULTRA is one of the last in the underground.

Thus you will find many of us in late night scrambles breaking into abandoned buildings, setting up power generators via truck, hustling "checkpoint" directions under the streetlights of abandoned streets...

Those whom inhabit our world are known by a facsimile of titles. There are multiple crews, various cliques – but the true-blooded ones, those who would fight to the death alongside any of us – this is "The Family."

The Family is less some weird Charles Manson shit then a bond. One by one we've grown, the mass feeding itself. We live a life of our own self-perpetuated myths, proudly embracing The Gutter. Society thought we were degenerates, so why not flaunt it?

We were hated by the police – despised by parents, teachers, preachers. We are the greatest collection of outcasts and misfits ever found – drug addled, cocky, unemployed, broke & half crazed. *We are elite...*

8 car snakes in the dead of night, 50 waltzing into a household or venue at a time – at epicenter "The East Side Crew" is the regime. It's our planet, our tribe, and everyone else has been assimilated.

The East Side Crew are the denizens of East Dearborn itself, born & raised. Those absorbed into our group are known as *"regulars,"* or *"randoms"* – to be branded "Family" is of an exclusive rank...

Cassum is the main focus here, and has been since day one of my re-integration, post-LSD. Never can he accurately be described by mere linguistics – a mutant of many forms, drugging his audience with a suffocating form of hypnotic volubility.

Or, as he so puts it, *"Only when I achieve death or captivity will I win, for I am The Martyr who wants to be accused."* I have ongoing opinions of him consistently subject to revision. Apart from myself, he is the most interesting & amusing con-man I've ever known.

Currently he is studying government regulations attempting to register the rave scene as an official religion in which he will be The Pope. It is our plan to create the "Ministry Of Sound" – a "*church*" in which you must "*donate*" a rotating sum in order to "*pray*" to the progressive trance emitting from the turntables.

Before the services begin one must "*donate*" a sum of $25 to participate in the "*holy sacrament*" of MDMA, for any individual that chooses to break our ritual is a blasphemer of the highest order.

Only members of the clergy – solely ordained by Cassum – can distribute the sacrament, a divine gift from God. Heretics are subject to Inquisition, hideous torture, violent excommunion.

I am to be the pastor of this church once Cassum moves onto the next major city, repeating his creation as the Neo-Messiah…

Cassum is insane for a variety of reasons. First, he is a pathological liar and one mustn't believe a word that comes out of his mouth.

He honestly has no idea as to what is real anymore & entering his mind in order to find out the root of the problem is like snorkeling through an ocean of raw sewage.

He also has the sixth sense, though muddled from chemical damage. He bounced around the United States with his father and most likely developed his tall tales as a result of isolation. His mother died of leukemia very slowly, finally buckling in '95.

This is an obvious source of dementia for him. Funny thing is the craziest stories he emits end up being confirmed by some random individual you thought may have been a product of his sloppy imagination. But until that moment occurs, you're never really sure.

We just go along with it, decode the wild exaggerations, and come to our own conclusions. There are hundreds blissfully unaware of his madness and he has conned the entire rave scene into thinking he is John Gotti. The end result of babbling all his delusions over the years has transfigured him into one infamous figure. He is a firm believer in *The Revolution*; he is the Acosta to my Thompson…

Nez, on the other hand, does not believe in *The Revolution* – he takes the piss out of me for it, *actually.* He's a skeptical voice of reason.

However, I am a man on a mission, and in order to save the world I must destroy it and remodel society in my own twisted image. It is an insane pursuit of liberal fascism with no foreseeable epilogue. It is the ultimate art expression…

Although he'll most likely utilize his black-belt training on me for describing him in such a fashion, Nez resembles a young, skinny, strung out Eminem. Nez has a hard front & knee-jerk reaction to anything that upsets the foundations of what he considers reality.

Like many of the others, Nez feels that I am grossly exaggerating the severity of my drug problems. This is total malarkey because I've regularly done more drugs in one night than the vast majority of Americans have done in their entire lives. My peers' extremism is volcanic.

If Nez really applied himself he could easily make a fortune. He's a cocky, stringy, quick moving hustler; quick shots & rum-punches, lots of elaborate handshakes. Smoking marijuana is a main goal of each passing day; he spins progressive trance for MKULTRA, Cassum's rave imprint...

Teeth wants nothing more than to fall in love and disappear. He is a giant pothead with extremely low self-confidence. Anytime he finds a girl he waits too long to make a move and ends up in the friend zone.

Every girl that he dates exploits his kindness, breaks his heart & leaves him further in the despair of his bottomless depression...

He rarely calls anyone and when people are over they are huddled in his tiny room smoking pot and playing *Tekken*. His behavior in any other home mirrors the same situation.

If it's a concert or gathering he'll be crouched against the wall talking about *X-Men*, never working up the nerve to initiate conversation with anyone foreign. He is a very honest man that detests drama, and knows everything about Pro Wrestling.

Teeth has regularly been caught by his parents & authorities with Mary Jane for the past 3 years. They've threatened to kick him into the street/incarcerate him constantly but he knows his father would never fulfill such a threat & the police just suck money out of him, employ community service slave labor due to his low-level, non-violent offenses...

Ricky, who has just turned 15, is the youngest of our crew. His acceptance exception is rooted in our association with his older brother Johnny, who's been an East Side staple all the way back to the "capture the flag" days. He is the little brother of the group, and one of the few voices of reason.

Ricky is unusually mature & perceptive for his age, on par with Cassum and I. He is rarely carded for booze/cigs due to his height & bad teenage mustache. Ricky claims that he has eaten LSD every consecutive weekend for the past year and a half. Many of our nights are involved dissecting television and society at large, producing conspiracy theories with assembly line fervor.

He doesn't like new people and is extremely paranoid. He hates Arabs even more than Cassum & regularly speaks of nuking the Middle East. He is skinny & strung out, slightly twitchy & oddly laid back. Ricky is Hispanic and enjoys skateboarding & Dragon Ball Z. He lives with his brother Johnny and his father, a retired FBI agent...

Johnny is a hothead and is constantly getting into fistfights in order to prove his immortality. He believes this because no one has ever disproved him. He is about six-three & hits like a sack of bricks. He is extremely quiet and observant and is dating Susan, one of The Twins.

Johnny is an urban legend around these parts. He's somewhat of a gang leader alongside his personal crew of thuggish-ruggish cohorts. They aren't "whiggers" in the wide-spread, widely used slang of Metro Detroit.

Here, even black folks say it – and it refers to lame, extremely honky suburban white kids going to insane lengths of concentrated application to forcefully become a bad, uncontrollably laughable stereotype of something they are absolutely not.

Now some white guy who's just kind of 'Hood, who's natural – well, everyone treats him like a man. No one says "whigger." Nah – here, in The 'Burbs of The 'D, they are seen as theatrical, absurd frauds.

This is to whom such mocking slang applies – suburban white kids arbitrarily deciding to go wildly out of character 24-7 as to permanently method-act that they are somehow legitimate Black Men from Inner City Streets is the stupidest subculture ever to emerge from America. *And somehow the jocks & preps ingrained them into the fabric of accepted, encouraged normality...*

Johnny's crew are authentic products of their environment. They are also giant freaks at heart with good intentions. And they are not a gang, just friends that got jumped too many times & decided to fight back.

Johnny is a pain to have around because if an officer of law enforcement happens to see you with him for any reason you're going to be stopped and searched immediately.

Actually, same goes for most all of us – we're all targeted and have been for years. Dearborn is a Fascist Pig-Farm that makes you want the terrorists to win…

We hang out at Ricky's a lot which is fitting because it's haunted by the residual energy of a violent alcoholic. Every odd year, in the fall, the disturbances kick back up. This happened just recently as Ricky and I were watching John Ashcroft push the Patriot Act on CNN.

A week beforehand Johnny had been kicked out for showing up drunk & breaking a bunch of furniture in a fit of rage. He stole Ricky's bike and rode off into the night, passing out in the park shortly thereafter. Susan was still there, intoxicated and cursing obscenities on the front lawn.

Ricky ended up dragging Susan into the street by her hair. She panicked and ran off into the night after he threatened to call the police, fearful of breaking her probationary requirements…

Ricky could never stand Susan in the first place, but really despises her now for convincing Johnny that he's the father of her child. It is painfully obvious to us all because the boy is whiter than Ron Howard. Johnny is in a serious state of denial.

So back to the present (*or recent past*). We're in Ricky's back room when we hear the front door open and close modestly, a few steps cautiously leading into the middle of the room.

We both think its Johnny breaking in to get the rest of his belongings & Ricky grabs a Louisville. The room is empty and the plastic wrap sealing on the inside of the window starts going crazy with a distinct hand imprint causing the commotion.

It halts abruptly and we then hear footsteps going downstairs. We go into the basement and the power-drill jumps off the tool shelf and lands in the middle of the floor; the cat freaks out and runs upstairs.

The manually operated dryer turns itself on and stops 10 seconds later. Ricky lifts the bat over his head, gives me the nod and I whip open the dryer door. All we find is a bed sheet cold as a corpse in mid-January...

When Ricky was 6 & Johnny 11, the entire family was in the back room eating dinner. Ricky's mom had this shelf full of music boxes, dozens of them – they all went off by themselves, all at once.

30 seconds of mute panic until all the boxes stopped in unison – except for one of a goofy Italian guy riding a weather balloon. It kept turning until the guy was looking straight at Ricky & stopped on a dime.

Other strange disturbances have happened throughout the years. Johnny says a knife was thrown at him once when alone in the house. This other time he & Carl were sitting in the living room and when Carl got up to get a glass of orange juice a hundred-pound bench press weight dropped from the ceiling, nearly crushing his skull...

The Twins (Susan and Samantha) are the great granddaughters of a Nazi war criminal that used to run one of the lesser-known death camps; he fled to the states after the fall of Berlin and lived under a false identity.

Their mother abandoned them years ago and their father is in prison for armed robbery. They live with their Grandma who is dying of cancer, waiting to inherit her fortune.

The Twins are always finding hapless people at raves and dragging them into our web of destruction so we have a new place to party and can roll in 50 deep with mountains of drugs.

We burn these places out until our new associate is either thrown out by their parents, gets evicted, or their residence becomes so "hot" that it's no longer safe. After the burn, they inevitably become one of The Family and aid our parasitic cycle.

The Twins are manipulative bastards that control Johnny and his thug crew with their feminine prowess. They are the main source of all drama. They like me because I'm all too aware of their scheme and refuse to be a pawn in their endless game of human chess...

Stoney doesn't like The Twins 'cause he had enough of them long before prison. He thinks that I am a terrorist & laughs at everything I say. Often we are up all night playing Euchre with The Regulars. We always train, 'cause in Michigan, Euchre is your best shot at scoring cigs/drugs in jail...

Simon is a world-class pothead & a collector of many artifacts involving heavy metal, Pro Wrestling & horror cinema. He rarely ever leaves his house except for a metal gig, or the goth/industrial club. I met him in '97 – this hardcore Marilyn Manson / NIN fan of the *Antichrist Superstrar / Downward Spiral* era – always with a trench coat, or leather.

Simon's dad terrifies my own stepfather Toby 'cause they were in 'Nam together. They are both equally insane and I am consistently trapped between both, relaying Semper Fi gamruck.

Big Paul is considered by many veterans to be one of the biggest psychotics to ever emerge from the war.

He's never really come back and sees Charlie everywhere he goes. He volunteered for duty and once his first tour finished he extended his contract another 4 years because he enjoyed it so much.

He was Sergeant in a platoon of recon Marines deep in the jungle. By the time of the ceasefire he had 55 confirmed kills and claims to have killed over 300 men.

The first time I met him he taught us the true meaning of the stoner term "shotgun," blowing lungfuls of dope into a pump shotgun chamber and cocking the bad boy so it shot right into our lungs.

Big Paul is on a tether because of a domestic violence call. He is often drunk and tells the same stories repeatedly. Paul sees me as Toby's son, thinks I am Charles Bronson and teaches me improvised munitions, hand-to-hand combat, automatic weaponry…

Dre is one of my biggest fans & says I'm his literary inspiration. He is an exceedingly violent rapper. Dre's has been shot 3 times, stabbed 12, has a bullet lodged in his head & is clinically schizoid. He is a living, breathing example of survival against all odds.

This spastic cartoon is short yet muscular, with homemade tats, short stubbly fro sprouts dyed green or bleached. He could stab you for no reason or bring you a bouquet of roses like a sweetheart.

He also recently come out the closet. We were all on Ricky's porch, passing Philly blunts, & Dre's like: *"Guess what?"* He grabs this butch g-thug dude white dude in a Lion's jersey & they jam their tongues down each other's throats, passionate & sloppy. Well, we saw it coming –

his basement room walls are covered in teeny bopper girly magazine photo-shoots of Justin Timberlake – *aaaand half-burned bible pages too...*

Carl doesn't have a psycho father to deal with 'cause his pops died from medical malpractice...

He is a Mexican/Mulatto mutt & Vic's 2nd cousin – the same Vic who began this web alongside myself and Cassum in 1994 and is no longer part of us. Carl finally won his lawsuit against The Hospital that malpractice-whacked his dad & has $100 grand; he's been blowing tons on Canadian strip joints with Johnny, Stoney & Dre.

Carl went there on a tangent recently, ending up at a massage parlor in Windsor. I was drunk, twiddling my thumbs naked except for a towel. This 20 year old came in topless in a g-string.

She laughed at the twiddling thumbs – she thought it was ridiculous cute, and that I was some aloof shy kid with no trace of dark, conquering eyes. I just made her laugh.

She busted out the oil & was ultra flirty. She seemed to legitimately be into me, although there was something else about her behavior that was legitimately odd.

I was broke and apologized for not having the cash to tip her proper. She laughed: *"Oh don't worry 'bout that honey. But I do need a favor, if that's cool. Like, for real. Real talk, dude."*

The massaging hottie pointed out the window: *"See that cop car out there, with the lights? The cop's investigating that parked right car over there – I just stole that car and dumped it here. I'm not even supposed to be working here right now! I didn't know what to do, so I sped to work and ran inside! I can't let my boss catch me here either!"*

I'm like: *"Holy shit dude! That's intense! It's ok, it's cool, I don't give a fuck – I'm pretty fucking drunk right now, to be honest."*

"Alright then – fuck yeah, you're on board!"

"Yeah man, no problem."

"So I'm just gonna hide in here with you until they go away. They were on my tail and – fuck man, FUCK – what the fuck was I thinking? I'm such a – dude, I'm so glad you're the one who's here."

"Ok, so should we start then?"

"Sorry, sorry, I'm just – I'm nervous my hands are shaking. I... Hey, I don't normally do this, but, uh..."

Now she was panicking, realizing that even though I'm being cool right now I might not be later on. If they do come inside & arrest her, does this whiskey drunk Detroiter get investigated? Do they threaten imprisonment unless he rats her out?

BING: *"Hey. I don't normally ever do this with clients, but... Will you grease me down to kill the time? Just until they leave."*

She worked her butt jiggle, then laid down sultry on the massage table. She had me grease her down – it was like modeling spinning clay, just waves of super hot voluptuous flesh, like endless oily pizza dough, rubbery & weird & blissful – while holding a long conversation about the awesomeness of *RoboCop*, and how our parents were totally insane.

We bonded, she rubbed me down, and – <u>POOF</u>! Vanished & didn't even make me pay! Since we both had to flee from each other & pretend it never happened, it was the purist, most "no bullshit" relationship I ever had – wild, passionate, bizarre & never to return. *It was soooo romantic...*

Once Upon A Forgotten Time

We found a home in West Dearborn (*the broke side of the fence*) cornered by a semi-major road with ceaseless traffic – constant sound systems, blown mufflers, drunken road rages & buffoons night & day.

It was like an old, rickety farm house that was the first on the property. It had been around since at least 1910; the chipping paint revealed 18 different coats, sometimes over 1940's wallpaper.

The house was purchased for a mere $37,000 off an elderly polish man whose wife had recently died & within a month we'd realized we'd purchased one of the most haunted attractions in the state of Michigan.

I sensed it the second we moved in and wanted to vacate immediately. No matter where you stood it always felt some PMS monster loomed over your shoulder. Ed was locked in the basement via push-lock; attic would make noises, cupboards would open, TV would turn itself on...

The mid-floor had two bedrooms – one for myself and the other for the adults. The walls were paper thin as were the windows; in winter it was freezing all the time.

The basement was filled with mold. Smack-dab in the main area of the basement the sewage would consistently overflow – water-bugs, millipedes and spiders galore. In the concrete floor there were raccoon tracks imprinted from the initial construction...

In the basement were two creepy little rooms with thin wood doors. One was my playroom, the other a storage area with rotting planks hammered to the sides of a cement slop-job cavern. The walls would leak when it rained 'cause they gunked wet concrete over mud. My little room Ed painted blue, and I had two old trunks of broken toys from Mom's and

Eddie's youth, weird stuff he'd picked from the junkyard down the street growing up in Detroit.

The bathroom walls were filled with rusted old razors from a drop slot never to be emptied. Directly across from the toilet was an attic doorway which would give pure chills every time you looked at it.

That door would only open halfway before it lodged the staircase, then you'd have to walk up a narrow, inhumanly steep & rotting wood staircase. From there you'd have to fish around in the dark for a single light whose wiring came from a circular switch you'd turn clockwise.

It was the ghost hive, like this strange unfinished slop of a living space that was never completed, with old closet stand-up racks of the dead woman's clothes. The attic was thoroughly insulated with newspaper articles from the great depression (*I actually found the showing times for King Kong*). The roof was steep and pointed, cobwebs & spider-hives, rusted nails jammed its sides like an Iron Maiden.

Half the boards weren't nailed down and you'd have to hop structural beam to structural beam in order to hit the small, rectangular cobwebbed windows. Underneath the loose planks you'd find obscure artifacts – unopened bottle of snuff from 1926 with receipt in bag, old medication, dried lipstick from '37...

We set ourselves up for our brand x blue light special Salvation Army lifestyle and Ed began a construction job.

Now, I was a nice kid at heart – well mannered, decent. But that devil on my shoulder wouldn't just whisper in my ear – it'd come raging out, this unruly yet still naively, cartoonish "*gross-out-the-world-leave-me-the-fuck-alone*" Punk Rocker vibe. I might as well been the kid from *Suburbia*, riding a Big Wheel with a mohawk. That's certainly how I saw myself back then – 100% that late 80's breed of "gross kid" hooked to *Garbage Pail Kids* & *MadBalls* & *Godzilla* & Underground Comics that were way too freakish & sexual & bizarre & violent then most kids should necessarily be reading – chiefly, how I learned to read & digest storytelling at a critical processing level.

While other kids were reading *Capt. America* I was into Dark Horse, Aircel, Caliber, Fleetway, Renegade, etc – ultra-sexual, high-brow punk-styled Indies meant for Mature Audiences...

Well, there I was – that Big Wheel riding loner, age 6 & of a certain breed that only kids from that era will remember. That kid, nor any of the adults in his world, could scarcely imagine The Internet. This tale & these years – they seem a fantasy world that can hardly been real deep into 2001.

Yet 1987 it is, months before my 7th birthday. I live in a new home now, a haunted creepy house, which is to serve as my residence until I am 18 years old, most likely, so they tell me, and to get comfortable.

In that house, also the Detroit house, also Grandma's – all I ever really was was some quiet entity hiding in a dank basement like a bunker, as if a war was always going on outside. Maybe that was the climate, as my grandmother died aggressively. The Russians were closing in, you know? And Central Command was of its last outpost, and I was just in the bunker, while all the last authority rushed around the floor above me.

I always felt centered and natural blending in with the silence & the shadows. And that childish punk rock kid in me just wanted to throw feces at the world until they said: "*into the bunker with you – permanently.*" So the whole world would piss off & I could be alone. I was already clinically thinking in the sort of way Charles Manson describes when explaining the sanctity of his solitary prison cell. I was all about escaping civilization via damp, cold darkness, spiderwebs & mold spores.

I enrolled in Whitmore Bolles Elementary School. During my first recess break of 2nd grade, I walked up to this kid Jenkins & slugged him in the face, asserting myself like a prison courtyard. The principal asked: *"why, why, why?"* in his office. I didn't have an answer. *Just felt like it.*

I quickly retreated into my own little world in my own head where I had no distinction of reality. I wouldn't respond to the teacher, who was terrifying. She had an obvious, shabby wig & humiliated me. I was still in that hospital with grandma, watching the lights flicker…

I don't remember much about that period except minor details. Trying to learn multiplication, a projection screen movie from the 70's about a lady with no arms that used her feet as hands… Teacher did this weird shit with meal-worms; we kept them in tubes of sawdust, recording their growth. We had insect races at the experiments finale.

Afterwards we were told to let them free into the playground wilderness. Wormy was the closest friend I had, so I brought him home. He got lost in the carpet & multiplied like crazy – we had 1000's of gray moth-like bugs everywhere – inside the thermostat, the Cocoa Crispies, the TV remote. They eventually died off in a seasonal affair…

This was about the time of the Mayfly Festival where Eddie's folks' lived. Every year, in May 300,000+ nasty moth creatures would hatch & fuck in swarming masses on car hoods & street lights…

The rednecks would have a parade where Ed would cruise his restored Model T. Just imagine an army of clowns on Main Street, crushing mating insect masses with floppy red shoes. I regularly had nightmares about these things penetrating my skin & devouring me…

The Mayfly Fest, like Fermi, was one of those things I didn't recall until much older. We visited one of Ed's construction buddies.

The city was host to Fermi – a monolithic nuclear plant that reigned over the landscape. Close was the guy's home, a trailer in a back road subdivision.

I was introduced to his son, and after dinner we ventured outside. I noticed a dirt road meters past the fence. I interrogated him where it lead yet he was unsure, as his parents forbid him to investigate.

Being the adventurous, manipulative bastard that I was, I coaxed him on an expedition. We followed the trail a half hour & came across a cinder block wall that seemed to extend for miles. Kid pulled a rusty, discarded bucket from a brush & set it up so I could hop over.

I dropped a good 6 feet down; the fall knocked the wind out of me. I lay on the loose grain of beach sand – something was slimy beneath my elbow. I got up, dusted myself off & silently absorbed my surroundings.

From edge to edge lay hundreds of dead fish half devoured by the acidic water; I'd landed on top a toxic carp. In the distance was Fermi, an enraged bull ready to charge... Years later I did research – Fermi was shut down during that period for environmental concerns. A second was constructed shortly thereafter…

It should be mentioned that I was a sexually-interested kid, or trying to figure out what was going on, at least. But lots of guilt & that endless head-slam of Catholic repression & one hellfire sin-screaming momma really warped what should have been a natural process. All of this stuff, it has led to a very confused adult life, a very disjointed sexuality.

What chiefly destroyed my ability to feel comfortable observing sex – well, this one kid found a stack of sticky old smut magazines in the trash & hid them beneath Ed's broken jeep.

All the kids from the area were looking at this stuff together, behind my garage, and I was the dumb-bell who got stuck being the caretaker. They just kind of dumped it on me, the hapless 7 year old who didn't know any better.

It was my first exposure to anything sexual really, apart from the "fairly dirty innuendo yet still clothed 'cept some nipples here & there" comics I was reading. Anyway, this stack of porn this kid brought over – all of it was extremely over the top: *double-dill crotch bouncing, anal fist-fucking whips, chains, bondage, cartoon erotica, the old "in & out"*...

Mom discovered the entire stack. She was really angry but I lied & said I'd no idea where the mags came from. She knew I was full of shit, but I refused to budge because I didn't want to let her down.

She kept saying, *"Just tell me the truth, I won't be mad"* but she gave up. I wouldn't budge. She was ragingly pissed off, but it was dead wall. I pretty much locked up the entire budding sexual process that day. I couldn't look my mom in the eyes & tell her I was looking at men shove fists up people's asses & freaks beatin' the crap out each other with S&M.

In time made me feel dirty & wrong about everything, even my want for gentle, normal human touch. I mean, yeah, ok, the above situation is pretty extreme for a parent to walk into with their 6 year old child, but my mom was excessively against sexual anything.

She was trying to make me some repressed, missionary-only type of nice Catholic Boy doing absolutely no wrong in the world, saving cats from trees & holding the door for old ladies & saving babies from burning buildings. She basically wanted me to be a Catholic Priest.

I worshiped horror films, as you know. Mom & I used to watch them all the time. All of the decapitation, disembowelment, torture and maiming was fine but the second anything sexual came up she either made me close my eyes & cover my ears or fast forward the sequence.

She'd rant about sex & eternal damnation. Every girl I ever dated was a whore, none of them good enough. This is a major reason I could never hold a relationship – her bitching voice in the back of my head…

There was this one time though, back in 3rd grade – I had a legitimate "thing" for a deaf girl. It didn't feel dirty cause she was so innocent seeming. She just observed & kept to herself. I used to communicate with her though body language; I was interested in learning sign language just to talk to her.

The deaf boys soon retaliated though because they felt I was trying to steal their special little angel. 5 of them ganged up & jumped me at recess. I was on the ground covering my face, getting kicked & punched, and all I could hear were angry, throaty deaf growls. They all started spitting on me after I was too beat up to fight back.

I wrestled my way out of it and ran for the bathroom to wash up because all I could smell was nasty, milky loogs. Inhaling the stench while running though – I gagged & puked all over the hallway corridor.

Nauseous in a puddle of half-digested cupcakes, the school bell rang. All kids came in from lunch & started pointing & laughing. My nickname thereon was "*Barftek.*" I never looked at her again…

In 5th grade I made friends with this girl who gave me a Mad Magazine button. We were both outsiders and liked each other, but everyone made a big thing of it. Everyone threw it in our faces that we were dating, even though neither of us declared that, and it made it all so horridly awkward.

We drifted out of pressure and it ended when she overheard me quoting Tim the Toolman Taylor in the lunch line. *"There will never be a woman President because they think with their hearts and not with their heads."* I made this kid laugh and then I turned and noticed her face. She stopped talking to me and moved shortly after.

On Valentine's Day all the kids were required to give each other miniature Hallmark cards so no one felt left out. They refused to give me any, risking discipline rather than associating with me. If I did get a card it would almost always say something mean.

In 6th grade my buddy Fat Joe asked what girl I liked when I spent the night at his house. He was the first real friend I had, him and this Elliot kid that wanted to be a boxer.

Well, I didn't like any of the girls because they were all so mean, but I didn't want to sound homo so I replied: *"Tonya."*

The next day the entire school found out, all mocking me. When Tonya saw me her face turned to a scowl and she alongside all of her pre-cheerleading friends ripped on me every day until middle school.

Then there was this ugly girl that wore gaudy grandma sweaters with big yarn ball flowers. I took her to the 6th grade dance to be nice, although I refused to sway in a moonlight sonata 'cause she smelled funny.

In 7th grade, she gave my number to her friend with Tourette's Syndrome. She began stalking me, calling all the time to rant about the Red Wings whom I knew nothing about except that Bob Probert was cool because he always beat the living shit out of people...

First time I established contact with the kids down the street I was riding my Big Wheel during the fall of '87. Soon as I cleared this long line of neatly trimmed bushes a psycho child lunged out swinging a sledgehammer and jabbering freakish garble.

I started crying and ran home, totally freaked, and my mom bitched out the kid's parents. That was Jesse, who later on became my best friend even though he was my worst enemy.

Jesse was named after Jesse James, the outlaw. His mother, Athena, later became my babysitter. She was this bitchy, chain-smoking, whacked out ex-acid freak that spent all of her money (*sugar daddies*) on "power crystals" and purple pieces of sheet metal that were supposed to re-energize your charkas. The house was full of cats & parakeets.

She found nothing of value in *The Simpsons* & hated it because they were yellow. She thought AC/DC sucked, she hated Judas Priest, and was convinced no good music had been released since Van Halen 1982.

She'd soak herself in tanning lotion & lay in the sun all day, rambling on about John Elway being the greatest American hero of all time, or read aloud snippets of Jim Morrison's poetry & life story to the kids on the block. The man was like Christ to her...

Jesse was a love child. The parents weren't married but lived together in separate rooms. His father was a high school janitor with this gray, dead eye from getting hit by a crowbar during a mugging.

Their relationship was like Peg & Al Bundy but if Al didn't have any self-deprecating esteem and just hid in the back room all the time listening to Stevie Ray Vaughn and playing blues guitar.

The only time he'd ever come out was to wash his massive black Ford truck in the driveway or hang at the all-night poker/euchre parties they'd host, watching hockey or football games with his janitor buddies.

Jesse's himself was a mean, back-stabbing, intelligent little bastard that played everyone to his best interest. He was always turning on me then becoming my best friend.

He, Danny Mitchell and I were the 3 oldest kids on the block & together were the commanders of the childhood operation.

Danny was this big fucker that wasn't too bright, the latest offspring in a long line of jocks that were a throwback to the caveman days. His nickname was "Monkeyface," to which he'd go into bleeding rages if ever called.

His pops, a tall & stocky Neanderthal factory worker named Hank (*ironically a near-carbon copy evil twin version of Hank from "King of the Hill"*), would build him intricate replicas of various assault rifles. We'd run wild in the streets with them playing *Predator* or *Aliens* – big M-60's with real bullet straps hanging down *Rambo* style.

Danny's life revolved around tormenting me. His vicious predilection for football was unchallenged & he was the poorest sport in the history of the game.

Even if we were on the same team & I scored winning touchdown, he'd kick the shit out of me for neglecting his sterling victory. I'd be doing the victory dance, then see him charging at me with beat red face & outstretched clothesline. He'd wallop me & I'd go down chanting "Monkeyface" – he was just too damn big & strong...

Among the many games Jesse, Dan & I played were a special 3 that I now lovingly refer to as "The Triad of Pain."

The first was "Bottle Rocket Tag." We'd run around the neighborhood with plastic tubes like miniature bazookas, lighting high-speed explosions at each other. Sometimes they'd miss and we'd start someones roof on fire, but would run in their backyard and garden hose it before anyone would notice.

The next was an innocent childhood sport entitled "NIGGER." This super-ultra-fun pastime was such: one kid would be deemed the "NIGGER." He then would have a 3 minute lead to run as far as he could to successfully hide from an aggressive pack of ten or more kids.

The second the clock wound down the hunt would begin. If caught within 15 minutes by the "Slave Hunters" the "Nigger" would have no choice but to take in exactly 2 minutes of full-blown lynching.

Yes, as in laying on the ground & being kicked/punched repeatedly while the other kids laughed like sadistic ghouls. I can barely remember a game where I wasn't the "Nigger." *We played this one a lot...*

Then, of course, "Smear The Queer." The object of this particular game was to hold onto the football as long as you possibly could with all other players trying to take you down to wrestle it away.

The game would then begin again with a new queer to smear. Well, Danny would just shove the ball down my pants so he could jump on my ribs and punt my stomach. If I tried to pull it out he would just shove it back down my trousers. I always took my beatings like a man...

There was another game though that I invented called PIGEON. It was like a high-stakes NIGGER but on bicycle. One kid would be the Pigeon, 3 to 5 other would be the hunters, all zipping through the neighborhood. I'd imagine myself as Ghost Rider on his cycle, a raging turbine of sulphur & skull...

It was after a Smear The Queer game when Danny convinced me to play tackle football. I'd avoided this but he promised we'd wear all the necessary equipment & he'd exhibit fair play. Hank would oversee the game, bringing along his Beta-Max video camera.

I figured since his Dad was coming, Danny couldn't do anything that horrific. We were, after all, in the company of a responsible adult.

We set up for our game; I was center & Monkeyface the nose-tackle opposition. He loomed over me like a brick wall, grinning sadism.

Jesse muttered *"hut"* & Danny toppled over me like timbering redwood, popping a vertebrae while knocking all the wind out of me, bending me in half like a twig with his mighty obese gut.

As I lay on the ground panting for breath & crying from the inability to feel my legs, big Hank – who to us would narrate self-explanatory action films – videotaped the entire episode: *"What's that? You can't feel your legs? You some kind of pussy or something?"* as all the bastard children surrounded me, laughing at my temporary paralysis.

I limped back to the Mitchell household where Hank proudly revealed the taping to the entire family. They replayed the tape to every kid from around the neighborhood for the next 3 years…

Ed hated Danny from the get-go. During a barbecue Eddie had urinated with anticipatory glee into a squirt gun and asked if he was thirsty. Coincidentally it was a scorching 104 degrees outside.

Ed called for drastic measures. He took me to a gun & knife show and purchased a WWII rifle stock. He disappeared into the garage that afternoon only to emerge with a .32 Caliber Remington replica, like the ones Hank made for Danny.

He was basking in the glow of his contraption as he handed it down: *"Tell Dan he can go to hell. If he gives you any shit, break his nose with the butt of your gun. I promise you won't get in any trouble."*

I thankfully accepted, running off to show the other children as he patted me on the back knowing he had done a good thing. It wasn't the masterpiece Hank would've produced – it was decrepit in comparison. Yet it symbolized a torch of defiance to a troubled boy...

Fuck, I'm jumping the gun – the whole Athena thing didn't begin until after Cathy, my first babysitter.

Cathy lived down the street and had twin girls that were 3 years older than me. I didn't like her too much and I really hated her kids.

Cathy was always at work so they ignored me or said mean things, and I'd just sit there alone. If the twins were around, I'd take these huge plastic jigsaw piece playground accessories and build a solitary prison cell. They'd knock & knock & I'd refuse to exit...

The last day of 2nd grade Cathy was in her car. She motioned for me to come close so I did and she pulled up a little, parking on my foot. Her window was rolled up and I started punching the glass and roof of the car. She sat there mouthing, *"What the fuck is your problem?"*

It went on like this for about 30 seconds until she rolled down her window and realized what was going on. She moved like lighting, flew me home and plopped my foot in ice water. It was squashed flat like a pancake but I didn't break any bones & it didn't hurt that bad.

I just sat there watching *Duck Tales* until my mom got home. Since then, my foot has gotten these random vicious cramps were it'll seize up hard and stay that way for at least 5 painful minutes.

Later that night I limped back over to Cathy's with a box-cutter & tried to slash her tires, although it was unproductive. The next day I was supposed to stay there, but I just went home & watched *Roger Rabbit...*

The Twins came over whapping the door & peering through the window, yet I hid under a blanket so they wouldn't see me. It was obvious I was present & Cathy came over, banging on the door freaking out.

I was crying in frustration, looking at her through the window. She kept demanding to know what was wrong and for me to let her in, tugging on the door handle from outside. I ran into the kitchen and scrawled the word "BITCH" on a piece of loose leaf paper with magic marker.

I snagged a huge butcher knife from the sink and ran towards the door in a rage. I held the paper to the window for her to read I kept stabbing my front door screaming and swearing in a head-sick rage, calling her a fucking cunt, a fucking whore...

I had quite a few moments like that back then. I'd acquired this plastic ninja star that had these suction cups on it and when you chucked it at the wall it was supposed to stick but never quite worked all that well.

Jesse and Dan stole it from me and I marched home and grabbed this rusty hammer from the basement. I brought it over and started swinging it at their heads, threatening to kill them. They were terrified & crying, and I just sauntered home laughing. Athena came over and gave my mom hell for it, who didn't seem to care.

Athena had this dead van that was always parked across the street. I brought over a can of gasoline and started dumping diesel all over it. I tried to ignite the blaze by banging rocks together like I learned in Boy Scouts, but it didn't work because they were from my mom's garden.

The next day I sat across the street watching Jesse's puzzled father searching for a line leak, just chuckling...

Boy Scout's didn't teach me much of anything and I only stayed in for three months. It ended when the den mother flipped out after her kid and I raced bare foot down the street in January.

She dragged him in by his hair, slapped the shit out him & forced the kid to take a bath while we were all in the basement mortified. We could hear water splashing upstairs – this kid weeping as she scrubbed him down, calling him a worthless piece of shit like his father…

I only wanted to learn how to make booby traps anyway, which I did on my own, digging deep holes and covering them with sticks and leaves like the Viet Cong.

At the bottom I put this giant board filled with nails I hoped to kill Bigfoot with (*I thought he was wandering my neighborhood because of this incident involving a raccoon smashing my window at night*) but since I could never get to Sasquatch, I went after Danny's younger sister.

The trap didn't kill her like I had hoped and she couldn't get out, so I started filling the hole with water from my garden hose, trying to drown her. She climbed out, Butchie beat me up and all was forgiven.

Despite trying to kill her, she was one of the only kids I actually liked on the block except for Jamison, who was obsessed with Monty Python and later was singer of my band Birth Of A Tragedy…

Another kid I was friends with was named Dustin, who lived a few blocks away. His mother had abandoned him to the care of his grandma, and his father was in prison. His nose always was running and any time he fell down in the summer he'd have mowed grass stuck to his upper lip.

Dustin was very strange and alienated, and would dangerously climb 30 foot pine trees to the very top and refuse to take a bath afterwards because he enjoyed being coated in sticky maple.

He was totally oblivious with no understanding of himself, always asking us to beat him up. We'd peg him with rocks as hard as we could, throw dirt in his eyes. Sometimes he'd just eat handfuls of mud.

I remember he was in my backyard, there was snow on the ground, but he took off all of his clothes so he was completely butt naked and had me spray him with the near frozen garden hose for 10 minutes while Jesse chucked rocks at him...

Athena's was one of the places I bounced around during those years. On occasion I'd stay with my uncle Craig at the Argyle House, my real home in my actual neighborhood that I always wanted to get back to.

He would teach me graphic design, spew the knowledge he acquired from the audiotapes. He was into advertising and taught me propaganda to force people into pathological purchasing habits. He always tried to make up for the vacuum my Dad left...

Now my Dad would still show up on occasion, maybe 3 times a year. Once randomly, the other two Christmas & Thanksgiving. He got remarried to the lady he cheated on my mom with and moved to Indiana.

Every time he showed up I either had a new half brother or met a new family member who I could never remember. Pops would take me to Coney Island, check out the waitress' ass, chain-smoke & pretend to listen to what I had to say. In 6th grade he moved back 'cause divorce...

So Dad started showing up more frequently because he now lived 20 minutes away. He made all sorts of promises, apologizing for not being around. We were communicating and enjoying our time together.

Right before my mom took him to court over neglected child support we saw *Jurassic Park* together at the $1 show. As he was about to drop me off I broke down and started crying.

I hugged him really hard and said I loved him & not to go away because my mommy was crazy & all the kids were mean to me and that I needed him more than anything in the world.

He told me that he loved me & we were a team & he wasn't going anywhere anytime soon. *That was the last I ever heard from him…*

I would also stay over my Aunt Sylvia's house a few days a week during the summer. It was in Taylor. The children were terribly sheltered; kind of like the Flanders kids from *The Simpsons* but replace Jesus Christ with Walt Disney. That's all we were really allowed to watch, and every possession was sci-fi or educational related.

There was not a semblance of the world's evil permitted to enter their minds. So susceptible were they that the end scene of *Gremlins* where Stripe shoots Billy with a crossbow made them wet their beds from night terrors so horribly the parents had to buy new mattresses. The third set of mattresses arrived when the *Alien 3* commercial started airing on TV.

The oldest cousin was like C-3PO, the youngest R2D2. They literally modeled themselves after *Droids*. We'd collect crystals, study paleontology, and game an awful lot of Monopoly.

When they played Nintendo they had every strategy guide and Game Genie code properly laid out so they could never lose, never experiencing challenge. We weren't allowed to go around the block or travel more then three houses from the parents sight.

They weren't normal kids; they were hypochondriacs with learning disabilities. They were terribly allergic to everything and would get badly sunburned after 20 minutes of exposure; these kids that never would've survived nature without the advents of modern science.

They used to own these really expensive power wheels that were big robots and rode them around the backyard all the time, which was directly behind this U-Haul industrial equipment center that would invariantly shoot huge bursts of diesel fumes. Just imagine watching these weird kids driving robots around while dizzy on operating crane fumes…

We were all obsessed with Nintendo. While waiting for my 8-bit system uncle Craig gave me his old-school Atari 2600. I played the thing non-stop for four days and it literally melted from over heating.

I was so crazed about NES that I would fantasize about it all day. This kid at the end of the West Dearborn block (*Pardee Street*) had a front porch that you could sneak up on silently. I was so addicted I used to stalk the family and watch them play *Zelda* through the porch window…

I read a lot as a kid, mostly comics. But not the usual Batman or Superman stuff. I was enamored by the heavy duty cold war satire punk comics I'd get from the independent store.

They had a "ten for a buck" bin with very graphic stuff that was usually kept behind the counter or only sold to older customers. The kids at the counter knew this, but would just wink at me and slip it by my mother, hoping to plant some fine seeds.

My favorite was The Punisher, because he was basically a serial killer that lived for revenge. Instead of swooping in with a cape and spouting morality tales, he'd just shoot junkies in the face or snap mafia guys' necks. He was my number one role model.

When I did read books, it was always about mythology, horror, the supernatural. My mother had fanatically barred me from reading anything involving witchcraft 'cause she had an unspoken past where fearful &

haunting things came as a result. I wanted an Ouija board from Toys R' Us, but she gave me terrified logic about not opening such doorways...

She never would talk about such issues, so I know nothing outside of finding her old Tarot cards which I'd attempt to read in the basement at age 7. She found me fooling with them, freaked & tossed them in the trash.

I overheard her say she thought she tossed them years ago after a reading came saying my grandmother would die. Coincidentally, she soon was diagnosed with cancer, and my mom semi-convinced herself it was all somehow her own doing, sinning by tarot cards...

My favorite book was about Vikings legends; I convinced myself I was a berserker (*later on I got really into all that black metal shit, which is probably of little surprise*). Following Odin's example, I'd attack the bullies out of hand. Clothesline them, punch or kick 'em for no reason, knock books out of their hands...

In retrospect, I guess I was the bully, and I was attacking innocent children for no reason other than the impulses in my head that said they were all out to get me and I was a Viking.

I'd come home every day covered in scrapes and bruises. Eddie turned me on to pro wrestling. He said, "*Between you and me, take notes. A good shot to the nuts and they'll drop like flies.*"

Now, the WWF stuff had been on in the background – at Grandma's, it was when MTV & WWF combined with Cyndi Lauper, Mr. T & *Hulkamania* – that huge moment & classic era of the industry. When I'd visit my father, my Grandpa was watching the old 1970's stuff – like the Jesse Ventura & Verne Gagne super-outlandish AWA stuff.

When Ed sat me down and made it a point for me to understand what was going on with the WWF, it all clicked – I was instantly hooked, for the rest of my life to varying degrees of attention-span. Mom & Ed thought the stuff was hilarious, because they – just like my Gramps – were raised on the 1970's Saturday Night stuff.

They explained how it wasn't "real" but it wasn't "fake" either, and that it was all a big show meant to entertain you, and even though it was decided already who would win or lose, the sport was making the greatest show they could. How the bad guys weren't really bad guys, that the art of their performance is making you hate them, because that was "The Joke."

They basically had me compute it from the standpoint of an adult knowing Santa Clause isn't real but explaining "The Joke" of Santa & what adults say to each other about Santa when the kids aren't looking.

Pro Wrestling was the same thing – except there were endless Santa's – so many, it fooled & clouded your vision, like an endless sea of red tape to cut & mirages preventing you realizing it was 100% scripted.

Even knowing it's a show, the art is like a magic illusionist such as David Copperfield – the wool is pulled over your eyes, and it was impossible to distinguish what was real & what was fake.

Pro Wrestling was a perplexing, hilarious carnival – and in the cheeseball 1980s, it was presented as a cartoon. It really was the closest you could see in real life of Comic Book superheroes battling each other.

Until *Batman* 1989 (which still had 2 more years before existing), almost every Comic Book movie or TV show attempted sucked – all we had was Lou Ferigno's *Hulk*, Reeves *S.Man* & that *Swamp Thing* movie. Pro Wrestling was the closest we ever got to seeing some epic battle between *Avengers* & *Justice League*.

Watching Bad News Brown whoop the competition filled me with the will to fight back. I wanted to know all the wrestlers, all their feuds – I came at WWF like a psychologist, enamored by every angle of the production. I watched it as if a crew member filming it, a stage-hand operating it, a scriptwriter consulting the writers team, as if a board member alongside Vince McMahon, whom no one even knew was the guy behind this whole crazy thing like a Willy Wonka the entire time, hidden in plain site as a mild mannered, bow-tie sports announcer.

I started Hogan-booting & body-slamming antagonists into the brutal concrete playground, expecting the Intercontinental Championship. This just caused the fights to increase in their severity. Every day I'd stumble home bloody nosed & teary; Eddie'd say *"Clean yourself up."*

I began to live for violence & enjoyed making the other children's lives miserable, indiscriminately – punching & kicking for no reason.

To freak them out, just for fun, in that angry punk rock shocking way – I'd slam my head into a locker as hard as I could, or take my Social Studies textbook and blast it into my skull. Knock myself into concussions for amusement, laughing ta the pain...

I hated everyone & wanted to ruin it for everyone. I'd sit in music class and make up my own lyrics like *"Frosty the faggot snowman/had a very stinky butt/he never used to like me/so I shot him in the face."*

In art I'd draw pictures of classmates and teachers being stabbed, shot, defenestrated or mutilated by Jason Voorhees. My creative writing demonstrated the same impulse. I wanted everyone to hate me as much as I did them, so I'd do anything to shock them.

When everyone came in from recess, I'd be in the hallway licking the floor as hard as I could, telling everyone how salty and great it was from the snow-melting rock residue.

During lunch I noticed a kid get in trouble, forced to sit by himself on the other side of the cafeteria. It looked great, so I had to. I kept sprinkling donut crumbs in this girl's hair but they just told me to stop. I started throwing food at kids and lunch ladies gave the evil eye.

Finally, I grabbed this kids t-shirt, stretched the hell out of its neck, and used it as a clutch so I could keep punching him in the side of the head. After that I was sent to the other side of the cafeteria to dine alone.

When they tried to reintroduce me after my punishment,, I attacked another kid. From then on I was permanently on the other side of the lunch room. I was so happy to be hated & alone. I was back in that hospital hallway with the flickering lights where grandma died; no one else existed.

I decided I wanted to be totally isolated so I ran over from cafeteria quarantine & threw a punch at some hapless, random victim. *They permanently sent me to lunch in an empty auditorium!* It felt great to be the most hated kid in the school. I'd sit there & laugh hard as I could, make loud fart noises that echoed throughout the empty halls...

The teachers weren't sure if I was insane or misunderstood. They knew I was smart because I scored in the top 10% of all students in the country on my MEAP and IOWA scores.

My mom used to yell at the principal and he thought she was crazy until she took off my shirt in front of him and showcased all my cuts and bruises. He sent out the word and the teachers started to intervene.

I got sent to Mrs. Clemence, the school social worker. I just played with naked Gumby men in lumps of warm clay as she asked me questions. They weren't scary talks; she reminded me of grandma.

Anytime I felt like getting into a fight or doing something nuts I was allowed to go to her office and draw or paint. I was given an endless recess pass as long as I didn't do anything psychotic.

From that point on I roamed the school freely. While everyone was at lunch I'd break into classrooms and go through desks just to see what was in them. I'd spit in teacher coffee cups & rub my dick on the handles, slop glue on their leather desk-seats like a Harpo Marx sabotage.

Then I'd go visit my friends in the defunct science room. It was my special place filled with jars of dead roaches, butterflies, toads, snakes in embalming fluid, and a preserved monkey brain. I'd speak to my friends clam as a happy eating PB&J sandwiches…

It was during those solitary winter months that I encountered my 3rd ghost.

I was in this bathroom no one ever used & out of toilet paper. I couldn't pull up my pants cause I'd get poop on 'em, so I covertly lunged out the stall & into the other, grabbed T.P. & was about to re-enter my throne when I got one of those radar blips – I heard this kid laughing at me. I whipped up my jeans, flipped around – nobody was there...

I started noticing that blip all over the building. Shit started getting weird with my belongings, things would turn up missing in my desk and locker, then returning days or weeks later.

It was like I had an invisible 6 year old playing pranks. Even now, sometimes it seems like the little bastard is still misplacing my keys…

Shortly after the Elvis impersonating rapist fiasco occurred...

When my mom stopped at a pharmacy to pick up medication, I bumped into this eerie slime-ball with greasy, jet black hair. He gave one of those dominant impressions of pure death. On our way to the parking lot we saw a car with Elvis bumper stickers & a license plate "MEMPHIS1."

2 weeks later on *Unsolved Mysteries* was a segment about this Elvis impersonator that raped & murdered women in Las Vegas. After the bad reenactments it showed pics of him & his car with "MEMPHIS1."

My mom called the hot-line – they'd received dozens of tips regarding his whereabouts in Michigan, and he was nailed in hours. From then on I thought Elvis was going to pull a Sideshow Bob on me. I used to have nightmares of him inside my closet, knife between his teeth…

As that summer carried on, Ed's drinking increased in severity; he'd been fired drinking on the job. I waited for the great hope that would stabilize his deteriorating relationship with my mom.

He took me to job interviews: *"Give the man starved looks,"* he told me. He successfully won over the chemical plant & on the way home we cracked open a beer for victory (*we always drove drunk together*).

A few days later I returned home after a rough game of NIGGER; Eddie was shit-faced on the couch, chuckling at a *Jefferson's* rerun: *"I had to quit that job buddy, the fumes were killing me."*

I went in my room, holding back tears waiting for my mother to come: *"IT'S US OUR YOUR FUCKING BOOZE!!!"*

Ed was halfway out the door when I ran up clutching the *Archie* comics he'd given me. They were the last artifacts of his childhood. *"It's ok buddy - You keep 'em."* He stumbled out the screen door, hopped into his truck & drove off, never looking back…

extracurricular

Where I work is Fairlane Grounds. With the exception of Davis, I'm the only white guy on the shift.

Like most jobs I've kept my subversive mouth shut in a ripe attempt of normalcy until 9-11 dragged me into the debate. Now I'm one of the most popular guys, especially among the Arabs.

I started working at Fairlane Grounds about a month before 9-11. I'd talk about terrorist groups with the Arab guys and they would joke: *"Ryan you are ok – but when the Jihad comes, we must kill you, haha."*

Nasser loves to bullshit about the insanity of Christians while Gamal preaches the wisdom of the Quran, hoping to covert me. He tells me I am his friend and wants Allah to protect me when America falls.

Ahmed, who is married to his cousin and saving to open a grocery store in Yemen, feeds me mouthfuls of the exotic, psychedelic plant Caad in exchange for rides home.

He barely speaks English yet I understand every word that comes out of his mouth. I'm his translator when we're together on Lionel's crew, who is this old black guy that stops to pray to this Virgin Mary statue every night 'cause his wife is dying of cancer. Old Lionel say's he'll shoot me if he finds out I'm writing about him.

Amar, who is an Iraqi refugee under political asylum, doesn't like any of them. He says they're all full of shit and especially dislikes Ahmed, who is always dancing around singing the Saddam song. Saddam Hussein executed Amar's cousin as a dissident during the Gulf War...

Our original foreman used to work us like a prison gang but was fired after a brain seizure. Under Michigan law he couldn't operate heavy machinery for another year.

Facey, my new General Foreman, thinks Amar is a pedophile: *"Faggots! Faggots I tell you - all of them! It is common in the Middle East – they fuck little boys. Just like Arafat – the Mossad got him fucking little boys on video. Anytime he goes on diplomatic missions it's in his contract that he gets little boys to fuck! Fucking pedophiles!"*

Facey is this paranoid black guy from Belize; he's got a strong Jamaican sounding accent & talks conspiracy theories. He brought in his photo album of hot South American chicks he banged, and laughed uncontrollably explaining the comedic stories behind his greatest lays.

He talks about elemental creatures arising from the mist, and having to deal with tigers in his back yard – a farmer he knew that raped goats by sticking them in a rubber suit with him so every time it kicked its hind legs back the fun was felt.

He keeps encouraging me to go after the 20 year old hot blonde girl I work with. She is the good seed of her twin sister, a nice drug-free girl that's in total Disney territory.

We have a thing for each other but she's joining the police academy soon, and I am a black market pyrate. Therefore, she will never keep the horrendous secrets needed kept quiet within my serious relationships, and it is forbidden territory in general.

But we did go to Canada and I booty-grinded her hard in front of her boyfriend in some sleezy Windsor nightclub. That was last week, and she just dumped him. I feel like the black goat of the easy sheep.

It would only end in travesty, and I do not wish to blacken her soul, not this one. Yet still, as the internal debate rages, Facey will lean into my ear with wide eyes & a smile: *"Go for her Rye-unn – she will geeeve you that pussy..."*

My other job is as a music journalist for Real Detroit Weekly – a free newspaper with an estimated 200,000 readers per week.

I knew I walked into a good thing from the very start 'cause my editor's office resembled my bedroom circa '96. He's a NIN/Tool fanatic that's never censored me.

It doesn't pay much but I'm gaining a lot of clout in the music scene. I get into any concert I want for free and I average about 20 free CDs a week. I have a bi-weekly column called "*Mentality Of One*" where I ramble on about heavy metal and whatever else I feel.

I also do one called "*Postmodern Dystopia*" where I run political snippets, bizarre facts, weird stories. It's the first political thing the paper has ever touched.

We mostly do advertorial crap for dance clubs, restaurants & concerts. I take great pride in tearing apart lackluster nu-metal albums and all of the major labels fear me while the indies love me 'cause I'm a walking encyclopedia of underground metal...

It's all part of *The Revolution* – "the entertainment division." My master-plan is to find as many quality unsigned acts as possible, promote the shit out of them, network like crazy, send demos to all of my contacts, and get as many bands signed as humanly possible. Right now I'm helping out a few dozen groups...

One by one we prop up franchises in every major city, a huge union of tribes. It is a do or die situation against those controlling the dials.

We have to take back the industry that's polluted the minds of the youth with Korn Bizkit, Puddle Of Creed, New Found Charlotte, Sum 182, & a myriad of other such dubious amalgams.

Real Detroit won't bring me in full time yet which is why I'm at Fairlane Grounds. I hope they do sometime soon 'cause I'm sick of crap jobs and want to get paid to sit on my ass & listen to Immortal...

All of the contacts I've been making will no doubt help out my musical ambitions. I'm playing drums in this band called Birth Of A Tragedy, though I'm primarily a guitarist. Jamison is the singer. You may remember him from earlier 'cause he grew up on Pardee Street too.

Also in the band are the Mackenzie brothers. Chris is an overly sensitive metal-head and his brother is flaming. They've been in about 20 bands that have gone nowhere, except Tortured Lovely.

They opened for Cradle of Filth once, the "Big Score Gig." Chris used to play guitar for Third World Amerika, my terrible, one-dimensional metal band in high school...

Unlike the million projects preceding its conception, BOAT isn't metal or industrial or punk – not exactly. We're a cross between Zappa, Mr. Bungle, Dead Kennedys & Tub Ring; real wacky & theatrical.

We're going to Albuquerque in Spring 'cause Mackenzie's mom runs a production house there with unlimited studio time. I'm unsure of this move. Besides, if one goes "all the way," why Albuquerque & not LA?

We run around like the Marx Brothers with as many stage props as a Gallagher stage-show. It is our plan, once famous, to unsuspectingly release a record of raw misanthropic thrash, death & black metal to forever corrupt the minds of the youth...

Jamison spazzes out, rolls around, smashes pumpkins over his head & rants gibberish monologues between songs. Talking to him is like watching a rock doc on VH1. He'll mimic celebrities, act out dialogues in character – one minute he's Sinatra, the next Lux Interior...

Birth of a Tragedy has no fan base. Among our age group, the places we play such as I-Rock, Paycheck's, the Harpo's locals – Detroit is a scene dominated by Pantera bands.

And again, among our age group and influence, no one has a real cohesive DIY process. Everyone is swinging in the dark, just playing gigs with whoever the local bar books, and it's like 10 of their friends, and people just show up and take off afterwards.

No one in the Detroit suburbs has a grip on promotion, and bands are selling tickets & getting ripped off to open for a major band, like this is important on a resume.

The Pantera bands do not "get us," and we don't know any weird locals on a personal basis. That's why I want to declare total war on the music scene and picket our own shows...

The only attention we've received is due to our bassist – she's the sole reason we made the cover of Jam Rag, the next largest after Real Detroit. She's this cute black-haired goth chick, army boots and fishnets, a little Twiggy Ramirez worshipper.

She's real quiet & takes panic attack pills all the time. She can't really play bass well & the Mackenzie brothers write all of her parts 'cause she refuses to write anything except for this really lazy Peter Steele rip-off riff she's constantly trying to force into a composition...

Splinters of Separation

It wasn't long after Eddie when my mom hooked up with her boss. I met him early into 5th grade after a grizzly bout of *Smear The Queer*. This tubby guy was lounging on the couch, talking like an 80's sitcom.

That was Toby – a cop & once upon a time racist bastard. This is 1991, when he was a complete asshole. Nowadays, 2001, he's dropped the N-bomb dropping asshole routine. He finally "grew up" in his 60's, after his daughter had black babies. But back then, he was a total fuck.

In those days, Toby & I never connected at any human level. We simply could not. Not only was his worldview the antithesis of all which punk rock stood for, he was extremely impatient, film illiterate, hadn't read a book since high school – and an ultra-conservative Reganite.

He had no taste in music, told nigger jokes, mocked the "freaky" & pissed endlessly about leeches on Food Stamps. He was so anal retentive he'd compulsively wake in the middle of the night to clean the house.

When he himself was a kid, Toby always dreamed of joining the Navy. When the 'Nam draft came he thought it a sane idea to beat the system by choosing his military branch of choice.

Despite his lifelong dream, at the recruiting station the Navy guy was on lunch and, hating lines, he refused to wait 20 minutes & joined the Marines 'cause they had cool looking uniforms...

He was in the jungle for a year and a half as a recon sniper, living in a tree and surviving off grubs, spiders & bark. He had 13 confirmed kills by the time he stepped on a landmine.

He was awarded a medal of honor and occasional paycheck for exposure to Agent Orange, which in turn gave his children scoliosis.

Whenever he goes through metal detectors the siren wails because he has so much shrapnel lodged in his calf.

In the early 1970's, he joined the Detroit PD as a beat cop, being shot at by snipers atop freeway overpasses. He was an undercover NARC befriending dealers for years at a time & had dozens of hits on his head. He got out & transferred to a desk job 'cause he was sick of paranoia.

Momma thought since I was into Danzig I would think he was cool for shooting someone in the back of the head & pissing in his skull. Not only did she need to alter her attitude and interests to accommodate him, but I had to fall in line as well. I had to shape-shift overnight, spic-and-span so he'd stay in the picture.

When she realized how deeply molded I was she swelled with anger. She'd no understanding of what my world was like, nor would she listen. In denial, she convinced herself of my perfectly happy childhood.

Fangs bared & temper flaring, she ruthlessly began her assimilation. She started cutting me down, physically attacking me for not changing too. I liked the wrong movies, listened to the wrong music. I had incorrect thoughts.

My mother projected herself nervously. She'd storm in the door after work and would viciously scream or erratically nurture me like one of her cats. The only real communication was via entertainment industry – movies & gossip, or gossip with the family, always like a dogmatic church lady shaking a finger, deriding everyone else while doing nothing but scowling, complaining & self-shaming. Always mocking the idiot co-worker or talking shit on our family & all their deficiencies.

If I ever brought up her chameleon nature I was a liar and a fraud – a terribly deluded child. Before Toby, I felt I could still go to her. I could still talk, if even a polite version of the truth. Even midst this rugged disrepair, we'd still have some fun.

She had a twisted sense of humor. She loved *Kids In The Hall*, *Monty Python*, *The 'Burbs*. Black humor triumphed between us. But none of that wasn't funny anymore because Toby didn't get it – "weird" was shameful, cast out like a leper...

She was a chameleon – a nonperson without a definitive personality. Now she was the Toby doppelganger, playing human chess to restructure me into what he wanted as a son.

They started taking me on "vacations" – thinly veiled weekend affairs. Toby would attempt to convert me to the GOP & a military career. He'd take me to Navy shipyards to look at Destroyers, hailing the murderous firepower, shit-talk Clinton for letting faggots in the army. He actually gave me George Bush trading cards, wrapped with a little bow.

The first was a trip to Washington D.C. We saw all the landmarks – The White House, The Smithsonian, The Magna Carta. Then they'd disappear into a second hotel room, leaving me to watch pay per view movies. It went on like this for a lengthy stretch...

One of the last things I remember before the illness was class baseball.

The teacher drew names out of a hat to decide team captains – myself and another kid who bribed me with Gretzky cards so he'd have the first two picks. The first choice was mine and I fingered the nerdy kid with the three craters running down his forehead like nasty, infected zits.

The pre-jock took the cream of the crop and then I picked the second best player in the class because I hated him and wanted to make him angry. Afterwards I kept drafting the worst losers until there was a team of fat kids, nerds, girls and weaklings versus a team of child pros...

I thought it would be like an after school special where the freaks would win 'cause we had the most heart. Instead we got our asses handed.

However, I'm still amazed at the level of playing that came out of my team – kids who never had any athletic inclination were practicing after school in preparation for the fight against the great, common enemy...

I was pretty athletic back then, or tried to be. I'd mess up the rules of the games though 'cause I never had a father to teach me. Captain's would choose girls over me in draft just to laugh at my pained expressions.

The kids always judged each other by the sports clothes they wore. I collected sports cards & sold them like currency, like a hustler at the tent of an Egpytian Bazaar – comics too, of course. But I wasn't "geeked" for sports – even though like everyone I wore team hats & shirts.

Since we were so poor I could only buy whatever was on the clearance rack – I'd get laughed at for wearing the bottom-barrel teams of every league. Once I convinced my mom to buy this White Sox t-shirt, who were blistering at the time with Frank Thomas. Some kid ruined it by sticking gum on the back because I "*wasn't worthy.*"

I should Mention Sid now, my buddy who was a natural born monster. He had bright red hair & a bleeding rage in his eyes.

I met him in 4th grade when he jumped me with a few others. His lackey hopped my back and had his arms around my neck. I threw myself backwards and crushed him into the monkey-bars, flipping him over my shoulders to the ground.

The next kid rushed at me & I punted him in the stomach, pivoted & kicked the other in the knee. Sid came swinging & I elbowed him in the face. A few more punches were thrown but I ducked & kept whapping these kids until they capitulated in retreat...

After that Sid & I were friends, sort of. He'd just float around like one of Bart Simpson's bad kid peers. By 6th grade we started teaming up out of mutual affection for malicious destruction, and by high school he'd lapsed manic bi-polar and would gobble handfuls of meds to get high.

He existed to fist-fight, shoplift, vandalize, sell drugs (*only cause it was illegal, not for cash*), procure explosives, commit computer fraud & burn the world through extremist arson. I have never met such a devoted Danzig fan, nor anyone as Arachnophobic...

I was a fanatic of a British comic book called "*Spellbinders (AKA "Nemesis The Warlock")*." Nemesis was an demonic looking alien that was a revolutionary fighting a covert guerrilla war against Torquemada, a genocidal Darth Vader figure.

I had this dream where I was fighting alongside Nemesis as a character called Hobbes that only existed within my imagination. I wore a white gentlemanly suit with black tie, had a large scar running down my left eye and was a diplomat of sorts.

When I woke up I wanted nothing more than to go back to the intergalactic *revolucion*. I began forcing myself to sleep at all hours of the day just to get there. And after awhile, I just believed it was real...

Since then, my dreams have been continuations of fictional realities. For instance, I may have a dream where I'm a detective solving a homicide. I'll wake up, forget about it for years, but then it'll randomly return exactly where I'd left off, like a movie on pause.

All of this dreamscape is connected in some way, and all the dream stories take place within it. Detroit is subliminally restructured as a labyrinth of sorts, a dark Metropolis in which Zug Island itself is the beating, blackened heart. Zug Island, the pulsating core of filth, the sternum of the inferno, the mad genius of the operation ...

Every day after school I'd torch newspapers, homework assignments, dead animals. I taught all the neighborhood kids the best methods of application. I'd head up to Sunoco, buy 50 cents worth of gasoline and get to work. This overwhelming desire reached its apex post-7th grade summer when Sid and I nearly set a local strip mall on fire.

We were on the train track viaduct fumbling around with this road flare I stole from my mom's trunk. We had gone up there to drink piss-warm 40's and all of the vegetation was brown and dead. Pieces of silk laundry were spread among the tracks, so we gathered all of them into a rusted old shopping cart.

I took a leak inside the mall and came back to discover a half-dozen fireman in full regalia blasting their hoses on a massive blaze that had taken out two trees and the dead brushes. Sid had chucked the lit flare in the cart, kicked it down the hill and just walked away...

I'd pick up a dozen plus boxes from the fruit market and drag them into my basement after school and just go ape-shit with a crowbar, thrashing everything in sight while jamming Nine Inch Nail's *Broken* on my boombox. Afterwards I'd set it all on fire for pure joy... The way the flame burned – *the purification of ash...*

Broken had a tremendous psychological impact on me. The first time I hit play I was horrified by the record – I thought Satan was trying to communicate directly, like its dissonance was going to replace my soul.

I hid the cassette under my bed and refused to listen to it for 2 months. But it was always there, taunting me to be thrown back on...

It was only after the Shattered Mary that I did so. I listened to the entire tape in one sitting, so unspeakably filthy and glorious: *"Don't Open Your Eyes You Won't Like What You See/The Blind Have Been Blessed With Security/Stick My Hands Thru The Cage of This Endless Routine/Just Some Flesh Caught In This Big Broken Machine..."* *"Gave Up Trying To Figure Out My Head Got Lost Along The Way/Worn Out From Giving It Up My Soul I Pissed It All Away/Still Stings These Shattered Nerves Pigs We Get What Pigs Deserve/I'm Going All The Way Down I'm Leaving Today...* *"Smashed Up My Sanity Smashed Up My Integrity smashed Up What I Believed In Smashed Up What's Left of Me/Smashed Up My Everything Smashed Up All That Was True Gonna Smash Myself To Pieces I Don't Know What Else To Do/After Everything I've Done I Hate Myself For What I've Become/I Tried I Gave Up Throw It Away..."*

I ventured into the basement at dusk, orange light pouring through the windows. I had those vibrations rumbling through me, all those warped sound-freak noises, all that hatred & self-destruction.

I stared at myself in the old stand-up mirror I'd trash picked. My eyes were a cold, receding blue. Sweat dripped from my forehead, my hair hung like loose grass.

I snagged a lead-pipe from the ground & attacked the mirror , shards flying through the air, spilling across the floor. I dropped to my knees examining a hundred selves in the fragments...

I was a devout Catholic, regardless of all. I'd pray every night, speak to God all the time. I wanted to be a priest, or more sincerely, a vigilante killer in the name of God.

When Jesse and I would play hide and go seek at this church his father used to operate the boiler at, I'd often disappear halfway through the game and be found praying at the alter. Theft had a certain resonance with me. At age 9 I found a faux-Roman coin looking earring on the floor of a department store and stuck it in my pocket.

The next day I asked my mom what God did to thieves. She told me all about demons and endless torture. I prayed to Christ for forgiveness but no sign came. I was going to ride my bike all the way across town in the middle of the night and slip it under the door to be cleansed. Massive, bottomless guilt stayed with me from that sole action...

When we received a cable-thieving black-box through Toby, I protested heavily to no avail. I watched my mother slip deeper into sin and hypocrisy. When I questioned her about it, she just laughed as if immune.

But I soon gave in, watching endless porn on the Spice Channel – hours upon hours of lesbianism & BDSM. My mom would still rant about sex as filth, about how all fags would be murdered by god, about degeneracy, about how all females were vile whores...

But when we started getting phone sex mags sent sloppily to our house all the time, I'd steal them for myself. I attempted to start wanking off but had no idea what I was doing, and my junk didn't really work yet. I knew I felt that itch, but was totally confused how it worked.

I was enamored by the bondage depictions – I'd aesthetically observe leather fuck pyramids as a critic would the Roman statues of a museum, cause it was all some weird comic book that I did not take seriously. I had no idea why any of these people would ever want this stuff to happen to them. But I guess this is what sex really was – some freak-show where you try to "out-do" each other like *The Gong Show*...

It was fall; I was wearing a blue denim jacket with the lapels up like an 80's rebel, hiding in the darkness of my room. Mom burst in screaming at me for no reason, slamming the door shut. The ragged vibrations sent the statue hanging above my doorway crashing to the ground.

In seemingly slow motion I watched it shatter – the Virgin Mary cradling baby Jesus – the porcelain splitting perfectly between the two icons. The symbolic nature adequately showcased the dreary current. I waited until she was in her oblivious television womb before I climbed out the bedroom window & wandered the drizzling streets for hours...

We started seeing Dr. Hendrik, who grilled me with questions while mother hovered in the seat next to me, disapproving and angry. I wouldn't talk to him, not after all the threats of institutionalization on her behalf. I sat like stone giving vague answers, only wanting to sleep so I could fight alongside Nemesis in my white suit.

A kid in the adjoining room started beating his head against the wall so hard it shook the timber. Mom, Hendrik and I all heard the other doctor and mom screaming for the other kid to stop, but the child kept crying & bashing his face against the wall. I was gut-laughing – sincere, deep hysterics; my mother fell into anguished sobs...

She started taking me fishing, bowling, horseback riding – all activities which Hendrik designed to make us close that rift. All of them were disasters 'cause I would only give simple answers when spoken to and she'd hold back tears, cutting me down, saying God would punish me.

I told her that nothing she could do to me would ever hurt me again. She began cursing, screaming & chucked a light bulb at my head. I just kept laughing at her like a demented clown no matter how hard as she repeatedly slapped me...

I stopped talking or dealing with her at all beyond a business level. I made the conscience decision to bury my emotions. I was the machine of anti-Zen, concentrating on the purist hatred & violence...

I used to go to the Boy's & Girls Club a lot 'cause it was a nice alternative to Athena's. None of the other kids from school or my neighborhood went there either, making it a neutral reality.

Most of the kids were black, dumped off as inexpensive babysitting. I'd never talk to anyone – just shoot pool, play Kayla, paint, or make ceramic dragons.

Sometimes I'd play basketball with the black kids who actually taught me the rules and I did ok. I'd participate in wrestling tournaments and did rather well, but I soon gave it up 'cause I felt like a queer wearing that skimpy skin-tight Kurt Angle outfit.

I went there off and on for about two years until I felt a too old for it. It wasn't girls that diverted me, but the promise of chaos. Plus they kept busting staff for child molestation...

When I wasn't at the Boys Club or wandering the streets doing random arson or vandalism, I'd be lost in my headphones listening to metal tapes from Columbia House & BMG. You'd sign a contract to get 8 albums free – but in return you'd have to order 4 more over 3 years.

I penned intro offers under fake aliases, paying them off with the cash I'd get helping Jesse on his newspaper route. If you were able to get someone to sign up to Columbia House, you'd get a bonus 4 albums free, which I was able to hustle out of 10 kids or so. Started since 6th grade.

Metallica's *Black Album* was the first record I ever owned, a present on my 11th birthday. I thought it was the heaviest thing ever made. So you can understand the mind-blowing experience I had jamming Sepultura's *Arise* the first time.

Even though Jesse bought metal records, it was only half-hearted. He never really listened to them & only collected as an excuse to feel superior to me. I was made fun of daily for loving NIN, especially by Athena, who thought nothing worthwhile had been created since 1979. Within a year, Jesse listened to nothing but Dr. Dre & the like...

If there was any one band we agreed on, it was Pantera, whom his uncle had secretly passed a "best of" tape to 'cause Athena was horrified of the language. *Holy shit was that band brutal!*

Everything savage about Sepultura was streamlined with hook-oriented chops & lyrics that spoke to us clearly. Anthems like "*Walk*" & "*A New Level Of Confidence*" did so much to help me find the will to fight back...

By 8th grade I saw Pantera live, my first authentic concert with opener Type O Negative. Touring on *Far Beyond Driven,* Anselmo was at his peak. I saw a political rally, a gathering of strength – the dynamic evidence of an uprising calling for a new society...

Anselmo was not a rock star but was a Five-Star General. His directly preachy rhetoric elicited brotherhood, vigor, indivisibility.

I snuck by security & entered main floor, thrashing around the mosh pit with huge skinheads happy to see a young bastard with so much heart. When it was all said and done, I mesed my neck up so badly from head-banging that my skull hung limply to my shoulders the next 2 days...

Jesse started hanging out with mean-spirited hood-rats – drug-addled white kids with no artistic grace in the damage they caused. They were blunt, ugly, numb-skull – and the first kids around me to openly use drugs.

Calvin was the main character, a blonde skater with a lengthy record at 14. Even though Calvin & I fist-fought often, he seemed to like me. Like so many of these maniac children, he'd slug me in the face then pat me on the back in the blink of an eye.

One day Fat Joe called giggling stupid with a weak prank call. It wasn't a big deal but Calvin was on my porch, egging me on, revving me up to do something to him as if he himself were the one insulted. So we went to kick Fat Joe's ass.

We banged on his door, I had a baseball bat in hand. We thugged him into apologizing, threatening to split open his head. I told him if he ever talked to me again I'd put him in the hospital. He didn't understand why. Shit, either did I – Fat Joe was my only real friend.

Calvin & I walked to a park and started busting off the fence caps with my Louisville slugger. The neighbor caught us – he had Calvin by the arm, lugging him forward. I drifted back & ran for it. They soon showed up at my house, 'cause Calvin snitched once he threatened cops.

My mom began checking all of my friend's police records – a practice repeated religiously until the end of high school and beyond. Everyone was an enemy, stealing or plotting against her…

Fast forward to 7th grade when Cassum & I have English class together. The teacher wrote these sayings on the board we had to copy & hand in at the end of semester or we'd fail the class. I had all but 5 & she humiliated me in front of the room, openly failing me to set an example – *telling me she was going to have me held back a year!*

She handed my notebook back with a smirk – *"BITE ME BITCH!!!"* I smacked her in the face with it & chucked it at her boobs.

Cassum, who I had never talked to before, exploded with laughter. The class was in shock; the teacher sprang up, grabbed my hair & dragged me to the principal's office by my ear…

The Principal exuded the radiance of a dirty old cabbie: *"It's alright kid – she's a fucking bitch. Just write a fake apology & I won't call your house*." And I got away with it too, until my mom met her. That was the reason we started seeing Dr. Hendrik in the first place...

Cassum & I had two other classes that year – math & gym. The math teacher was always breaking down, crying & running out of the room 'cause she couldn't handle the pressure.

She slapped me in front of the class, then realized what she'd done; I used it as blackmail to get a B- 'cause I knew mom would never have believed anything higher.

The kid that sat next to me in that class never said a word and one day he disappeared without a trace. Turns out he went home, grabbed up a needle from his mothers sewing kit & stabbed his puppy in the face until it dropped dead. He was committed and no one ever heard from him again.

It was also in that same math class that I decided hop a boxcar to Atlanta. It was a Friday; I was to stay with Aunt Sylvia & the robot kids that weekend as regulated by adultery.

I got a bathroom pass & began wandering the school working up the gall to leave. I panicked, deluded, and tried to find the room with all of the toads & snakes & monkey brains from elementary.

I needed my friends – I needed to sleep so I could join Nemesis in battle. I was caught erratically trying to break into a janitors closet & sent to the principal. They thought my uncle was molesting me or something...

That summer I was sent to a week long camp against my will for yet another adultery vacation, beyond protests from my family for my mother to stay home. They knew I was drifting far out but she wouldn't listen.

It was during isolation at camp when the sickness began creeping in. Sitting in this bed-bunk cabin – breathing in the darkness like a vaccine, staring into the moon; *thoughts fragmenting, that cold thing in my gut*

churning, pain & humiliation subsiding in erratic thought vibrations to a
grim sense of nothingness & misanthropy...

The period leading from then until my suicide is a black hole... Coming
into my bedroom, "Burn" by The Cure – everything crimson, sparrow
shadows across the walls... *Smelling things that weren't there, hearing*
voices, shoving pieces of metal into my skin... Throwing knives in the
basement, cutting my arms with razors as angels glide the velvet sky...
Holding a brochure from the "Alliance of the Mentally Ill," circling all of
the disturbances listed, praying someone would expose and commit me...
Fighting Danny on Jesse's lawn – he was jumping in the air, landing on my
stomach knees first; I was spitting blood... *Contemplating suicide to*
dethrone Satan and liberate all souls in torment... In gym class naked
backed into a shower corner, laughing jocks whipping me with wet towels,
praying for God to have mercy on their souls... My bike is stolen and I
nearly am jumped by a mob of 20 who all laugh & spit in my face...
Running over the corpse of a pregnant squirrel with my bike until fetuses
spray all over the pavement... Bedroom walls breathing, mutating,
constructed of fish eggs... *Drinking bad gin & smoking plastic...*

ONYX

"How does it feel knowing that with the slightest twitch of a muscle I can slit your throat?" Onyx is slowly running his index finger across Kluck's forehead, which is beaded entirely with cold sweat.

Kluck, the fearless drug-beast who's legendary in the hardcore, death-wish, opiate abyss of the rave scene now appears to be nothing more than a deer caught in the headlights of a Mack truck.

I'd attempt to fudge this psychological scenario but Onyx just slammed a 5th of Mohawk and is in the prime of his abilities. *"That's how the magic works,"* or so he claims. *"THINK FAST – what do you do?"* Kluck is petrified, butcher knife three layers into his skin.

"FUCK, YOU'RE DEAD!!" Onyx blindly chucks the cutlery over his shoulder and hops to his feet – *"Now we fight."* Onyx grabs the masking-taped boa staff and tosses Kluck (*whom he keeps referring to as "Space Monkey"*) a similar weapon, dragging him outside for a duel of vicious self-discovery.

I'm remain on the davenport which reeks like "The Drunken Master" (*a.k.a. the babbling, incoherent man who's been hammered for 15 years straight*), eavesdropping through the cracked window. *"Alright, come at me!"* Onyx demands.

Kluck begs to be discharged from this test of stamina. I hear a hard, wood-to-skull thunk before Onyx shouts, *"Wrong answer! Come at me!"* The plead-hit-thud pain carnival clods onward 2 more minutes before Kluck retaliates full force.

It sounds like Big John and Friar Tuck are going at it out there. I crack a smile knowing that I have done a good thing, for once dawn arrives, Kluck will have completed basic training. Another soldier of *The Revolution* will be unleashed among the rising sun of a glorious new era...

How I came to meet Onyx is another story entirely in itself. Kluck, on the other hand, is a "Regular" – an associate of the East Side Crew...

I never actually dealt with him beyond a business level until earlier this year. The entire crew was present, rolling face or snorting K. I opted for the K & occasional blunt because I had a real sweet tooth for pills and knew if I ever got really into them the way the others did, I'd just as well be signing my death warrant.

The essential trap of ecstasy is such – MDMA, upon first roll, is a simulacrum for reaching the deepest sanctums of repressed emotion. As the pharmaceutical aberration burns up your entire stockade of serotonin in one massive wave of pleasure, all aspects of the mind-fire dharma graph to your soul, pure and true.

The beauty of life's forgotten promise brings tears of joy as each emotional jolt is light-years beyond the speed of pain. Everyone that comes near is your immediate best friend.

Rolling together you'll examine the arcane contours of your souls in unison with a childlike exuberance – sharing dreams, anecdotes, emotions never thought possible. All inhibitions fade; the peak invincibility & absolution...

...And then the big comedown, no slow tapering off. You're ascended to a purity burning so brightly you'll curse the world for its cynicism and grimness then instantly it's raped of you – *a sharp, stabbing pain in your gut, that horrible soul-abduction.* Dehydrated & dead tired, you'll fall into a deep sleep.

The next morning the world you thought you'd escaped will have returned tenfold as grim. The aftermath lingers for up two days – this magnified, bi-polar hell, stomach-knotted arctic & viciously stabbed by horrid currents...

But no big deal – just one long day of sleep & 24 hours of darkness, right? You'll try it again, just once. You know what to expect now so it won't be all that bad.

But when you do it the next weekend the peak isn't anywhere as close to what you experienced that first time & the aftermath is twice as worse. And then the fourth, fifth, sixth...

By the tenth roll your brain is so physically scarred from the MDMA that your serotonin levels will never replenish themselves anywhere near their originating state.

That's the trap, the source of addiction – *to claw your way back to that first night*. Eventually, ecstasy becomes a necessity to feel *anything*...

Friends and family will notice a definite change in personality; you'll ignore it pretending nothings wrong. You're brain will scream for it, every atom & molecule lusting.

You close your eyes and all you can imagine are white gargantuan pyramids of Liberties, Boomerangs, Triple Crowns, Big Macs, White Fish, Ying Yangs, Pikachus, Zorros, Giovannis, Motorolas, White Rollex's, Blue Teepees, the killer Red Mitsubishi...

I've always preferred K. With one rail it hits the viscera, charting its way to the cockles of the heart, pumping through the arteries with steadfast fuzziness.

The monolithic crest of an exotic tsunami crashes over the right side of the brain, paralyzing the nervous system with sedated glee. You are no longer confined by conventional physics. Gravity becomes a moot point

& your jerky, flailing movements cut through the air like a fork through dripping margarine.

Gross distortions of physical perception are soon to follow. Your limbs stretch & contort like Reed Richards; uou make a drastic attempt at communication but the words only strengthen the wall of noise hovering mid-air like thick, South African jungle humidity...

Generally, in confusion, a drug person will run up to you and shove a bump under your nose with a shaky key. You'll knock it down like a beast and this will continue until you reach the introverted pit of warmly enveloping despair, free-falling like Alice.

And once you hit those murky depths – *when through tunnel vision you can only vaguely make out your friends mutating into giraffe's or other trans-continental wonders* – you'll discover the terrific wonders of the dreaded & glorious "K-Hole"...

All it took was one single impulse on my behalf to forever alter poor Kluck's life. I cannot remember how this conversation began, but I quickly darted at him with a litany of analytic questions: *"What was the defining moment of connection that transcended your relationship with your father beyond the vague conception of parent and son?"*

"Do you feel physically repulsed or attracted to any certain shade of color? How old were you when you first realized that you were going to die and what impact did this have on your childhood?"

The room stood in slack-jawed at the intensity of my pursuit, and how nervously he kept running from my questionnaire. People were unsure if this qualified as comedy or disturbing mental attack. Regardless, I pursued him relentlessly until Nez demanded I stop because he was on acid and I was making his brain hurt...

Later that summer at Johnny's birthday party it was an average night, resembling one of those hotel sequences from *Fear & Loathing In Las Vegas*. I remained sober to play the *"Psychedelic Referee."* No matter how bad a trip can get, I can reverse it. And if all fails, play fear chaperon.

Anyway, I'm plodding through this electronics diagram book I bought off Ricky for a $1 because he needed a bill to snort coke with. I notice Kluck on the front porch deep in an "East Side Trail Mix" affair (*"a K-Hole in which you can move"*) and abandon my pursuits to go full psychological throttle on him.

I'm hopping around the front yard like a Kangaroo, doing cartwheels, running around him backwards in circles jabbering nonsense like I'm being broadcast from the public access channel in reverse.

Every once in awhile I'll demand to know the meaning of life. Another 15 minutes of kangaroo hopping passes us by before he finally breaks down: *"The meaning of life... is... surrr-vye-vullll."*

I force him into my car & we cruise the ghetto blaring *Their Satanic Majesties Request* & Meshuggah's *"Future Breed Machine."* I kept screaming *"SAY IT!! FUCKING SAY IT!!!"* and he began shouting *"THE MEANING OF LIFE IS SURVIVAL, THE MEANING OF LIFE IS SURVIVAL!!!"* It's been 3 months, and tonight's events are in accordance to Onyx, who is the 10th step in my clandestine "13 Step" program...

Onyx is the cause and effect outcome of a random occurrence. If I'd never randomly showed up over Brandon's to smoke pot in the summer of '99, then this whole scene would have been erased.

See, Brandon was on bad terms with his parents because he couldn't hold a job, sucked up their money on psyche meds & court fees, and lingered around at the bottom of a bottomless depression.

It wasn't really his fault, because he was nuts to begin with. He got molested as a kid, later developed bi-polar depression (*schizoaffective*), and spent a chunk of his teen years in Boys Home after an attempted murder charge.

Brandon later lost cohesion due to the brain damage he suffered after committing suicide in '97. He went further down the spiral after doing a year in prison over a bogus rape charge...

But back to the near past, when I'd got him kicked out. He was 23 at this point. Although I'd been friends with him since he was 18, he could never come over my house because my mom was ultra-intrusive, obsessively checking all of my friends police records.

She of course forbid me to associate with him, which was laughable. He lived next door to Smitty, only 3 blocks from the Pardee house, so he was in consistent circulation.

Brandon has remained the most loyal motherfucker in my entire history. He's probably the only person I really trust. If they were water-boarding him at Guantanamo, he still wouldn't squeal.

I could hand him a billion dollars, leave for a week, and when I'd come back he'd hand it right over, minus a few bucks he'd use to buy a bag of Ranch Doritos & Mountain Dew (*the ultimate combination*)...

Brandon wasn't always the way he is now. Before dying he was just one of the good old boys. We used to smoke dope all the time and make goofy movies with Smitty's Hi-8 camera.

He was a brick wall – if anyone even attempted to fuck with any of us they might as well have been going up against a full-scale riot. Jason Voorhees was his absolute hero.

Anyway, back in '97 we were in Smitty's garage getting stoned and Korn's "*Daddy*" came on, which is a depressing number about child molestation. Brandon was whiskey drunk & time-bombed. He started ranting about how he was dragged from the streets and raped by a black man in Detroit when he was 5. He nearly ripped the door from its hinges & ran off into the night, vowing to kill *"that nigger motherfucker."*

The cops found him swinging punches at thin air, sobbing, not knowing what was happening. He'd get so lost in his terrors the current world would disappear. The empathetic officers brought him home.

The next day he downed 3 bottles of sleeping pills + his anti-depressants. His parents found him & rushed him to the hospital where he was pronounced legally dead for 2 minutes.

They revived him and he remained in a coma for a week. Once he snapped out of it he was the Brandon we know today – *different; Zen-infused, obsessed with witchcraft & Buddhist philosophy – stricken by intense brontophobia...*

Brandon began drawing pictures of God all the time.

Of course, this wasn't Jesus or Virgin Mary or Allah or Vishnu, for he'd witnessed divine symbolism. That whole tunnel of light ordeal occurred, but when he popped out the other end there was this massive triangular shape turning clockwise ever so slowly; all light & darkness sucked inside of it in slow motion, counter clockwise. In the middle was this vacuum, drawing all energy within it...

He was just floating towards it bodiless without the slightest trace of fear, remembering things that had occurred during his life. It was the most beautiful experience he ever felt.

Without warning he was sucked back with the velocity of a reverse coaster; everything went black. That's when he went into the coma... What Brandon saw was the ancient Sumerian symbol of *The Abyss...*

No one was really sure how to react to this new Brandon. We knew he wasn't lying, although he sometimes exaggerated stuff the way a little kid would. Yet he was never so serious.

He had no fear of death & welcomed it once his mission on this earth was complete, although he could never figure out what that mission was, and just went back to smoking pot all the time shortly thereafter...

So I got Brandon thrown out of his house because his mom caught us getting lit. I bought him a motel room in Prostitute Alley & he disappeared into thin air for a good month. I thought he was dead or in jail until I got a phone call, Brandon rambling on about this haunted house.

He was staying with a former co-worker from this goofy Hawaiian themed restaurant; Brandon was now working as a bouncer at this strip-hooker joint where there was no stage & all dancers (*walkers*) had black eyes, track-marks & stretchmarks of a multi-year triplet shitting marathon.

Brandon's new place was a dominant impression of pure evil; a massive three-story twice the size of any other house on the block, street bordering a clanging industrial plant. Brandon swings open the door & drags us upstairs – has us to stand in the corner of the hallway 'cause we'll feel a demonic presence pushing against our lungs.

This random kid we're with does as instructed and grows pale. I do the same and it kind of feels like a weird sense of gravity – like a lesser form of that Gravatron carnival ride.

Brandon goes on to tell us about everything – *the sightings, the videotapes*. Says he first noticed it when he was looking into the corner of the living room & saw something that resembled heat coming off asphalt.

The coke-head that lived upstairs had a Hi-8 camera with night vision and they filmed the occurrence. When they watched the tape it looked like one of those floating head sketches from *Cool World*, like faces mutating into weird shapes, but purely heat-mist. Then the strange noises, misplaced items, opened cupboards...

The coke-head woke up to someone was knocking from inside his closet. He pulled his handgun and opened it up finding a man sitting Indian style on the floor. He started shouting at the intruder to sit right there as he called the cops, threatening to cap him.

Guns drawn, the fuzz barged into his room but no one was there. They thought he was insane and refused to answer any of his recurring calls about the invisible people trying to break into his house, beating and tearing from inside the walls...

We came back the next day. Soon as we were about to knock on the door the porch light came on, the patio window flew open and we heard a stampede of individuals running around downstairs. The coke-head yelled at us from the upstairs window because no one was there. He was trying to sleep and was pissed we were making such a racket.

We showed back up 2 days later. This time I knocked on the front door which had a window in the middle. You could see the stairs leading to the upper flat and a man run down them. I figured it was the coke-head and as I went to grab the doorknob it started turning from the inside.

I clutched it and turned it all the way, slowly opening the door so I wouldn't hit him. He kept pulling it back as well but as I stepped in to say hello the door touched the wall. I quickly jerked it back & no one was there. I looked at Irish who was plenty terrified. We went into the front room where Brandon was confused because he'd just locked the door...

We intended to capture the beasties on film and conducted multiple tests. Music has a tendency to provoke them, especially deranged noise, so we played selections from Mortician, Bethlehem, NIN's misunderstood masterpiece *The Fragile* – this had no effect. We beat on pots & pans, used New Testament scriptures as rolling papers, sarcastic witchery...

We took a break; I sat on the couch filming into darkness with green night-vision. When I tilted the cam down I caught a shadow zip across the distance like a mini Greyhound. I jerked my head to catch it, as did Irish. I continued to film, pointing towards the bathroom.

On camera there was this "Lite Brite" face on the shower door, like those colored 80's pegs. I thought it was a reflection of the night vision but while stationary the glowing smile enlarged. Its eyes brightened, enlarged as green blocks. Then it just vanished. I kept filming.

Across the open doorway, the entrance to the lavatory, and these vertical white lines started appearing, like slanted rods. They grew larger and more solid, like prison bars made of bone. They too had vanished instantly. When we reviewed the tape the spectacle was captured...

Brandon mentioned couch cushions making patterns of their own in the fabric imprint. I had everyone get off the couch, set the tripod, and took a short recording.

With night vision you could see the imprint of a child's hand. We turned off the camera and left the spot alone. 15 minutes later there were three long bone fingers. 20 minutes later it became a symbol, like the bone design from that rancid *Crow* sequel...

And, of course, Brandon accidentally taped over the footage while recording a vodka-bred striptease in the living room... The Mexican & coke-head abandoned ship, and when Cassum & I tried to move in the landlord refused. Brandon ran off with a stripper who knew Onyx, ended up on the Urban Priests couch where he's remained to this day...

Moral of the Story: *While marijuana might not be the dangerous gateway drug it's reputed as, it sure does have a nasty reputation of taking you to some really weird places...*

Onyx, just like many of the weird characters I have met over the years, defies the descriptions of mere linguistics. I thought he was in his 50's but he's really only 31. His shoulders are ever-endowed with his pet sewer rats Comedy and Tragedy, which scramble inside his trench-coat.

He's sort of like the Hitchhiker from *Texas Chainsaw Massacre*, except with a genius I.Q. & obsessed with human psychology instead of grave robbing, mass murder & cannibalism.

From 13 to 19, Onyx was confined to a laundry list of mental institutions. By 20 he worked the streets as a prostitute. By 23 he'd advanced to BDSM Power Master with a large clientele & made a living torturing people. Now he is retired & lives off State Assistance.

He can't get a real job because the tax bracket of minimum wage will prevent him from receiving the medication necessary to control his epilepsy, alongside the mountains of crazy pills which regulates his more sinister urges and schizophrenic hallucinations.

His monthly allowance after rental & utilities is only $50 dollars. The money he earns on side is from cutting grass, bottle returns & the endless rummage sale of his front porch, most items which he garbage picked & sells to neighbors.

Onyx met his wife – a 53 year old overweight schizophrenic woman – 2 years ago & they were married within 48 hours. She is constantly doing my astrology & arguing on Jesus' behalf. She believes I may be The Antichrist. Her mind has no filters & makes anything real...

While Brandon crashes on one couch, Homeless John "The Couch Gnome" sleeps on the other. Black garbage bags filled with his possessions surround the davenport like sand bags on the beaches of Granada.

Homeless John's been drunk for 15 years straight, and no one seems to know a thing about him except that he always wears red flannel shirts & filthy brown pants & never stops talking, as if socializing at a party to invisible guests wasted as he is.

Always laughing & smiling – yet even though he seems eternal bliss, you just can just feel the hideous trauma behind that grin. The reason he never stops talking is 'cause we'll "*miss the most important things*." He is a low-volume radio in the background, communicating to ghosts of past.

He gets up at noon, slams a half pint of vodka, and rides a 25 mile bike route of snatching bottles & strange artifacts. Not long ago he found an entire pound of weed in a shoe box on side the freeway...

Aunt Tommy, one of Onyx' heyday prostitute buddies, rents the back room. He's in his mid-30's but looks 70, because AIDS. Brandon's just kind of waiting for Tommy to croak. He feels dirty about it, but doesn't have much choice 'cause no real job will hire him & no landlord will rent due to his sex offender registry...

Onyx wants to return to the power master business but can't until he receives access to the $5,000 worth of whips, dildos & butt plugs stashed away in a rent-a-center that for some reason he can't get into.

He wears snow boots all the time and is a massive alcoholic. He takes down a half pint of Vodka in one gulp, chases it with purple Slurpee, hits a smoke, and he's good to go. He claims that there are little hairs in your throat that are essential to the process of vomiting and when you take a drag, it neutralizes their function.

He was a prospective writer until his grandma died. They buried all of his writing in her casket because his aunt thought that's what he would've wanted. He can't dig her up because the grave is in plain view from the police station across the street.

He is trying to write a book, or rather each one of his 14 personalities are. He carries a notebook for each personality, which is the main reason he can never complete a project. D&D is life or death...

Onyx calls himself "The Urban Priest" & gives free psychological exams to anyone that brings him booze. He is one of the most perceptive individuals I've ever encountered; in 5 minutes he knew my psychology inside & out. He's like one of those kids that used to take apart clocks just to see how they worked. Humans are the ultimate toys to him.

Onyx is anorexic in physique; filthy, rat-like – his skullet untouchable. His scummy teeth, gaunt face and pasty white skin make him resemble a Spanish conquistador.

He is a freak in the truest sense of the word, constantly over-glorifying the RPG characters he's created over the years like medieval fables you'd tell children before tucking them into bed.

He labels himself "*Mad Max in a Walt Disney world*," although I find the term "*Marquis De Sade in a Martha Stewart hell*" more fitting.

His trailer is filthy; in the heat of the summer all of the rotting meat, slimy dishes, dirty clothing & changed but not tossed kitty litter bags forge an effluvium so vile sometimes you have to run outside and puke, or be hardcore enough to adapt.

Onyx just simply does not care – he is the most glorious madman I've ever known. He is constantly bugging me to bring him more puppets. We are blood brothers of *The Revolution*...

ZHIVAGO

Committing suicide was the last thing I remember before everything went fuzzy. Trying to, at least... See, at some point, something happened. I can't remember what it was, but something went horribly wrong.

My mom wasn't "all there," you know? She started to get weird. I started to battle her mind, which had grown increasingly nonsensical, erratic, demanding, ill-tempered, cold as ice.

Like she had some kind of brain injury, legitimately, but no one would listen. It may not have been a brain tumor, but its was a something or other. And I was the only one seeing it, even if I was blocking it out or the severity with which she was increasingly "dreamy."

And I can't remember completely what happened, just that she was scary. That her behavior was very... floating & bizarre. She began sleepwalking a lot. Sometimes in the middle of the day, at random.

And she was very... scary. She began "checking out," not knowing what was happening. There were gaping holes in her daily routine and how she was functioning. And the worse it got, the more I blocked it out.

But something happened. An event I made myself forget went down about 5th grade, then things get fuzzy in my own head, with my recollections. My memories... they grow dim, totally introverted & dark – the labyrinth of a diseased, struggling mind...

The river of cognitive dissonance – it kind of ends for me when I tried to kill myself. From there, I remember fluidly & vividly. I had to basically sever whatever my life was beforehand & start anew. But it came in as psychologically an unhealthy a way as one could imagine...

8th grade was well underway, and I'd slug home through gray skies & dead trees, bloodied & beaten from student attacks. I'd rush in my house

& snag *The Downward Spiral*; like a vortex it'd consume me during the hours preceding her return. *Broken* had warped me, but *Spiral* forged a new soul. Every lyric was personal; each fragment an isolationist tome...

My mom had confiscated my cassettes, hiding them in her closet, claiming my behavior was a direct result of their influence. Music was all I had, the only thing keeping me going – literally.

To deny me of this release was to egg on suicide. She stole my cowboy boots cause they gave me identity, she hid my clothes...

I wrote down the lyrics to my albums & hid them in my shoes, between my mattress, anywhere they could be stored away like a prisoner hiding drugs. If she found them she'd immediately shred 'em, yet when I read them I could vividly hear the songs replay in my head note for note.

Soon as she walked in the door I'd force myself to sleep, my diseased mind, going deeper & deeper into unfiltered wastelands. I literally felt that I lived *The Downward Spiral*. There was nothing that existed except that record & the internal world it had impressed.

All action became a rite of escape; every waking moment nightmare – *always fragmented voices from thousands of directions screaming, screaming, always screaming, always wanting, always demanding, always distorting, always violence, always the lie...*

It all bled into one pivotal moment, a vast nefarious. Mid-Sunday, snow falling, freezing room, dead winter, empty house, room a thrashed mess. Magazine & comic cut outs taped to the walls – the bedroom of a 1994 teen with Ghost Rider & Maxx & Spawn & onlooking him...

I hit play on the final track of *The Downward Spiral*. I grabbed my knife. Knees planted, shoulders shrugged, examining the peeling linoleum; *the incalculable loneliness...* I brought it to my wrist, rocking, awaiting the end of the track to slash the arteries... *dissonant noise, shades of red; an obelisk of scrap rusting into oblivion...*

I couldn't do it; I collapsed on the floor, letting the cold linoleum suck my soul from it's discarded body. Yet eventually, after an hour of silence & catatonia, whatever was left of the kid pulled himself up.

He wasn't so much human anymore as he was some entity piloting a body – some ghost man who no longer even thought himself human. All that was left was a thing, "a watcher" seeking revenge...

Manic Depression is a physical disease where cerebral mechanics dysfunction & chemical imbalances are in irrational flux.

Thoughts & emotions jerk wildly without premeditation – a revolving door of panic, euphoria, fear, anger, depression; all compounded between the soaring extremes of full-blown mania & rock bottom depression. At times, all described sensations can fluctuate a full breadth in the span of 20 minutes.

The schizoid aspect (*if inflamed*) is identical to having a trace amount of LSD in your system. It's like being submerged underwater – no matter how hard you tread you never break the skin.

The undertow pulls fathomless, an abyss of fragmentation. You slowly drown in the convolution of your own mind...

Every dream becomes a nightmare, and eventually, the nightmare becomes reality. *You see sound. You hear odors. You taste vision.* You're scared to reach out because there are doctors with needles and electrodes waiting on the other side.

You pray to God but it's turned on you. No exit, no cure – just hospitals, prescriptions, re-education. Suicide becomes an obsession for death is the only true escape...

Thus enters Vic. Although Cassum had been friends with him for years, Vic didn't really trust or talk to anyone.

He also, as I later found out, had no intention of opening dialogue until I'd proven myself. Emerick, a psychotic death metaller, was the main benefactor in this.

I could never tell if Emerick was my best friend or worst enemy. We were constantly getting suspended. In math class he wrapped the phone chord around my neck and started blasting me in the head with the receiver. The class laughed wildly, shouting I was a worthless faggot.

I speared him over a desk and we were suspended for the rest of the day. Emerick would just start punching me in the face for no reason then demand I go hang out with him all night.

We stopped being friendly at all after my mom called his house looking for me one day. He was stoned & perplexed and decided to call her a stupid bitch, hanging up.

She overreacted and sent the pigs to his house to give him a stern lecture. Her intrusion started a blood-feud that went on for years, because he thought I'd personally sent the cops...

Prior to that, discounting all of the random floor moppings (*about 25 kids in total would jump me, kick me off my bike, knee me in the stomach, chase me down the street. In the hallways they'd punch or kick me for no reason. Spit in my face, call me a worthless faggot for wearing an Iron Maiden shirt*) were two incidents involving this huge Italian kid who had his growth spurt real early and was 6"3" at 13.

There was a food fight in the lunchroom and the Italian kid was on the sidelines trying to protect his new "No Fear."

I chucked my peanut butter and jelly sandwich into the crowd and it sped past its mark, splattering his shirt. He charged full force and speared me over a table, slicing my leg open on the metal stool.

300 children burst into laughter, calling me a stupid fag. I demanded further abuse, throwing my hands in the air but no attention...

In English class a story in which the phrase *"Filthy Dago"* appeared and it went around as a short-lived joke. The next day I was eating toothpaste out of the squeeze bottle in Science class and the voices in my head were laughing, demanding I shout DAGO aloud. I did so, rather amplified, in the midst of a quiet class taking a pop quiz.

I started laughing really hard and everyone looked at me like I was insane. In the hallway the Italian slammed me against a locker and said if I ever mentioned *"a goddamn thing about his race again"* he'd destroy me. I think I told him to kill me when he had his hand around my neck.

It was only after fighting this giant Arab kid that I finally earned Vic's respect. The Arab was a boxer – I kept dodging his fists, launching a few shots which caused another suspension...

I met Vic during an auditorium ensemble where we watched this 1970's Boston Tea Party reenactment film. We kept cracking jokes that made no sense, laughing spastic & never exchanging a coherent word.

That weekend I stayed at his house in East Dearborn & we kept laughing uncontrollably at everything – the absurdity indescribable.

Cassum lived a few blocks away and as a group we wandered the streets blasting KMFDM on his boombox, yelling gibberish at confused Arabs. We didn't make any serious conversation that entire night, and when I woke on Vic's floor my lungs hurt from humor...

Vic was Cassum's right hand man. They composed a two-man gang that would sell the pot Cassum stole from his mother. Although Cassum could scrap, Vic was the arsenal. He was this muscular Mexican/Irish hybrid and identical to me in numerous ways – a nonperson because his father was nothing but a source of fear to him.

The dad was a Marine in 'Nam and didn't talk much, just made Vic and his younger brother re-shingle the roof, paint the rooms, put up drywall. It was their form of rent so the parents could one day sell the house off and retire in style. He was an exceedingly dark, distant character and I saw a lot of it in Vic...

On Monday Vic was altered, brooding & smoking a cig with Cassum during lunch. They started asking me all of these weird questions about poltergeists & shadow people – *supernatural occurrences, split personalities, premonitions of war...*

One day a film would come out featuring a character that all 3 of us could easily identify with – *Donnie Darko.*

Whenever we'd talk about these freaky subjects, our experiences, all our strange "sixth sense" things, we'd code-name it Zhivago – a secretive word to explain something we'd head off to privately talk about, doing bad things to our minds...

My 14th birthday party was a sleepover mixing Vic, Cassum, Danny & Jesse under one roof.

The night began with *Akira, Hard Boiled* and *Dawn of The Dead.* Cassum bought me a Marilyn Manson t-shirt even though none of us knew anything about the band except that *Portrait of an American Family* had just come out & Reznor had produced it.

Jesse and Danny were their usual asshole selves, insulting the films and acting superior. Once the lights went out we turned heel and pelted them with markers, empty pop cans, pizza crusts.

They were whining and we were laughing at them. Vic called Jesse a bitch and Cassum was egging on Danny to fight him. They looked to me for support but I told them to fuck themselves and threw them out of my house in the middle of the night.

Jesse kept saying, *"Just give me back my tape man."* It was the self-titled Rage Against The Machine debut and Cassum retorted with: *"What tape? This one? Oh, you mean MY tape? Great album isn't it guys? Ha ha ha!"* Jesse went home defeated & I never invited either of them over again. They were forced ghosts.

Vic told me, *"Those guys are complete assholes. How long have they been treating you like this?"*

"My entire life."

"Fuck 'em – they don't exist anymore. You have us." We made a pact to forever have each other's backs, no matter the circumstance. That simple promise – it was the only thing that ever meant anything to me. The Old World was dead. Whomever "Ryan" was, he was just a corpse…

We started to gang up on all the shitheads that ever caused us grief. Cassum snuck up on this fat douche & started blasting fists into his face. Vic came from behind and clocked the back of his skull. While he struggled to get on his feet I kicked him in the stomach hard as I could with my birthday present – *shiny, steel-toed Carolinas…*

This kid pushed me in art class. I threw him into the metal book-stand and shot a knee into his face. In wood-shop I chucked a handful of sawdust into one douche-bag's eyes.

A kid dumped milk over my drawing at lunch & I belted him in the stomach. I approached another in gym class, tripped & drove his head face first into the wrestling mat. At the water fountain I cracked another in the face – *pegging with hacky sacks, stuffing beans down backpacks...*

The scum that gave me the most grief in elementary walked up to Cassum & Vic in the restroom. He told Vic to put his head in the toilet so he could flush him. They laughed & when he cocked to swing they drove him headfirst into the urinal, kicking his skull into the porcelain. He was crying with bloody lip & chipped tooth, covered in piss...

I started talking to Smitty, a nerdy kid with thick glasses, acne, poor social skills & clearance apparel. Some fat kid was harassing him so I clobbered that fuck with his own trumpet – Smitty whipped off his shoe & began beating him in the head with it...

Smitty lived a few blocks from me & didn't have many friends – a loner that hung with his brother & father. His pops was the type of guy you'd want to go fishing with, toying with CB radios & jukeboxes.

The mother was a terrifying monster, obese & miserable. All she did was cut the brothers down. 2 weeks before 8th grade ended, Smitty's dad died from a heart attack while they were camping...

We started getting into drugs. Cassum downed dozens of prescription pills & mini-thins & wandered off during class – the cops busted him for truancy & a sack of weed. He was kicked out rest of the year & grounded most the summer.

The second his dad let him out he got busted with Vic & vodka at a carnival; some kids they were feuding with snitched 'em out to cops, they got arrested & sent home in the back of squad cars. We'd just pissed in the church's confession booth too, and I snuck away quietly...

I smoked pot for the first time with Smitty & his older Sister. All it took was a few drags and I was assaulting him with a blue whiffle bat jabbering: *"House #2!"* repeatedly. He fell over gelatinous, laughing uncontrollably at the basketball he was dribbling. Marijuana immediately adopted a ritualistic air in our group...

Vic, meanwhile, ate peyote at Fallon's house. While Fallon & Cassum were stoned & watching TV, Vic wandered away tripping his face off & disappeared for 3 days! We kept making excuses for him – one day he was *"spending the night"* at my house, the next Smitty's, Cassum's.

By Day 3 his parents were furious. Cassum & Vic's younger brother searched frantically, all over East D, not knowing what they'd tell the parents. *Dead? Coma?? Rubber Room???*

Miraculously, they found him last second, laying face-down in a field inside Detroit, covered in flies. He was exhausted, covered in filth, scrambled, still wearing the clothes he'd disappeared in...

After the solitude of Peyote & wandering the industrial areas of Southwest Detroit for 3 days without food or water, he was a markedly changed man – and more convinced of Zhivago than ever.

He wouldn't explain the trip, cause it was all quite mortifying to even contemplate – only that the last he remembered was stepping out Fallon's door & seeing flaming skeletons marching down the streets. He ran to the train tracks – a force pulling him into the heart of Zug Island.

That's where he lived, for 3 days of demonic visions – residing in abandoned factories, oil refineries, train yards... He was soon institutionalized & deemed borderline schizophrenic...

We hung at Fallon's on a regular basis; we viewed him the way *Beavis & Butthead* did Todd. He was 25 & full of wild stories, convinced of his own myth. According to him he was a black-belt that had once taken down 25 grown men at the same time. He had swords & nun-chucks & would practice in the back yard, slicing effigies & cardboard boxes.

Said he once dived into hostile waters & fought sharks with his bare hands – said he beat the shit out 5 cops & stole their squad car, ditched it & ran 20 miles through the woods to escape...

Fallon "knew" an occultist cat burglar that stole the authentic human-skin Necronomicon from a German museum. Fallon claimed he had the spell for immortality – which required guzzling 2 gallon's of blood from a virgin's first menstrual cycle...

One night his roommate was fumbling around in search of a bong in the dark & Fallon went crazy – put a katana blade halfway through his arm & straight into the bone. We watched iron-hard Fallon led out in handcuffs, sobbing 'cause it was his 4th felony – *5 years & no parole*...

And then, we all met Brandon who'd been released from juvey. The charge stemmed from a fight he took way too far in middle school. He moved in 2 houses from Smitty & the Cleveland Street Posse was born.

We were one hell of a unit and this basic set-up was to last the rest of my life – *the most bottom barrel misfits, losers & outcasts forever united in our mutual hatred of the unjust world*. We were a support group, a street gang – *a volatile tour de force...*

Brandon reintegrating after 3 years of lock up, Vic out of his mind from way too many psychedelics; Smitty recuperating from the death of his father; Cassum dealing with his mother's slow death to Leukemia...

The only other individual to enter our ranks was Robinson. He'd moved from California and didn't talk much, just sort observed while living in the candy-coated art world inside his head – the original anime fiend that wanted to be a comic artist just like Cassum, Vic & myself.

As the years went by he further transmuted into living Manga, obsessed with everything Asian, looking like an anime character, gluing gems on his forehead like Sailor Moon.

Most assumed he was queer due to his designing of clothes & drawing *"Precious Moments"* caricatures, but never would he admit it. He swore he was straight, and proudly smeared sprinkle glitter on his forehead, wear skirts, paint his nails & smother on gothy mascara...

The ladies loved him though – they swooned. Tons of them hanging at his house. He was just *"swimmin' in pussy,"* as they say in Deee-Troit, but unlike every Detroiter, he refused to capitalize.

See, the human-manga thing was a progressive metamorphosis. This early Robinson we knew was like a blonde haired, blue-eyed surfer type with NIN's shirts & chin length hair & quietly into Jesus Christ.

Later on, he got neck-deep in the fringe Christian stuff, like offbeat Evangelical groups maintaining that certain Scientologist air.

He was saving himself for marriage, you know – totally straight edge too. He had girlfriends – smoking hot goth idol or rave queen types – but never, ever would he bang them.

They kept leaving him, one after another, cause he'd never put out. And then he just goes back to drawing cute Precious Moments people with big heads, listening to techno & extreme Christian metal, waiting to get married to finally fuck.

The parents were giant hippies. They seemed whacked from way too much mescaline in their Winterland heyday. His pops looked & acted like a mellow, gray haired Owen Wilson. He was obsessed with Gentle Giant and would give everyone back rubs.

Basic cable wasn't allowed in the house, only a VCR for film. Robinson had two younger brothers as well, and they all lived in a house I subconsciously assumed resembled the Sharon Tate residence. Maybe this is why I was always reading the kids segments of *Helter Skelter*...

Robinson always went along with my bizarre pranks. Skinhead Mary & a female pal came over and I greeted them outside, waved hi and a lead pipe fell from the sleeve of my army jacket, clanging on the cement. Robinson was barely noticeable through the screen door, cackling in darkness. We let them in, acting deep in the throes of an anti-life trip.

His 11 year old brother was twirling a butcher knife at the kitchen table, entranced by its shiny chrome. We pushed the girls into Robinson's room and his sister flipped on the stereo, pulsating a snow channel at max volume. We flip on the light and his 7 year old brother is bound in a potato sack thoroughly wrapped with phone chords & rusted chains.

He screams for them to run for their lives as we jab pillow sacks over their heads. Robinson holds them down with his knees as they scream bloody murder, all of us whelping them with spatulas & whiffle bats...

The summer of '94 ended with the death of Hewitt, a popular girl in school society. Although she hung out with kids we used to fight endlessly, she was from East Dearborn and an acquaintance of Cassum & Vic.

One month before high school begins, Hewitt was getting drunk with her cheerleader friends. They decided to dart across a major 50 mph road, flighty and smashed, and Hewitt was macked by a Grand Marquis doing, ushering in an unending funeral of grim monologues, candlelight vigils & roadside bouquets.

Hewitt's death permanently scarred the popular kids and a dark air fell upon the freshman crowd heading from O.L. Smith into Edsel Ford. Of everyone, I was the only of our group having to go to Edsel.

Vic, Cassum, Smitty, Robinson & every unmentioned character I associated went to Dearborn High. I was again alone, left to defend myself in a volatile atmosphere of unknown characters…

That summer also included an ill-fated trip to Sea World & Disney Land with my Mother conjured to settle our differences. It didn't work out because I didn't want to be around her for a variety of reasons.

Of course she never understood what was wrong, because I would never tell her, because I never wanted to hurt her even though she would never listen to me anyway.

She nervously dragged me around the amusement park in Florida heat, fake laughing at everything and trying to coax me along with it. I remained mute for the most part, giving basic answers.

At Epcot Center an elderly Italian woman bumbled over a curb fell flat on her face. A group of punkers pointed and laughed, mocking her. I started laughing and momma went off.

Later that night, in our motel room, she said: *"It's like my baby fell through the mirror and out came you."*

She only saw my father, never me – but what I got to see was a kid feed a tennis ball to a dolphin. That was raw, quite actually. Afterwards a 5-year-old boy runs by in dripping wet swimming trunks, crying and spewing blood everywhere. It was so Jodorowsky – he'd broken his nose on the giant slide & his father was rushing to catch him.

We rendezvoused with Toby outside of some key and rented a boat. I didn't see any alligators, but I did accidentally ran over a manatee at

35 mph. The motor chunked it & I heard it yelp from underwater, blood bubbles popping the surface. I actually feel kinda bad about that one...

Back to the Hewitt thing. A short time after her death, I was over an acquaintances & we decided to hold a séance. We lit candles & attempted to channel Hewitt – the flames extinguished from a gust of wind where no open windows existed. The kids got freaked & we changed the subject.

That night I had a dream of her walking through the halls of O.L. Smith. She was in a white dress searching for her friends, peering in classrooms only to see students she didn't recognize. She was lost & afraid with no direction or escape.

Hewitt would come in and out of it, like momentary flashes in R.E.M. – not fully there, just a floating impression of saddened confusion. She went in the bathroom and saw herself in the mirror, face half-rotted & decomposing like a corpse...

Years later I asked Robinson's little brother about it, since he was attending O.L. Smith at the time. I asked if he ever heard any ghost stories about the place. He mentioned the "girl in the white dress," the one in the mirrors with the mangled face... *I've always contemplated burning that monstrosity down in order to set her free...*

I was convinced the first day of high school would be like *Dazed And Confused*, asshole jocks running around with paddles. Surprisingly this reality was welcoming, not the prison O.L. Smith was.

Being weird was actually a plus for once in this barely post-grunge age. Edsel was crawling with freaks and it wasn't long before I had plenty of support from the Juniors & Seniors whom I primarily hung out with.

The assholes from middle school went their own way, concentrating on being accepted by the older jocks instead of fighting me for once. My electives geared towards art & creativity and my social worker was dropped because I hadn't been in any fights...

Now I could go on forever about the weird characters that came through the woodwork in this particular setting, but it is only important you know a select handful – Helen the Pimp, Skinhead Mary, Crazy Steve, Schreck, Salem & "The Three Witches" (*Melissa, Joanna & Miriam*)...

Helen the Pimp was the first gal I ever was crazy about – the first "Lunchbox Girl" – childlike & animated; slender, beautiful, sharply communicating lavish psychedelia. She dug my bad teenage poetry and was always slapping "Physically Fit" award stickers on my notebooks...

Skinhead Mary was her best friend, a strangling fresh-lady that shaved her head not to pledge allegiance to the skin movement but because she liked the look. She was anorexic & self-destructive; *acne & braces & hints of sexual molestation*...

Her family was off-the-boat Romanian, but she was very ashamed of this and would always pretend her mother was someone else. I could place her in a Bjork video at ease, always at Robinson's with bleaching hair encrusting beneath heavy strips of tin foil.

I could never work up the strength to make a move on Helen. In art class, I read her *Alice In Wonderland*; gym we'd bounce off rubber walls ala Arkham. We'd read *Helter Skelter*, spouting lines of slippie wisdom...

In Gym we were assigned to basketball teams but revolted alongside Skinhead Mary, shredding tiny orange bibles and crumpling the pages into a basketball. In the middle of the game we formed a third team, gaining Salem as a nose guard.

Eventually, the jocks realized what we were shooting hoops with, and threatened to fight us. We went back to our rubber room, all 4 of us, bouncing off the walls.

Helen was soon expelled for showing up to school while suspended & getting stoned in the parking lot. I was so infatuated with her, and then one day, she was just gone...

Crazy Steve was obsessed with Bloodhound Gang. He had bad, crooked teeth & light blue eyes huge with hysteria. His car sound system intimidated, and we'd get high and ride around at 3am blaring my *"Sound of The Whales"* cassette tape.

Underwater mating calls would bump so loudly the suburbanites would flick on their porch lights and gaze into the night, unable to distinguish whether they had dream the turmoil.

Crazy Steve graduated when I was a sophomore and joined the Army as a demolitions expert, honorably discharged over a meth binge on the shooting range.

Before lapsing into a rather long k/snow/meth/speed/ecstasy/LSD saga, he told me: *"Never join the military. All they do is find people with no self-esteem that desperately need to be a part of something and brainwash them into believing the Government is God and all morality is defined by killing in the name of it."*

I said, *"Yes, but you learned how to blow shit up real good right?"* His face lit up, *"Fuck yeah!!"* We cackled like hyenas into the night, this great man teaching effective methods of kitchen napalm production...

Shreck was one of my biggest influences. He was real Slavic looking with long features and messy, half-curled blonde hair which he never bothered to comb. His father was a military man and Shreck spent most of his life bouncing around the U.S. He read books through most every class, obvious he thought everyone was a moron.

In his eyes I was a lump of clay without adequate direction. He took me under his wing and taught me the eternal importance of the punk rock movement. He introduced me to Abbie Hoffman, Richard Bachman, Timothy Leary; *Jesus Chrysler, Minor Threat, Man Bites Dog...*

In acting class we'd slash up auditorium seats with his switchblade and slop graffiti over the rest. The school paper actually printed an article on our domestic terrorism, calling for someone to turn us in for $50.

Pissing on classroom floors, spitting in teachers coffee, leaving gobs of mayo on their chairs & stretched out Trojans on car antennas... I only got busted for small time shit, never the hardcore delinquency.

One of my favorites was when the principal read a drawing I did aloud while I was baked in his office – a picture of a stoned smiley face with a blunt hanging out his mouth. *"Mr Bartek, could you please explain 'yummy, yummy, yummy... I have... mun-chies... In my tummy.'"*

Shreck saw to it that I was educated in all the subcultures of the world. But as he explained, *The Revolution* is not one single goal, pursuit or movement – it is a collective term for nearly all dissent combined and each man has to forge his own personalized agenda.

The aimless spiritual vacuum I maintained from the death of God was now replaced by a zealous passion for rock n' roll calamity. The master-plan was slowly unfurling, shaping itself as my environment continued to become malleable to my sadistic whims...

Shreck was aced from my existence when he showed up to school out of his mind on 4 hash brownies, stumbling around barefoot demanding to know *"who the fuck"* stole his shoes. He was swiftly expelled and his father moved them out of state. Never heard from him again...

And *The Three Witches*, whom nicknamed me God. They were a triad most everyone assumed were lesbians, although there was never any proof except for the Spatula incident.

It was a drunken night and when everyone but Miriam was passed out, Joanna came into the room with the kitchen utensil, cordially sat down & began masturbating with it. When word got out everyone began calling her *"Spatula Girl"* and we'd pass her demanding pancakes. She never caught on and started calling me *"fork-head"* in return...

Joanna was tall & thin, always on the lookout for a metrosexual dude. She was the odd one out. She claimed I once prevented her suicide by calling at the right random moment...

Melissa was short & slightly plump with long black hair, but a pretty girl nonetheless. Miriam was pure Irish; ass-length orange-red hair & sparkling green eyes. Melissa was real flirty with everyone, real sexual. Miriam was far more reserved & delicate as her ballet routines.

Melissa's was our main haunt. She had the entire upstairs, walls covered in magazine clippings, Jim Morrison/Clockwork Orange posters; the smell of burned incense ever strong.

An armada of candles, incense & sexy lingerie strewn about; whips, handcuffs, chains, fluffers, runes, tarot cards, occult books, comics & music zines in disordered jumbles. Most nights were chain-smoking & discussing paganism/witchcraft – tarot, runes & palm orientations...

Melissa's boyfriend Salem was a hardcore Satanist since 12. When he wasn't in a Deicide or Venom shirt he was a total nuisance – they had to alter the dress code cause he kept wearing fishnets, corpse-paint & feather boas to gym. Salem made a big scene demanding to wear high heels in the gym class run, since there was no dress code stipulation forbidding it.

When I flew the flag of die-hard Satanism, we actually ran for Class President/V.P. under the *"New Satanic Age"* platform.

Even though we weren't on the ballot, we pulled in 100+ votes as write-in D.I.Y candidates, then started a "student newsletter" called *The Order of Baphomet* in which we faux-interviewed the principal in regards to his chronic addiction to pedophilia, incest & bestiality...

There is no denying that Salem was the one that got me hooked on all the LaVey shit. It wasn't far into 9th grade when he handed me *The Satanic Bible*. I read the entire thing twice over before the dismissal bell rang.

Everything I truly believed in was right before me, and with our collective descent into occultism in general, it was the final building block in my worldview and attitude for some time to come.

The good Doctor had conjured an exciting & inspiring mix of pure propaganda & adequate semi-cornyness which I couldn't deny, and thoroughly ruffled the feathers of every adult & especially the other teens at school I so detested.

Admonished was indulgence instead of abstinence, earth bound existence over spiritual daydreaming; the destruction of hypocrisy & self-deceit – self discipline, reliance & undefiled wisdom; kindness, respect to those who deserve it & vengeance over turning the cheek....

The war against the leeches, the drones; absolute master-ship over the culture of fear by reveling in all aspects of fear – no sin, no damnation but what we define... *the human ego as the center of worship; that man was the center of his own destiny and, in effect, his own God...*

Satan was not a literal being, but a term for all thought & human experience deemed "evil" by the greatest war criminals of the human soul.

After all, the Christians & Muslims had mass murdered non-believers for centuries – we modern pagans lived in *their world*, rooted in *their* perpetual crusade which ran deeper than any political or social cause. To directly combat religious brainwashing was not a banal attack because a complex spectrum of injustice endlessly spiraled from its roots.

Shreck's belief that all subcultures/movements in the underground fought for the common thread was well implanted in me. Acknowledging now as I did then that anti-puritanicalism is not the *only* answer to the problems we face, I did not see any philosophical, moral, or intellectual regret in concentrating on this particular target.

Other individuals & groups could focus on combating different social or political aspects – crushing mad religion was my personal stake in the war effort. My belief was in contributing to a global movement by my own individualized methods & tactics...

It didn't matter that we were isolated – the counterculture existed worldwide & this was abundantly clear from the magazines we read, the music we listened to, the media we were exposed. We were but one link of a never-ending chain. It was impossible to win this war – but it was crucial we died trying. Our dignity superseded any material concern.

Having been hooked on the Norse legends & my Celtic roots, I felt an even greater commitment to rid the world of the spiritual-fascist influence. I'd lay awake at night with visions of my ancestors brought into chains, forced to choose between honorable death at the hands of the dishonorable or assume the religion of the invaders.

This is why this Satanism injection held such meaning to me – not only was it rebellion against spiritual injustice, I felt that I essentially fought for my Celtic Ancestors. No Druid or Celt Warrior or Pictish Tattooed Freak would put up with Jesus. They'd be so bummed. Thus, not only would I avenge their loss, I'd destroy modern mental slavery...

Magick is the *"art & science"* of using human will to transform reality, and when an individual becomes egocentrically linked to the concept of a self-made god – no matter how noble or idealistic the intentions – there is but one honest term for it: *BLACK MAGICK*.

Was I truly though? I took Magick way more serious then Anton LaVey's propaganda cult, which was just organized atheism with theatrics to it. But I did not understand what True Magick was. I had a stronger grip then most Americans force-fed Hollywood & all the cheesy things of Witches everyone hears as kids – but I was still far in the dark.

The Tarot made no sense to me other then a disjointed thing. No one knew "how" it worked or it's underlying blueprint, because it's impossible to grip tarot unless you know the Kabbalah, and no one bothered to tell me this or anyone who read Tarot Cards I meant. Theyt were always amateurs half-memorizing cards & relying on "How To" manuals.

If someone had tried to pitch me the Kabbalah back then, I would never have listened, because Kabbalah was Jewish stuff & I was a heavy metal guy protesting against the Judaeo-Christian mental conditioning. Furthermore, no one ever tapped me on the shoulder & told me: *"Dude, here's what's up – Qabalah with a Q is the Magickal version that has nothing to do with the Jewish or Christian God whatsoever, Kabbalah is the purely Jewish version, Cabala with a C is the Christian variant, and Qabala without the H is The Anarcho-Magickal version...*

At 14 I thought Egyptian Magic was ludicrous & primitive, and dismissed it outright. I thought the Golden Dawn was God & Angel magic tied to Jesus – and their images used the Star of David everywhere, which I didn't know was a Babylonian thing, an Astrological Magick thing....

I didn't know who Hermes was, and thought Alchemy was 100% about transmuting minerals to Gold, for $$$. The Norse Runes were cool, but they were limited. Vikings make great literature – but you don't wanna be one. The Druids were not very clear either, except as Green Wizards – and I didn't care much for gardening...

There are as many definitions of Magick as there are Operators of it – and it's agenda & formulation depends wholly on it's Engineer. There is a term called "Syncretism" – while generally used in political context to describe amalgams of ideology , it is also used among Occultists.

Syncretic Magick/Paganism/Alchemy describes a self-styled system that pulls from the whole of Magickal theory. Basically, you are a One Man Magickal Order of your own imaginative construction.

A Syncretic Pagan, by design, is a kind of Anarchist loner among other Witches, Wizards, Druids, Magicians & Magickians who prefer restricted, more constitutional forms of their "Magick Workings," per se.

The question, though, was "Agenda." The deluded 14 year old I was – that night I lay in the darkness, arms behind my head, watching shadows dance in hopping candle light. I felt supreme & invincible.

Bleak visions overcame me as beautiful opera. Piles of books ablaze – the fist of revolution & every falsehood buried; their charlatan traditions made myth of ancient. They created me, and I would unmake them; *freedom, liberty, the volcanic nexus of civilization…*

Zelda

It has been said that love is a gimmick which makes sex respectable. A degree of validity may exist in such a quotation, but the Sphinx riddle I retort is thus: Can love make absolute *filth* respectable?

Sex, in all earnest, is a generalized terminology – oft marginalized by low-ring slurping acrobatics & lackluster missionary visions...

Can filth in itself be a substitution for love? Is there any differentiation, other then the mutual lovers' own truncation of values? The "Eye of the Beholder's" per se?

What would the *Marquis* have to say about all of this? The answer remains elusive, but one thing is for certain – no single human being has ever set me on fire the way Zelda has...

We became properly acquainted only as I entered the most venerable of all prospects – substitute high school janitor. Only 2 years liberated of teen hell, I'd returned to scrub those same toilets clean.

Zelda never had a shot at what many would consider a normal brain. A heroin addict single mother was her only sense of family. Her best friend was her grandfather, deceased by 5.

A dozen homes, a father she never knew, an uncle that taught her all she knew about music (EDM), intense Christianity slithering throughout her childhood. She had wanted to be a nun actually...

Zelda lives at her "grandparents" house, who are not her grandparents but the folks of her mothers ex-boyfriend. Both of their children died in their early 20's to heroin overdoses within a 2 month span. Surrounded by fish tanks & kittens, that she tells me all upon the phone...

Zelda isn't a person; she's more a walking, breathing emotional impulse – a beacon of love in a world of whores, angelic body matched by her disordered mind. She is the freest human alive.

Her liberation shines every time she catches wind of a lightning bug – the way she rushes off and all else disappears. The way she'll glimpse an alley cat & every thought drops...

Zelda is the most attractive, vibrant one of the reproductive species to ever grace the earth. Her big, blue anime eyes – her wild, mischievous smile that lights up like a million candles – the dynamic strands of hair dyed every color of the rainbow – the gleeful feet that squiggle in sheer joy, the seductive nature of her curves that can bring a nation to its knees – the humor & mind she possesses that drives me mad...

So gentile is her nature I wish nothing more than to float away with her delicacy. Her ability to let go completely, to feel completely, strikes me with envy and awe.

I have been wounded; I have lost the ability to dream, to imagine – to *feel* completely. But it is not a mortal wound; I am healing. She heals me. She is beautiful and I am but a curious observer...

I first met her on Robinson's porch, July 2000. It was a bright-blue afternoon and I caught gentile footsteps creeping the stairs.

I bolted through the screen door and locked eyes with her – one of those infinite zangs which resound across the entire universe.

I'd crossed paths with her before, back in '99. I was cruising in Pinkeye, Billy still rolling on X from the previous night & chewing a pacifier, blasting 45 mph down suburban streets with the volume cranked on *"Drums A Go-Go."*

We dropped by the annual carnival and this cute young thing was working over a caramel apple.

I fished her in to smoke some dope, and to the tune of Ministry's *Deity* we were flying through side streets, doing u-turns, screaming obscenities at Jesus Christ...

She began appearing in the rave abyss; nothing ever came of our attraction until an experimental rave with 2 distinct rooms (*one happy hardcore, the other satanic gabba*).

She was fooling around with Simon, though it was going nowhere fast. They broke up that night and she floated off like a hurricane dandelion. Simon told me, in disgust: *"The more you know her, the more you'll hate her."*

That night ended in a house in the boonies at 5am, 20 of us huffing on a nitrous tank. Zelda was on mushrooms, bug-eyed, laying in an empty bathtub. I locked us in the restroom and we jabbered for an hour about naked, screaming, Anime bondage schoolgirls.

By 8am we were alone, devouring blueberry muffins at the bagel shop & having a brutal staring match with a drunken vagrant. I invited her over for a tour of my new residence and we soon leapt on each other, my Hawaiian restaurant theme song CD spinning in the background...

Thus the frenzy began... Mad Love, my pals. Every inch of me cried out for her to homogenize my milk, toot my trumpet, cream my wheat, shape my play-dough, toggle my boggle, scramble my eggs...

And for once sex was comfortable; it was *pure*. All the shame and degradation of my upbringing had been mutilated, butchered, left on the side of the freeway among ripped up tires, spark plugs, muffler shards.

I realized why I could never go through with any relationship or be comfortable with anyone for more than a few weeks. That repressive monster was always in the back of my head, truncating hope like machine instinct. But I took a sledgehammer to its ugly face.

I was liberated; a man possessed. We'd mambo through flea markets, glide endlessly to Rossini, Brahm, Chopin, Tchaikovsky – jump up & down on my mattress like spoiled children, create Lucky Charm soufflé's, spin in circles until sea-sick hypnosis; snarl like pyrates at elderly men while waving butter knife swashbucklers, run amuck in Hooters laughing at tight orange buns.

She'd keep me up all night on the phone speaking pure majesty, orchestrating happy hardcore symphonies on her Casio, delighting me with every wonderful splinter of her soul...

And Jesus 2000, her proposed cable television show...

We were to co-direct this magnificent program featuring a poor, receding hairline Jesus living in a shitty cockroach infested Manhattan apartment.

The only purpose his Jesus powers served were to cause him further dismay. Every lottery ticket he would purchase would be a winner but when handed in for its just reward it would evaporate into thin air...

Every sports team he'd root for – even if openly cheering against them to trick his powers – would lose pathetically. He was impotent & could never score with Hairy Harry the She-Male, his dire love interest.

Jesus 2000 is always defeated because he-she is always hoeing him out on a Saturday night for a midget with no arms or legs called "Wormy." His only friend was Hermaphro Bill, a half-human/half-alligator mutant in the sewers that would give him bad dating advice like Wilson from *Home Improvement*...

But it does not stop there, no sir-ree-bob – Jesus 2000 is like Magneto with oncoming traffic. The automobiles just fly at him, as do cans of Spam. Every time he steps into a lake to swim hundreds of leeches pound his scrotum; when he cracks an egg a half formed chicken plops onto the frying pan; every watermelon houses an angry bee hive.

And every time he goes to McDonalds & bites into a Chicken, a tumor sprays white yuckness all over the dashboard of his 1986 Festiva...

We liked each other *waaaaayyy* too much but... *she had a boyfriend.* I felt no ill harbor, yet after awhile she backed off & so did I... But then at it again... And gone... *And again, again, again* – intense circles until she snuck off to reside in a candy-kid commune... Twiddling my thumbs, counting the ticks of the clock: *"Zelda, Zelda, return to me, for my heart shall explode, my soul shall swirl down the shitter bowl of nothingness"*...

Deep in R.E.M, I had another jigsaw premonition regarding her. Actually, there were always strong premonitions. You see, it is an angle of my curse to know certain things about an individual long before they occur.

Originally I'd intended to pull a guardian angel scenario, keep an eye on her. What might that bad juju be? *Overdose.* Yep, the <u>BIG H</u>. I was madly in love with a girl I had pegged for certain death...

The dream... We were on a rusted fire escape in an alley somewhere deep in ghetto Detroit. In shadow-heavy blackness she was naked from the waist up, latching on to me shaking and crying, fluffy zebra raver pants leaving her wide open for ridicule. I look at her arms and half shot syringes hang out her arteries, vein holes gaping like tiny mouths. She's begging for help, for forgiveness as I'm protecting her...

Islamic zealots rush towards us with drawn golden swords. They stab me as I coat her body like living armor, but the blades are flimsy & harmless, limp macaroni as they prick my skin.

I hold her tight and gaze into the sky. The moon is full & bright, blood red – Islamic Star clearly defined in the middle... And I wake to the sound of steel crashing into a mountain of concrete, the pulse of fire, the mortified screams of thousands – *the age-old glimpse of snowing ash...*

I try to contact her for the next few days but she refuses to speak with anyone, even me. I finally get through on September 10th and she tells me she's been stealing heroin from her mother's purse and snorting it everyday for the past month.

This has been going on in spurts since she was 12. I freak out, write more of my novel, panic at even greater volumes then run outside. Like a man possessed I demand that if God has any balls he immediately bring on the cold turkey Apocalypse...

Last we spoke I explained how I'll most likely be running to Denver because at the mile high altitude the nuclear radiation won't be able to touch anything and that she should pack all her necessary belongings and flee with me.

She abruptly refused my offer, welcoming a horrifically painful death alongside her family rather than a post-apocalyptic romance with me in a barbaric world of nuclear winter & genetic mutation...

The RISE & FALL *of*
The Prozac Nation: *Part One*

Thus my work began, and the world I chose to create produced a vortex so chaotic hundreds were warped in the chain reaction...

The conflagration which festered so long within me had oozed into physical reality, culminating in a doctrine of intolerance. There was a term for our new tribe: *"The Prozac Nation."*

Quite simply *"Us"* versus *"Them"* – *the total elimination of all basic deficiencies in the collective body...*

The circles go far into the past and well into the future, but the opening of said Pandora's Box was centered right there, in that volatile moment of flux & metamorphosis – one lunatic design turned contagious, igniting a domino effect of many a cannon already loose...

My entire life had been a cocoon, continually shaping through a multitude of nightmares both inner and external. If there was an out, I'd long ago dynamite-encased the entrance.

The scales had tipped of my own volition, leaving the logical world flimsy and opaque on the continually receding horizon...

If ever a glimmer of hope existed, it was snuffed through my own dark consent. Whereas before there remained a ruthless struggle between solid ground & the sickness – *a constant juxtaposition between reality & the terrors of Zhivago* – there was now no distinction whatsoever...

So what then, after a terribly deluded child sacrifices himself to visions of the apocalypse? *To multiple personalities, shadow people, trance-states, drug-revelations, auditory hallucinations, astrological occultism?* All of this, encapsulated in the shell of an 18th tier underdog trauma victim? A laughable 14 year old wreck of egotism & derangement?

The term "wannabe" is adequate. It is the phenomenon of a crippled child who looks in the mirror and doesn't at all like what he sees. The reflection trumpets only its distorted prism; in eventuality he embodies it. I was a train wreck of compartmentalized emotions so sharply defined they took a life of their own...

When I speak of warping the world, of transmuting society, the mirror comparison is of the most importance. It was the ground zero campaign of all efforts, the finest way to push extremes & incite transformation.

In the quest to inflame one's passions, or to exploit them towards total havoc, all they need is the right voice whispering in their ear. The right push to help them break the chains. And there is no more potent a voice than that of the one who initially drops the gauntlet.

It's the concrete law of the self-remodeling chameleon. There always has to be a lightning rod conductor of a human being, a hurricane force of charisma with the right magnetism to take that hold.

The one that is so extreme in everything, so able to capture the attention & perfectly phrase those hidden desires beneath their lonesome struggle, that that person becomes the archetype the mirror gazer had lain in wait so for long for & thus allows themselves to be fully seduced by...

To pretend I was this superman would be an utter lie. But to admit that I was a brilliant actor in my own tragic play is fully assured.

Ryan was a 15 car high-speed pileup of a human being; he was average in almost everything – skinny, weak, pimply, alienated, mocked by peers and adults alike. Girls laughed at him, bullies picked on him – a third-in-command underdog treated like a passenger & never a leader.

But when Hyde took control, no one was laughing anymore.

Those introduced in the coming years would never know the worm existed. Mr. Bartek was an instant legend; an abnormal freak of steel-hard confidence & passion with a masterful domination over whatever human element precipitated – proud & strong, vengeful & arrogant.

Women took notice and men feared me – and all sad mirror gazers desperate to escape their cursed shells saw that very hope in me.

I was them – I knew what buttons to push, the surgically exact precision to fit the accord. To make them understand the abhorrent injustices of the surrounding world – to reexamine every detail of their perceptions, to comprehend the darkest purities; *to do away with the human dilemmas of guilt & morality and live as Gods upon the earth...*

The purpose was not to be some Fuehrer but instead create a million little dictators of their own fanatical persuasions. Just churn 'em out & sic the bastards loose. One colony begets another, one cell births the next. One gigantic network spreading with the rapidity of cockroaches...

The world of the stage, of our dreams & fantasies would be no different than the constant reality we'd face everyday. There would be no deviation between private and social life, no deviation between the artistic dream-state and physical manifestation.

Over time the network would swell to behemoth proportions. That this network didn't exist didn't exactly matter. If all subcultures fought for the same general goals but in different ways, then the network already existed, even if unrecognized. We were all components of a larger struggle that's DNA was the counterculture itself.

And surely I was not alone in my fanaticism, and surely there had to be others, and surely if we grew strong enough, traveled enough, pushed it hard enough, this pipedream would become reality. Surely there were other fanatics in every major city of the world, all brimming with the same ideas, pushing for the same general transformation, and we would no doubt link up to them in due to accelerate the process.

There was only one term to describe it – *"Pan-Tribalism."*

I viewed these goals as something inherently international in their makeup, although I had by no means any way of establishing such communication, nor would the older freaks on top of the subcultural pyramid of power ever take some psychotic 14 year old seriously.

I may have been young, and I may have been crazy, and I might have been grossly ignorant about a multitude of things – but I had a solid theory, guts of steel & a Nietzschean will to power.

"The Prozac Nation" was the tag for these humble foundations of empire which we'd build from the ground up, starting in Metro Detroit, and would exhaust its purpose & title once we could link the construct to larger communities who were theoretically pursuing the same general goals.

It was only after years of constant demagoguery that many took me literally, yet at that point what most would consider youthful daydreams towards conquest of empire simply becomes unsettling. It did not matter if I was able to convert. With every seed planted the web would spin itself in return...

Vic in particular, with no real sociopolitical devotions or hardcore anti-Christian outlook, simply shrugged off these ideas as a growing phase. In fact he was thoroughly annoyed by them, even more so as we grew older and he'd adopted pragmatic working class views.

Or as he used to say oh so jovially, *"I'm not your puppet motherfucker, so leave me out of this Satan Prozac bullshit. I don't care what crap you feed those morons – you just some crazy shit-head to me."*

My frequent tirades about a utopian construction became a topic to roll his eyes to, because for Vic there was only the nightmare. There is no question that he agreed with my hatred of the world, as did Smitty and the ever-gentile Robinson, who both sympathized with my outlook yet I could never consider die-hards.

Cassum always was a total zealot, albeit maintaining a vicious antagonism towards Satanism as "*total crap*." Brandon was an unstoppable blood-brother from day one as well. Salem too, albeit winging towards the satanic/pagan wing of the occupation.

It is also fair to admit that apart from the general psychosis enveloping all of us, we were in many ways normal kids insofar as our outside activities were concerned.

While the crew at Melissa's certainly indulged in rituals, we weren't sacrificing animals or having crazed orgies (*although I should have pressed the latter*).

Nor were any of us actively planning on killing people, stealing cars, consorting with the mafia, robbing gas stations, trafficking hardcore drugs, breaking into houses, assaulting people, counterfeiting money, mugging easy targets, committing arson, or the like...

But as for now we still did a great deal of average teenage things. We went to concerts, hung out in bookstores reading zines, went to the movies religiously sitting through 2 or 3 features in a row at the $1 show.

We'd dig through comic shop archives for hours, listen to records and discuss music, drudge through the clothing racks at Salvation Army, play street football, draw pictures, laugh ourselves silly with goofy jokes or make dumb videos with Smitty's HI-8 camera.

I was enamored by cheap records I'd pick up from thrift stores and sit around listening to polka, swing & mariachi vinyl for hours on end...

When we did get violent, we mostly fought ourselves to toughen up for future rumbles. We'd take turns defending ourselves against 3 others at a time, learn the best ways of dodging people or using their own body weight & propulsion against them. We'd demonstrate exploiting any opening or the finest offensive strike combos...

Vic began calling me all the time, mentally slipping – weird hours of the night explaining the nightmares. Always acid or demons, how he would trip & run through East Dearborn jumping fences, climbing garages, fighting dogs like *Weapon X*...

We'd walk those cold streets sharing anecdotes & dreams, dragging each other into a mutual abyss of fear. With my concentrated embrace of the "*sixth sense*," the more I opened myself up to the invisible world around me, the more I became a magnet for forces which I could not explain, or wished to explain away...

Oh yeah – I should've brought up The Gray Van last chapter. We were all being followed by an unmarked gray van with tinted windows. It had some kind of connection with the school system, our parents, the military...

Vic pointed it out in the middle of the night. I woke up to take a piss and he was staring out his front window like an attentive sniper. "*Look over there – don't open the shade too much.*"

The Gray Van was parked across the street, motor running, silently observing. He said it used to follow them everywhere when they were kids. Now it was back, parking outside our homes in the middle of the night. Cruising by our parties, examining our crew as a whole...

We had several theories... First, it may have been a private investigator collectively set up by our parents to find out what the hell was wrong with us. After all, Vic witnessed the driver of the Gray Van hand over a gray folder to Cassum's father.

There was definitely something going on there, a conspiracy with the school system. We'd hand in papers and on many occasions the rest of the class would get them back except for us – the teachers were hanging onto things, spying on us, spreading information.

I had once walked by a room full of 7 teachers who were talking about us in a meeting while everyone was at lunch. I only overheard a little, and booked when one of them realized someone was outside the door. I tried to tell my mom something was up but she'd flip out & say I was insane. I half-believed she was slipping drugs in my mash potatoes...

Then there were the Army recruiters. Several individuals we were associated with had gone to their center considering a military "career." They had a list with all our names & they'd request information, digging in our dirt. They knew what we were going to become before we became it.

The Feds were always crawling East Dearborn. We all knew about the Jihad and were convinced it would eventually happen. Would our home turf turn *Die Hard?*

Most the Arabic businesses in East D had bomb shelters; the blueprint for this huge Mosque they were completing for August 2001 had an underground shelter for 20,000...

We'd iterate our concerns that terrorists lurked our hood, but our parents & teachers said we were completely paranoid. It was, in fact, one of the delusions Vic received shock therapy for.

So eventually we just kept our mouths shut, neurotically preparing for the possible, theoretical zenith battlefield in which we'd defend East Dearborn to the last man standing...

Smitty was going through many revisions. It was a hurricane of change coursing his troubled spirit as he kept gobbling acid, getting into fights, chain-smoking, smoking pot heavily...

He'd become enamored by heavy metal, taking the lyrical messages to heart, utilizing them to become stronger. He'd eventually have that CFH logo (*Cowboys From Hell*) tattooed on his chest...

Smitty lost a lot of weight from doing plenty of push ups & sit ups. He ended up bringing an entire new crew into the picture – more preppy than anything, but they weren't soulless. They were into metal & horror movies & drugs but just looked kind of normal...

And thus enters Kelly, brought to my attention by Smitty & Vic. She was their mutual love interest and we were to meet her at the corner gas station where Smitty and I would get a kick loosely mimicking Jay & Silent Bob.

It was a foggy night, it just rained; unseasonably warm for September. She was standing in the parking lot taking drags off a Marlboro Red. She was involved in the occult arts – *I could just smell it on her*...

Kelly resembled Shirley Manson and had a glass eye that was light blue, scars all over from a bad accident. Later that night I got a phone call even though no one had given her my number.

She was to be my first girlfriend though it only lasted a few weeks cause I knew nothing about dealing with girls & was too fucked up to feel close to anyone except Helen, who I still could never work up the courage to make a move on despite mad love inertia tendencies.

Kelly and I only went on four dates. The first we hung around a coffee shop chain-smoking and she put her legs on my lap. At that point it was third base. My mother gave her a ride home and once she left the car mamma went on a tirade about what a worthless whore she was…

At Robinson's we were alone in this black lit basement where I put my arm around her for about 10 seconds until the screaming voices in my head made things horrifically awkward & uncomfortable…

The third date we went to a comic book show where we held hands, another first for me. One of the guys from GWAR rolled by on roller skates in a thong bikini and grunted at us. Iron Man just kept trodding his heavy boots of lead…

On the last date we saw *Periscope Down*. In the dark of the theatre the voices kept screaming at me that I put my hand up her shirt or she'd leave me because that's what guys did with girls in movie theatres, or so said movies themselves, my only real father.

So I did, mechanically – I fished for a nipple awkwardly cause I thought I was supposed to, and it wasn't good because she just sat there frozen. I stopped abruptly & remained relatively quiet until her mom picked us up. As far as I knew that's what boys & girls did at movies…

There was a big scene the next day because Smitty & Vic thought I'd treated their friend like a whore, and for this exact reason she didn't want anything to do with me.

I called & apologized but it ended anyway, although I didn't mind 'cause I was horrified by the entire thing & just wanted her to go away…

And she did so until Easter '96, after a much-needed church defamation campaign. We met for coffee & spoke Revolution. She'd become a quasi-goth Mother Goose; the female strange-lings flocked to her. We concurred to unite our sustained efforts of Freak Empire & "The Prozac Nation" was brought to a new level.

Finally I was being taken seriously, with someone who truly understood my noble visions of the iron broom. We began invading Pharaoh's Golden Cup, which served as our town hall...

Pharaoh's was a dark and dingy "all ages" local music venue with hieroglyph styled wall paintings that had exploded due to the post-Seattle boom and the resurgence of punk in the mid-90's.

It was a time when anyone & everyone that knew how to play three chords, could keep a halfway decent beat or roll around the floor screaming into a microphone was handed a gig. Coincidentally, every freak kicking around the area from age 10 to 25 did so.

There were so many bands crawling Detroit it was lunacy: *The Blood Sledge Electric Death Chickens, Bloody Dung, Telegraph, The Scholars, AFA (Another Fucking Abbreviation), Facegrind, Demise, Juan Valdez Love Machine, The Freeloaderz, Secret Service, The MIB's, Riot In Progress, Don't Ask, Nobody Good, Mad Henchman, Pickle, Pezz, Universal Stomp, The Nobodies, Sideshow X, The Hillside Stranglers, Passenger To Nowhere, Multigrain, Gutterpunx, The Parasites, Factory 81, Skazilla, The Epileptix, The Piranhas, Detroit Choirboys, Cryptic, The Independents, The Dendrites, The Trash Brats, The 3rd Degree, Spinfist, Fuzzbox Twins, Bones of Contention, Panic Attack, Neck-Back-Sacro-Illiacs, Tonsil Boxers, World of Hurt, Drizzle, Wafflehouse, Lost Direction, Misanthropy, Laceration, Suburban Delinquents, Endless Rage, Bizmark, Cast In Fire, Thicker Than Blood, Gutwrench, Rootbox, Bedford Drive...*

The Spaniards were among my favorites. Without a single practice they booked a show of pure misanthropic noise. They played for a half hour, vocalist rolling around in sawdust & hay. On stage there was a Farmer Jack imposter, arms crossed, unmoved for the duration like a

London guard. A hooded KKK trooper came out and did some break dancing moves, drummer sporting Mickey Mouse ears...

Pharaoh's was run by this mafia looking Italian guy sporting black turtlenecks & a slick leather jacket; he'd give Machiavellian advice to any that would listen. He knew the inner-workings of the floor, kept tabs on everyone. He knew what bands to mesh, how to keep inertia rolling.

He'd sit at the front door talking to everyone, extracting information for that little black book he always carried. He knew what kids were the main instigators of their respective scenes and made a point to hire them for odd jobs.

As a result a myriad of dynamics were at play – SHARPS, goths, punks, mohawk boys, emo types, rockers, metalheads, grunge folk, industrial obsessives. Pharoah's was connected to the Mosquito Club – a 21+ joint with a lot of traffic from smaller national acts.

The older crowd mostly hung at Mosquito, like big hair chicks with tassled fringe leather, but you could still get in with a fat no-booze X. Still, the youth were in abundance – both venues hosting endless 8 band gigs of our growing spirals.

With the duel onslaught of Pharaohs' & Mosquito so much D.I.Y. activity was going down that a dozen indie labels started out of that place, a zillion musical projects started up, and bands from out of state were streaming in & swapping gigs with locals throughout the Midwest circuit.

If there ever was proof of my infallible Pan-Tribalism, Pharaohs' represented direct evidence. I was right at home & networking like mad, filling up my own little black book – finally taken seriously...

By summer 1996 everything was in motion. Receiving a computer for "*school work*" I was now hooked into the Internet for the first time.

The second I realized I'd had the power to extract any bit of knowledge from the vastness of human civilization, any prospect of dragging me from that monitor was futile.

I saw, in one fatal stroke, the birth of cyber-anarchism. The world had forever changed, yet the adult world remained oblivious...

One day a knock rattled the screen door. It was Ed; he looked like he'd been on a bender ever since. He was unshaven, unkempt – his teeth a scummy yellow, like that of an elderly smoker.

He plopped himself on the rickety table he'd trash picked years ago & nervously blew through the majority of his 30 pack Budweiser case in a half hour...

Ed related tales of desperation sung with the underlying layer of severe alcoholism. He spoke of dropping acid as a youth, the mystic visions associated with Jim Morrison, the perils of cocaine sweet tooth – but most of all, the loss of my Mother...

Before mother pulled up he told me one last story. It was about a time he was lusting after his friends' niece. He said, "*I would have sold my soul just to have sucked the cock of the guy who last fucked her just so I could score a taste of her sweet cunt.*" It was last I ever saw of him...

There was a concentrated effort to get past all the crap mother did to me & just be friendly. We hadn't talked much in years, even though I saw her everyday. When we did talk, it was on a business level, yet still there were those fleeting moments where it was like before Ed left.

We were going to the cinema every Sunday but that was about all we had going – sitting in a darkened theatre and giving her the "PG Rated" version of my life along the ride. Anytime I ever tried to tell her anything she didn't want to hear she'd literally put her hands over her ears like a child and shake her head "*no*."

The only other connection was through gossiping about depressed millionaires who neither of us would ever meet, random television commercials. She learned not to fuck with my music anymore or lay any bullshit on too hard, because I wasn't scared of her anymore.

She basically came to the decision that I was rotten & set in my ways like a grown man. So she ran off with the Toby while I did god knows what while she wasn't looking, preferring to live in her own version of reality where I was a nice kid that watched a lot of horror movies, read comics & drew pictures all the time.

I had no option then to just struggle through it, since threats of boot camp or mental hospitalization.

She wanted Toby & us to be unit, which just wasn't going to happen. He completely killed it when we drove past some black guy sitting on a bench, and excited like it was some family activity time declared "*Hey, let's call the cops on that nigger!*" with a lil' zinger "*whudda-ya-say?*" rib-jab. My mom laughed and said "*Oh you're such a horn.*"

Toby, Mother and I drove to South Carolina for bonding but all it did was drive us further apart. I was scribing zombie literature which I attempted to share along the way, but mother started reading it & scolded me. Toby rolled his eyes holier-than-thou…

We went to Busch Gardens in Virginia, then I almost died in South Carolina. I was floating along the coastline when tidlewave dragged me under, belting my head on a rock. I nearly went unconscious. I struggled to get myself back upon the beach, gripping handfuls of mud.

Dizzy, whirled, I was dragged under twice again... When I made it to the hotel room I was so badly sunburned I'd water blisters all over my back, like an amphibian mane. I felt like I'd been worked over by a Singapore cane job.

We stopped for grub at a diner in Ohio. I was half awake, groggy from painkillers, and all I wanted was a burger. In response to the waitresses, I filled out the order in a slow, confused mumble: "*Umm... Cheese... And...*"

I was about to ask for pickles & Toby – assuming I was mocking her – totally unloaded on me, verbally ripping me apart...

And Davin, that guy, who'd been hanging at Smitty's – short kid with a big nose always climbing trees barefoot. I found him at Edsel. Sometimes we'd walk home after school.

He'd tell me all sorts of weird shit about "*eyes turning to hourglasses,*" demon entities out to kill him... He was on a Zhivago kick, but was seriously legit crazy.

July 3rd around 2am, atop a parking structure. Davin had been in a void-state, gabbing about suicide but none of us bothered to acknowledge him. It was pretty lame. Davin jumped on the ledge, outstretching his arms in some pansy martyrdom. He was mumbling gibberish about flying...

I dragged him down & kept slapping his face: "*Kill yourself on your own goddamn time fucker – I'm not about to get curfew violation over your sorry ass.*" Heartfelt support, you know – Course 101...

Davin stabbed me in the back when, in jealousy, he told Helen The Pimp I went on a lengthy, nasty rant about wanting to fuck her. Which was true, of course – but I certainly never talked about it. He made this up to both chase her off from me and rope her in for himself. I was appalled.

She was hurt & angry, quoting ridiculous lies. The bastard had devised a shameless grief-cock strategy! Helen was furious! She wouldn't listen & my perceived betrayal fermented a nexus of heartbreak!

Had Davin never set me up, we would've surely been an item – my first real girlfriend! It was a nightmare of no return!

I stormed over Smitty's intending to slug Davin in the jaw – but I was moments tardy. Turns out Smitty was so independently sick of him that he'd literally just thrown him out the house by force, threatening to beat his skull in if he returned!

Davin soon came back anyway, hammering on the door window & sobbing for us to let him inside. *"Please,"* he pleaded as paltry heel manager – *"you guys are my best friends!"* We heckled him through the glass, extending middle finger salutes.

I pulled the little roll-down shade over his tearful face, then we drank scotch & watched *Gremlins*. Throughout the rest of high school I'd make it a point to randomly sucker-punch him in the hallway or just spit on him. He never took a swing…

It was because of Davin's existence, at least materially, that I overdosed on pills. I was big into No-Doze, Mini Thins, snorting Ritalin – Davin supplied me with 3 full bottles of Prozac, 200 in all. I started eating the shit like candy, for a week straight (*maximum normal dosage is 30*).

It was such a great high, yet so unfortunately sensitizing. After 13 days of this my stomach knotted up, a cold internal wind. In nausea I made it to the bathroom and collapsed.

My heart stopped beating. I was concentrating on this ant scurrying across the tiles, fascinated by its anatomy. Everything was getting white & blurry, time slowing down, yet debating this insect was far more important in my final moments then considering any form of regret...

15 seconds later my heart kicked back in & I projectile vomited a massive stream so brutal it popped a blood vessel in my eye.

I had Brandon's brother give me a lift home, and I was sick for the next 3 days. I was a wreck of overly-sensitized emotions while detoxing – I nearly started crying while watching *The Relic*, realizing the kids were going to be gobbled by the pre-Cambrian beast. I swore it off...

And Kaitlin, sweet Kaitlin, whom owned my soul completely – the only girl I've ever known that could recite by heart every line of dialogue from Dawn of The Dead...

Kaitlin's best friend was an Australian chick whose father immigrated for a short-term work contract. It was at her apartment complex where Kaitlin & I first met.

Brandon & I were in the parking lot as they approached. She was a very pretty girl, highly Sicilian looking. Slender features, thin lips, cute little curved nose.I stretched out my hand for a shake like a door-to-door vacuum cleaner salesman & asked if she'd ever "*circumcised a circus seal?*" She began laughing.

I looked around crazy nervous then shouted "*AIR RAID!!!*" I dropped to the ground covering my head, avoiding the gunner ships. The girls toppled on me, then Brandon timbered upon us all. While squashed, Kaitlin pinched my ass (*though she'll never admit it*)...

A year later she started popping up over Gio's house, when we'd all drink & play euchre. She started calling all the time – and every day after school, I'd call her at exactly 3:30pm. And she was always on the other end, waiting without fail...

The RISE & FALL *of*
The Prozac Nation: *Part Two*

*"Prick Your Finger It Is Done/The Moon Has Now Eclipsed The Sun
The Angel Has Spread His Wings/The Time Has Come For Bitter Things"*

Antichrist Superstar was released October 8[th,] 1996 with Nagasaki-like precision, unfurling a collection of anthems that created an explosive zeitgeist – a near-flawless shock & awe campaign of mid-90's alienation…

In its proper place & time, *Antichrist Superstar* was a formal declaration of war. It wasn't even so much about Marilyn Manson himself – it was the *ideas* he propagated openly in pop culture – messages that all of America heard loud & clear (*though, of course, did not understand*). Every sleazy idea seeped into the fiber of mainstream, nimble as firestorm.

Even those who thought Manson was a total cornball yet still theoretically supported what he was doing – they were a disdainful target for "normal people." The was a very real, albeit historically brief, line that was "drawn in the sand," per se.

Religious parents often treated it like an "infection" – scores were committed to institutions, sent to boot camp, shipped of to Christian re-brainwashing centers.

Many were harassed by police or arrested because the stereotype – in some cases stalked by the police, as if gang members. Constantly, all over the USA, kids were either suspended or expelled from schools for supporting this band or rebelling against student dress code.

In repose, our multi-tribal barrage united under one general banner of open revolt, whether or not anyone wanted anything to do with Manson. Mr Brian Warner just happened to set it off as a conversation piece, or rather symbol, that all conservative parents could point their finger at. That was his point as a Magickal Alchemy – to make himself a symbol that became a mirror that reflected whatever the onlooker *wanted* to see. That was a key thing to his approach – using taboo subjects to get attention.

So in reaction to the weird spell that this Cosmic Alchemist / Chaos Magickian rendered upon the mid-late 90's, we all became absorbed by this strange pop culture disturbance that Americans, by & large, simply did not like or appreciate. And when the parents want something like this to go away – especially religious folks, cops, etc – it just makes it grow.

The only one who could ever mess this whole thing up was Marilyn Manson himself – and it seemed that this "Classic Manson" – this sleazy, creepy, super-dark Manson – wasn't going to be going anywhere anytime soon, unless he somehow croaked young. As far was we could tell, he was going to "stick to his guns" & not water down, ever ever ever.

With this psycho-rocker pushing it as far as he could, long as he could – theoretically for life – it seemed that this Dark Era would last much, much longer & the heat would just keep growing.

Wvery malicious, tragic character it seemed was now running around the nation in a Nothing Records based temper tantrum, egging on God to bring Armageddon & dancing on the smoldering edges of society.

Manson's rise was perhaps a psychological ramification of Kurt Cobain's suicide. The vast majority of youth had been immersed in the Seattle sound. Cobain had unintentionally framed a sense of identity & unison for millions of pre-teens before traumatically taking himself out.

Nine Inch Nails' *The Downward Spiral* came out days before the suicide, priming the deranged transition. All those day-dreaming kids, all those little lunchbox girls – they latched onto Reznor in Cobain's absence.

With *Portrait of an American Family,* Manson became a lower-level influence within that echelon, having been Reznor's protégé. With

Antichrist Superstar, Manson became the breaking point, replacing any trace of Cobain – the wildcard who brought the dark era to fever pitch.

Antichrist Superstar was a gospel of reverse absolution; proto-black metal for the unwitting American outcast. It entranced the youth with an ideology nearly identical to mine – a LaVeyian, Pan-Tribal war-cry. It was the ace I needed to cement my morbid worldview into active reality...

October 15th, 1996 was the first show of the *Dead To The World* tour, crash landing at State Theater Detroit.

I was pressed against the stage when Manson walked out – he was an 8 foot giant in his platform boots, wrapped like a mummy in medical gauze, corpse-paint splattered over his face. Soon as the first few measures of *"Angel With Scabbed Wings"* screeched the entire place exploded.

Manson was absolutely filthy, begging the audience to spit all over him; flailing his trouser snake, rubbing broken glass all over his chest, wiping his ass with the American flag & demanding revolution.

At one point Manson took the podium as a quasi-fascist dictator ripping up the *New Testament* with 2,000 hypnotized teens throwing up their fists in unison, demanding the rise of The Antichrist. It was beautiful.

Salem and I were drenched in sweat outside the show, among Miriam and Melissa awaiting our ride, when the tour bus pulled up beside us and beckoned our buddy Kevin on board.

Kevin used to hang out at Pharaohs with us sometimes. He wasn't a midget – he had a deterioration disease that made him 3 feet tall. The roadie brought him on the bus where Manson personally signed him as an actor for some upcoming music videos.

Kevin appeared in the *"Tourniquet"* video as the little granite man, as well as the video for *"I Don't Like The Drugs"* later on, in 1999...

I was in English class when Crenshaw stomped in disgruntled & anti-social, limping his gimp ankle to a loner seat in back. His trademark uniform – red-laced paratrooper boots, army fatigues cut into shorts & a *Filthpig* T-shirt. A poorly dyed black Mohawk draped down his face and a junkyard of scrap metal glistened from his neck, ears & fingers...

Crenshaw was a Native/Caucasian hybrid from Downriver (*the hill-jack territory from South Detroit to Ohio*). He moved to Dearborn to stay with his mom after his tattoo artist father attacked him with a baseball bat. His mother remarried a Christian music producer and had 5 other kids.

We soon hung out & created dozens of prank flyers – missing buffalo signs, death warrants, phone sex hot-lines, eulogies, epitaphs, satanic verses – nailing them to telephone poles, mailboxes, car windows.

We head down railroad tracks towards the strip mall and found a fresh lump of magnificent roadkill.

Twas a squirrel sliced in half from the train wheels so perfectly it could've been the handiwork of a gifted & delicate surgeon. I named the poor bugger "Chad" and impaled its upper torso on a stick.

Crenshaw jumped into a shopping cart and I spun him in donuts as spectators gazed in bemusement & confusion...

As I pushed him towards the odious reality of Dearborn High School we approached a congregation of jocks in the middle of an outdoor gym session. They headed towards us with threatening honky stride – but Crenshaw began swinging Chad around in a frenzied circular motion, rambling gibberish.

They realized what it was and turned ghostly white – they backed off unsettled and the coach drew near. I pried Chad from his knuckles and chucked it into the road before coach could call the police...

Crenshaw was a complex character that seemed to fear absolutely nothing; an apocalyptic ferocity manifested into a highly tuned art of self-destruction. Not only did he detest every naive student but he'd made it his mission to blatantly promote it using bold antithetical aesthetics.

He wanted to attract the most negative reaction possible towards him at all times. He loved to be hated & wanted to destroy everyone's day from his sheer state of being. He'd walk up to the popular kids, supposed tough guys & slam them into lockers or knock books out of their hands.

Hysterical, considering he was a skinny, weak shit that could barely walk straight 'cause the muscular distrophy in his legs. His hardcore exterior was so poised for war that he intimidated all the squares.

He felt very strongly that whatever you wear is a costume and it's important to be creative (*and offensive*) as possible. He'd get suspended for coming to school in dresses with upside down crosses carved into his skin. I'd have to say that my favorite get up was a black trash bag and nothing else. He ripped holes in it for his head & appendages...

Crenshaw was abnormally street smart – his great ability was to erase all boundaries so that every environment he existed in would be the same as his private life with no distinction. There was no plastic face, no hidden personality – just honesty, brutal as possible, ridiculing everything he saw as false, stupid & materialistic in the modern world.

He also had serious beliefs in occultism, satanism & witchcraft, and became a fixture over Melissa's, soon hooking up with Miriam. He felt just as strongly about his ancestral Native American heritage as I did about my Celtic roots, and in the same vein, saw his rebellion & rejection of the modern world as being inextricably tied to the memory of his ancestors.

Crenshaw and I began dialectic psychological warfare operations on the unwitting populace of Edsel Ford. We'd stand on our desks in the middle of class preaching philosophy, politics, polemics – the anti-life in all its splendor. We'd build staple altars and perform ritualistic insect sacrifices for Mesopotamian Godmonsters. We'd saunter the halls speaking of our vicious STD'S – *the itching, the pussing...*

We'd build snowmen & women in *menage-a-tois*, hijack full boxes of holy wafers from Catholic discount stores to commence our own mock communions, steal edible undies and fool cheerleaders they were Fruit Roll-Ups. Devour tequila worm Popsicles for students to see – at lunch smash ketchup & bananas in Ziplock bags marked "ABORTED FETUS" & suck 'em out with Tropicana straws. Crenshaw would shove safety pins through his skin, hook car batteries to his tongue or nipples in auto shop...

I began taking video classes at Dearborn High, the sub-level video class beneath Gibson. He was a retired music promoter that used to run the Grande Ballroom in the 60's and The Greystone in the 80's.

He was responsible for both The Stooges and The MC5 getting signed to majors and was known as The Man you'd come to if you were looking to gig in Detroit. Gibson knew them all – Leary, Morrison, Hendrix. He was actually with Janis Joplin the night before she died.

He was loaded and supplied the equipment, making the video program among the best of its kind nationwide. He'd an army of student henchmen that were skinhead converts (*"Gibskins"*) because he totally believed in the SHARP Movement (*Skinheads Against Racial Prejudice*).

Vic and I were excited to use the editing equipment that was of a professional television studio; we had Hollywood in our eyes. The first short we made was called *One Dark Night* – sort of a *Reservoir Dogs* meets *Halloween* epic.

It was a silent film involving a handful of gangsters who had just robbed a bank in the typical Tarantino "skinny black tie" suits. We ran into an abandoned house to hide from the pigs and examine the loot – a glowing suitcase (of course).

One by one we start getting picked off by Robinson playing a psychotic half-zombie cultist. It was a splatter fest & by finale Vic blasted Robinson with a shotgun. He had this giant blood pack taped to his back – when he flung himself against the wall it exploded everywhere – his entire basement looked like a used Maxi-pad...

Before filming this particular short we encountered police friction. In broad daylight Smitty, Vic & I were walking towards the shoot in costume. We had a prop handgun & Vic whipped it out loudly going off about killing people, laughing up a storm.

Soon as we walked into Robinson's 10 squad cars pulled up – K9 units, battering ram, pistols drawn – *a full out raid*. Just mentioning Gibson made them back down...

Over sophomore year we continued to make shorts. One of my favorites was *Chili On The Rouge* in which I played Philip, a Chilean foreign exchange student that Vic (*as a dope smuggler named "Master David"*) brought to the USA for sweatshop labor.

I slept on a stack of hay and was used for various slave functions (*cooking drugs, breakfast, gardening*) until Master David decided to have me murdered to cover up all evidence. After being beaten half to death by his goon squad he had a change of heart, rescued me, and we made up drinking Vodka beneath the full moon. *Genius...*

And Kaitlin, sweet Kaitlin... One look in her eyes coupled with the right zang of electricity & it was all over. Her hair, her skin, eyes, curves, fragrance and lips...

I still swoon to the thought of her; the dark princess, unable to sleep at night lest she'd watched enough graphic violence and been able to curl up next to the blank snow channel of the nearest TV set.

Kaitlin was a talented pianist and excellent painter – a walking dictionary of movie quotes & especially the horror genre. Her room was a mosaic of newspaper clippings – intricate amalgams of words & images. We were always headbutting each other, filling up coloring books, doing horrifically dirty things with salad tongs.

We had a great time tormenting her Ecuadorian foreign exchange student whom Kaitlin's stepmother thought would be cute to adopt for a brief year, like a begging puppy from the pet store window.

Shortly before Halloween we were married in a mock ceremony. She promised to have my abortion, whom we would nickname "Gus." After its mushy baptism we'd cart it around in a stroller hand in hand among all the young couples, our bloody lump of joy firmly preserved by the embalming fluid of a filthy mason jar. Our baby pictures consisted of butchered rabbit Polaroid's mailed from France...

I no longer remember the first time we hooked up – something about stolen bowling shoes & French kissing behind a dumpster.

The following day I slammed a pint of vodka & accidentally popped my ankle in & out of socket. I didn't feel it but when I got home I puked everywhere & passed out in my own vomit. My mom caught me & I was grounded for 2 weeks, hobbling around.

In my absence Kaitlin floated over to this other guy – the first real jealous freak-out I'd ever had, to be honest – but I quickly got her back.

But then the dude showed up 20 guys looking to fight me! When I came out on the porch to confront him, he shrank in size & retreated femininely. One of his "boys" knew me – and once dude ran away from his abandoned attack half his lynch mob stayed there with me, getting' me stoned!

I continued to follow Kaitlin, and not long after the most beautiful thing I ever experienced up to that point happened to me – she just put her arms around me & we sat there buzzing in the back of our skulls.

Just quiet, comfortable silence laying on her bed in the blue of winter moments before sundown. No one had ever physically touched me before in such a way. All that pain, it was like she absorbed it. For years I would fall asleep to its memory...

Everything was dandy until her best friend moved to Australia. Kaitlin broke down in a monsoon of despair & started cutting herself up again. Not for attention but 'cause of the indescribable release.

Her arms would be a mass of red, scabbed up lines; she cut off most of her hair & later shaved the sides to make a wide semi-mohawk.

She began dressing more extreme, drinking all the time; gobbling acid & mescaline. She developed a bad case of mono – she'd be like a corpse for weeks at a time, then right back up into destruction. She kept lapsing in & out of severe sickness, unhinged from hallucinations. She left me reeling when the white-coats kidnapped her...

I'm not sure if there was a suicide attempt but I knew it was in her history. At 9 she threw herself down the stairs during a fight with her mother. She blacked out and woke up in an institution, not sure how it happened or where she was. Ever since she's had a tendency to flip out when waking up somewhere foreign at night, vomiting from panics...

Once out she backed away – she dumped me in a self-destructive frenzy & started fucking around with dark characters from Pharaoh's. Yet no matter what happened, she'd still call me everyday at 3:30 pm, or at random hours of the night telling me how important I was to her.

It was a constant bi-polar swing from my girlfriend to the consuming mess, leaving me scarred in a situation where she loved me so much she couldn't be with me. And I could not let go, and it did nothing but amp up the factor of personal insanity.

Kaitlin finally settled on Maurice, a cross-dressing Goth type that was Irish/Cantonese. He was all fucked up cause of his father's suicide. His father lapsed into paranoid schizophrenia, pulled a gun on the brothers, and was sent away to the asylum. He got out & soon after soaked himself in gasoline & struck a match...

Although I sympathized, I despised him cause he was constantly grabbing at my ass & being uncomfortably sleazy queer & he *was a serious heroin addict & acid-head, as nearly all other weirdos from the Livonia/Redford/Westland area that hung at Pharaoh's...*

Although it isn't crucial to intimately know this grotesque collection of misfits, it is important to understand the inner workings of the crew we amassed from campaigns towards solidarity in the inferno of Pharaoh's.

Seth was semi-leader of the Livonia faction, his house the main HQ. He was 6 foot 3 with long black hair, skinny physique – identical to Manson sans corpse-paint with a real hard-on for chain-mail, leather gloves with lead-implanted knuckles, trench-coats & medieval weaponry.

At 19 he was screwing most of the girls, and there were probably 30 loonies that bounced in & out of his domain. When absent, they'd normally hang at an abandoned mental institution nearby; Seth's floor was covered with stacks of inpatient profiles in manila folders.

They'd also infest the haunted "Northville Tunnels," this huge system of underground bunkers created in the 50's during The Red Scare. They were long-discarded, but creepy as hell, and many people had died exploring them by falling down unseen holes 20 feet deep; some were murdered outright by junkies or devil worshipers (*or so they say*).

No one ever knew who these "devil worshipers" were, but they'd leave pentagrams drawn on walls with animal blood & black wax. They found the severed head of a cow with nails hammered through it's tongue.

When GG Allin would play Detroit, the Northville Tunnels were his favorite place to hang out. Some of Seth's older acquaintances used to give GG tours of the place or shoot dope with him there.

Carrie was Seth's heartthrob, about as tall as he was with a Jester-like smile. She had chin length dyed black hair, and usually wore black dresses with army boots alongside a metal ammo box for a purse.

She was very beautiful, perceptive, gentile, artistic – pure Irish with the spirit of a pagan nature girl who'd get most her kicks from tombstone stencils.

I don't think she minded Seth's sex pursuits with other ladies because she was into girlies as well. Carrie once gave me a necklace as a gift, with little silver crabs so I'd always remember her as "*the girl that gave you crabs on your birthday*" ...

Heroin Mickey supplied all the dope. He dished out smack at Pharaohs, and caused a chain reaction where nearly 30% of that scene ended up abysmally hooked. 70% of the Livonia faction were booting up...

Late '97 Heroin Mickey was hit for a B&E and ran on bond, hot-wiring a Ford to Texas only to overdose at a motel en route to Mexico...

Daisy took her name from Manson guitarist Berkowitz and was really into Satanism. She was one of the few that I talked to on a regular basis. She was trash-punk all the way – ripped up clothes, crazily died hair, nutty looking eyes. Forever drunk and high, her jokes were poorly delivered & her actions totally obvious.

The parents were ex-hippie Born Again Christians. Eventually she was too, after a rave party in '00 when she ate 12 globs of liquid acid and snorted a mountain of K & crystal.

Every time she closed her eyes Satan was trying to pull her soul away from her and every time she opened them Christ was fighting on her behalf with a golden sword. Therefore, of course, it was totally real and not a drug-induced hallucination...

Stalker John whom Kaitlin briefly dated. She dumped him soon as Maurice was released from rehab. Guy walked 30 straight miles overnight in the rain to plead for her love.

He showed up at her high school, stalking her between classes, and ran away after she called the cops. He wrote her love letters for a good year afterward even though they dated 2 weeks.

Riverside Tony, bossman of "The Riverside Punks," a Prozac Nation affiliate composed of crusts, mohawk boys, vandals and thugs that were a central force in the Pharaoh's world.

He was the hardass that ran the security, and was always breaking up or instigating random brawls in the parking lot. He was 17 and rock solid, wore wife-beaters & carried a baseball bat like a walking cane...

Maurice II, the little brother. He was a nice kid, only 12 and shooting dope. I liked him a lot more than his brother, who was still making my life a perpetual hell with Kaitlin.

He'd hang out with us at Pharaohs & would be one of many cruising around in snake-like auto caravans that sometimes stretched up to 24 cars any given night. By early '98, Maurice II pulled a B&E & was condemned to a tether...

And Stella, a 26 year old darkling hottie in every respect; she usually worked the bar at Pharaoh's. If you would've thrown some Hilfiger on her she would've been Prom Queen of her entire school district.

Shaved eyebrows, corpse-paint & a flair for the cheer-leading outfits she'd steal from the open garages of Suburbia. I think she was one of the few that didn't get into the needle or bailed from it before too late...

Crazy Tim was Seth's buddy; one of the oldest at age 20, but he had the mind of a 15 year old. An avid comic collector, he was really into Iced Earth & 80's Power Metal – tall & goofy with long blonde hair...

Crazy Tim was always off center – he got into Manson because of *Mechanical Animals*, seriously dug the Vanilla Ice rap-metal album & thought Michael Graves' Misfits were superior to the Danzig era. Really?

In August '98 we picked up Vic and smoked a joint in the alley around Smitty's block.

Out of nowhere this 1990 Buick barrels down the alley doing at least 40 mph. It turns the corner and disappears – 30 seconds later, it comes back at least 50 mph & misses us by inches. It flies into the street and pulls a hit and run after it slams into the passenger side of a Taurus.

We're baffled because we're still locked into the first 10 minutes of stonerdom when everything is at its fuzziest, funniest, most confusing peak. We run to the accident and this old lady is having heart palpitations.

She hands us her cellphone and Vic dials the cops. The car pulls around the other end and parks with the engine running. I start booking towards it – Crazy Tim yells: *"Run Forrest Run!"*

I nearly fall over laughing and this crazy lady jumps out, hops a fence, lands on her head, struggles to get up and books down the street. I think about chasing her but instead rummage through her car, steal $20 out her purse with some loose change & walk back to the guys. The old lady is fine now and we abandon her because we're baked and desire Slushies.

At 7-11 I realize it's illegal to leave a crime scene so we come back & the cops have hit-&-runner in custody, 6 times the legal limit. We're absolutely stoned & the cops keep telling us we're heroes.

Her whiskey breathed husband runs up not knowing what happened and I tell him, *"The cops just started beating the shit out of this crazy bitch with their nightsticks – it was awesome!"*

Vic follows me up: *"Yah dude, she's all fucked up – bleeding everywhere n' shit."* The husband freaks & we exit silently. Later on we were called in to testify but she plead "no contest" at the last minute...

With all of those maniacs dive-bombing into the junkie shitter, Kaitlin's father sold the house & moved them right into the center of the problem. Kaitlin now lived down the street from Daisy, Seth & Maurice...

Around then, I had one of the most powerful dreams of my life. I "awoke" in the middle of a rusted playground at midnight. It was small park, like a median in the middle of a great metropolis where not a human dwell, where the only light was from burning fires in the distance.

The force of gravity halfway existed; my movements were light, drifting easily. It was as if my entire environment was in slow motion but I was normal speed.

A great abandoned city surrounded me, all of the buildings windowless, dead & black; one dead skyscraper in the center of it all, as if its blackened heart. A soothing voice came from the distance.

"*Hello Ryan.*" A 19 year-old kid emerged from the darkness in a black leather coat, black slacks, dress shirt and tie. He had short black hair, a freshly shaved clean-cut face, and hypnotic, light blue eyes.

He looked pan-sexual perhaps, like an otherworldly trans person without any makeup, like some smooth-skinned, wraith-like alien with near human likeness. The Devil asking me to politely take a walk, arms folded behind his back. He told me that we were in Hell and everything written in the Bible was horribly incorrect because God *Itself* wrote it...

According to this dream Devil, God was actually an entity from another dimension that created humanity as an endless source of consumption. Christ was it's disciple, tricking man into believing it existed so when a person died they'd give their souls unflinchingly. God would then digest the mind & essence as a sort of endless battery supply – as if Galactus devouring planets.

To continue the Judaeo-Christian belief, it employed the angels to form a series of coincidences & miracles. That was their job until this Lucifer I now spoke with turned on It, attempting to destroy god for it's lies. God couldn't kill the rebels because in doing so it would only destroy itself – so it cast this Lucifer from HETH (*heaven's apparent title*).

If a soul did not maintain faith it would enter HELL, a mass construct of all the old memories & emotions held over from the past lives of all who entered it. Both its existence and the continued longevity of souls were based upon the vitality of energy flowing into HELL; unless a spirit could adapt it'd eventually fade from lack of said energy.

This was accomplished through spiritual cannibalism – souls devouring souls. And it was The Devil's curse to be trapped in this realm, both Hell & God mirroring an endless heroin-like addiction of death...

The Marilyn Manson concert in Saginaw marked the beginning of summer. It was a reaffirming scenario given hysteria by 300 Christian protesters, an army of pigs & paparazzi + 5000 die-hards flooding a convention center.

The decapitated corpse of a sparrow was found in front of the mini-arena. Someone tore its head off, drew a pentagram in the sidewalk with its blood alongside the cryptic message *"FUCK CHRIST"* ...

Soon came Damian's suicide. Soon as Vic, Cassum & a few others walked up his driveway they saw a gunshot flash from his bedroom window.

I never met him but Vic & others knew him well. He was kind of reserved – a nice guy with an unwavering belief in God. The moment it all flip-flopped was when he ate bad acid – he was found ranting & raving about shadow people sometime later. For days he was still hallucinating, thinking demons were out to get him. He was institutionalized & released a few weeks before ***...

Damian's death brought many local punk & metalheads & freaks together – the original *"East Side Crew."* Most these guys were older & would soon filter away, but it was a Grand Momment in time...

A similar incident happened to another acquaintance from WDHS, one of Kelly's now-disbanded Witchcraft Coven. While asleep at night "something" attacked her *of shadows*.

Her mother found her screaming, completely out her mind, talking Shadow People. She was committed to the asylum & remained on heavy doses of psychiatric drugs until she dropped out later that year.

I had a freakish moment as well, of notable paranormal intensity. I'd seen *Spawn* at the movie theater, then went home to a pitch black, motionless house and entered the bathroom.

On the toilet looking directly at the attic door – pants around my ankles – something behind the attic door starts launching Mike Tyson style punches at full force from the other side, the door rattling off it's hinges.

I whip up my pants and kick open the door, breaking the lock – it swings all the way open, hits the wall; no one is there! I jet outdoors & pace my neighborhood chain-smoking & talking to myself until Smitty found me in shock. I stayed at his house that night...

The Fabio war was another bizarre situation of Vic's endlessly wacky summer. He was institutionalized a few days then once released his ex-girlfriend died after getting hit by a flat-bed truck.

The next week his appendix exploded and his parents made a big deal about calling an ambulance 'cause it would've cost tons of money. He nearly died on the way to the hospital.

By the time it nearly healed up he was chopping wood out back with a double bladed axe. He was stoned and didn't realize how much strength he was putting into it; it got stuck in the log and he yanked it back – blasting the axe right into his forehead!

One inch deeper, he'd be dead; one inch lower and permanent eye-patch! One iota stronger, and a fractured skull!

The axe in the bone of his brow but stopped short of cracking it – no permanent damage! Vic got 7 stitches above his left eye – afterwards, he looked like some hard-ass ninja super-hero!

Then came Fabio – a super-smelly, gas-station owning cologne-douser; covered in gold, with a Mustang & thug friends – tough ass drug-dealing types. He & two buddies cornered Vic in the street. They were about to go at it when out of nowhere this crazy fucker with Charles Bronson sized balls interrupts.

Vic looks over and there's this crazed looking Arabic punker with a dark blue Mohawk built like a tank. He's got an Islamic star tattooed on his forearm and a HATE tat on his knuckles (*no LOVE on the other*).

The punk attacks! He busts out one guys' teeth, hops over the mustang, uses jumper cables like nun-chucks and beats the fuck out of Fabio like he's an old punching bag. *And that's how we met Caylin…*

It was mid-summer when Crenshaw got his first car – a dilapidated 1987 GM Station Wagon ghetto-cruiser-deathtrap which we spray-painted black. You could hear us rumbling a mile away blasting the likes of Skrew, The Misfits, Birmingham 6, Bile, Ministry, Black Flag…

We drove to his homeland territory to hang his cousin (& *best friend*) Byron, lived with his mom at a tiny apartment in the "poor white trash" projects, snooty honkies might claim. They were descendants of Mark Twain. His mom was real nice – a skinny, burned out hippie chick that Crenshaw considered his second mom.

Byron was 15, with a tough build & blonde hair slicked into a ponytail. He was likable – not the brightest, but friendly & loyal. The reality of 7:101 became a HQ for our Edsel High School pals…

Crenshaw and I always had a strange chemistry. He'd be the first to do something radically shocking then I'd back him up with intellectually stimulating anti-speech soliloquy that would put us both in an uproar – pushing myself further towards extremism & catapulting his defiance.

We were equally destructive influences on each other and by September '98 the shoplifting sprees began. It wasn't long before I'd become a full-blown kleptomaniac. His trunk was soon packed with gadgets: beepers, cell phones, CD's, t-shirts, instruments, books, jewelry...

I began telling classmates I could get any CD they desired for $5. What began as a small time scam became an enterprise; we were now accepting full pages of orders daily.

Since we lacked the manpower to comply with the wild momentum of supply & demand, I suggested keying in some low life thugs on our business...

My first choice was Sloppy & Sid – they were like a deviant Abbot & Costello. Sloppy moved from Japan; he grew up on a military base near Tokyo. He was a hyperactive chubby kid; after a failed suicide attempt to slit his wrists with a Bic pen, he started hanging out with Sid & his friends – devilish hoodlums who'd beat him up & steal his grandfather's booze...

From then on it was a cakewalk. The further I ventured into the world of retail fraud conspiracy the deeper I penetrated the realities of the lives surrounding the Rivergreen Projects.

We began hanging out there nearly every day of the week. It became a perfect balance for our disorderly conduct – an epitome of broken dreams, harsh realism, anti-exogamy & centralized chaos.

The apartment itself was legendary in Rivergreen folklore. The walls were so heavily coated with THC through years of heavy smoke that grown men would seriously lick the walls to try & score a buzz.

We spent many nights conversing with strange mutants and loving every second of it. They were all minor miracles in their own unique ways. These magnificent specimens burst in & out with hurricane charisma.

The usual characters involved Redneck Dean (*a clueless hillbilly that'd arm wrestle you drunk & tell you how much you resemble his son*), Marvin & Mullet Ray (*who claimed to been ICP's high school bullies*).

Pegleg Pete who had a prosthetic leg. He used it primarily as a beer bong – and had once taken on 3 cops with it while dusted to the eyeballs on meth...

Marvin was either appallingly ruthless or extremely cool. He had mood swings like a pregnant woman and talked in a mumbling thug tone. He would rip on me for being unemployed but would always toss me smokes and fries from McDonald's. He'd get drunk and do cartwheels in the living room and break and smash whatever the hell stood in his way.

Of all the characters at 7:101, my all time favorite would have to be Crackhead Ruthie. Ruthie was this helpless, babbling rock fiend that would try to sell us cold, wet sausages and stale animal crackers.

One time we forced her to smoke pot with us while in a crack stupor. Her mind was clearly locked into that campground beyond the sun.

"Ruthie – sing 'I love Pena Collates' – show us your vocal talent!" She then went into a hacking spell that may have actually been her form of creepy mirth and out came *"I LOVE A PENIS AND A-CUM-A-CUM-A-CUM!"* in an undeniably uproarious black tone.

We began roaring with laughter. *"Ruthie, what does God look like?"* *"Shit, God be lookin' like E.T. right now!"* *"Ruthie, who did you vote for?"* A strange amphetamine transmission hit her and Ruthie began screaming *"HEIL HITLER! HEIL HITLER!"* & giggling pure insanity...

It was late '97 when I made the decision that what we were theoretically doing just simply wasn't cutting it. We had kicked & screamed and did as much as possible to make the pillars of our community collapse but it seemed to have absolutely no effect.

I figured if we couldn't make our slice of America fall apart through our feverish delinquency than I would have to take it upon myself to do so manually.

I started to bring a wide assortment of tools to class each day so that I could disassemble as many desks, chairs, lighting fixtures, door hinges, pencil sharpeners and sockets as possible.

Kids were sitting down and collapsing with their desks – the whole school was falling apart...

I was sealing my 3rd mason jar of freshly plucked screws when Crenshaw approached strung out, resembling a cadaver. He spent the evening in jail 'cause the record store we hit the hardest installed security cameras underneath the used CD racks.

When the cop searched him he dug through Crenshaw's pockets and ripped his finger on a razor blade. The jig was up and he had something secretive to tell me: *Miriam was pregnant.*

War began within The Prozac Nation. Seth and I were butting heads – but when I hooked up with his love interest Carrie, jealousy overtook him. It was bad enough that she dumped him, but wandering over to *that guy?*

I hadn't planned it 'cause I was still totally oblivious to women. And Carrie? She was smoking hot in my eyes. Too good for me, assuredly. I never would've tried 'cause I never thought I'd stand a chance.

I had confidence in my ideological dealings, my "business pursuits", but I was still awkward & shy with girls. I saw my inter-personal dealings as a matter of revolutionary business with fellow comrades.

While I was ranting my delusional view of Revolutionary Utopia, pushing this agenda – what I really was on was "a date," because in the really real world kids were just kids, and not revolutionary soldiers.

So when girls hung around waiting for me to make a move, I never caught on cause I was on my own planet, and terrified of them on any level outside *The Revolution.*

It's how I ended up hanging out with a surplus of 30 girls, many who were drop-dead gorgeous. I'd get their numbers, we'd go on these distorted dates, and I'd never make a move, just babble about overthrowing reality for weeks on the phone, and they'd assume I wasn't interested and "give up" while still "shooting the shit" with me on a regular basis, which in turn I viewed as ideological solidarity, not friends being friends.

When girls did make "that move" I wasn't expecting, or were plainly telling me to do so, I never would, because I simply would make myself ignore it in favor of my fantasy world.

And if they did make that move, it would rarely get further than a few days, because I hated most everyone & didn't wanna absorb their energy, feel their feelings, all that gross shit.

To show emotion was to show weakness, and detachment was elite & substantial. I was incapable of showing affection 'cause all I saw were monkeys & puppets, except for a handful that were *real people,* because they too were elite.

I had so many opportunities where women threw themselves at me and all I did was stand there like a dummy – *Kaitlin even!*

For all I tortured myself, she'd tell me things, ask I be something else – and I'd ignore it as if she never said anything! My anxiety doomed me – it clouded everything.

As I look back, these are some of my only real regrets. I could have ran around in a perverse whirlwind tasting every color of the rainbow had I been able to snap out of it. I was a pussy magnet and never even realized it 'cause self-deluded international revolutionary psychosis.

This irrationality is generally inherent in the pathology of the totally alienated – the compulsion to constantly destroy all achievements because success is intolerable.

And because failure is equally intolerable, one finds themselves lost in a meaningless struggle where the most resounding victory & barren defeat are often one in the same...

When I began talking to Carrie on the phone mid-'96, I figured it was business. We hung out 3 times, the first at Daisy's where she and Carrie molested me with outer-course.

But in typical scarred fashion, I never made that move, although I thought she was stunning. So it fizzled 'cause she thought I wasn't interested and hooked back up with Seth for a year.

By fall of '97 Seth went bye-bye, and I had randomly called to see how she'd been. She came over with this lame goth kid she was rebounding with, who annoyed us with his stories of jumping off a roof to commit suicide but waking up on the pavement with 2 purple bruise hand-prints on his chest because "Christ" had prevented his fall. When he left us alone, we just started making out on my bed.

Seth was furious 'cause the 16 year old loopy dictator had stolen his nearly 20 year old goddess. Third day officially together she came over.

As we were getting ready to go out, I leaned over & kissed her on the couch 'cause that's what they did in the movies and on TV. She slammed her tongue down my throat and just lunged on me – 5 minutes later both our pants were off, and I'd finally soiled my royal oats.

I was officially de-virginized and it took zero effort. I wasn't sure if I should act differently towards her, but I did need a Marlboro Red. As we drove around that night, nothing had changed. We drank coffee & talked normal. I went home & listened to vinyl of *Dark Side Of The Moon*

We went out for 2 more weeks, but I was still terrible at this romance thing, with no clue how I should act or what I should say. On this rocky ground, I mentioned to Seth Carrie's crush on this girl they knew. I didn't know it was a secret thing & he passed it along, to stir up shit.

Carrie was pissed – screaming at me over the phone. I just snapped and told her how funny I thought it'd be to gut her entire family. And that was that. Thus, she left me for another woman, actively avoiding me until the end of time.

Seth and I got over it though – we were still cool. We shouldn't have been, technically, but we both just really liked each other, even though technically we should've been bitter enemies, and it was always clearly leading to that irregardless...

November 1997 – the main hub was now The Zone, a little coffee house in East Dearborn. Dark atmosphere, neon red lights, art lining the walls, leather furniture – packed every night with every character you've read about thus far plus 200 others unmentioned due to the complexities of this epic, sordid tale. The Zone was the apex of our tiny Nation.

In the final days of December Kelly & Seth began dating. They weren't at it long when many of us were at a local band VFW hall gig. While 50 of us were inside getting trashed, Kelly & Seth had gotten into an argument in the parking lot, with Maurice watching the whole affair.

I was on the steps with Caylin; Kelly stumbled inside crying 'cause Seth allegedly punched her & bolted. Caylin and I freaked out – he amassed a 10 car snake to drive to Livonia & put them in the hospital.

They never were able to track them down, but I called a ban on Seth & Maurice from ever entering Dearborn again. If they were seen, they'd be stomped. A similar threat was put on my head in Livonia.

Caught in midst of it all was poor Kaitlin, the closest person to me on any real level, who refused to believe Kelly's story & stuck by Maurice, who in turn claimed Kelly was drunk, started slapping the shit out of Seth, and that he simply pushed her down with moderate force to escape and left her crying on the ground an intoxicated, angry mess...

Days after, Kelly claims Seth tried to rape her while passed out drunk – the alleged reason for the parking lot argument. I knew this was bullshit because she would've castrated him – not tooled around with him for days.

I drew the line in the sand and demanded she recant this absurdity, which she never did. Soon after, there was a scene at The Zone where Kelly slapped the shit out of Crenshaw's new henchman Billy, breaking his glasses. Internecine followed on almost every level...

The Pigs raided The Zone & padlocked its doors on New Years Eve, legally retracting ownership of the building. They claimed the owner had been selling wholesale cocaine and marijuana out of the basement to justify a warrant, but all they found was an 8th of pot in the owners pocket and a 10 strip of blotter acid on this random dude.

There were no big time drug deals going on there; they took it away from us 'cause it was ours...A new central location never came to surface & a dozen factions broke apart, all at war with one another.

The focus was now with Crenshaw. We went through a period of revision within our Edsel group & basically excommunicated those we could no longer stand.

Salem was gone – Melissa too, mainly 'cause Crenshaw had gotten involved with her while still with Miriam, which caused drama.

I got involved with Melissa for a brief moment, and although I sincerely liked her & felt I could've started a real relationship. But I submitted to the inferno of Crenshaw who wanted her gone, and I also hadf snapped at her in a loopy, uncalled for way, which was my fault & it very much wrecked things between us. She chastised me for, and slipped away.

Others either graduated or moved elsewhere. Those left standing were Miriam, Sid, & Sloppy...

Ted & Dirk also entered the picture. Ted was mousy, quiet & semi-anorexic. He came from a broken home involving severe alcoholism, physical abuse & religious dogma. He was always very depressed & wore shorts plus a single t-shirt no matter the sub-zero temp outdoors.

Anytime someone would speak of death he'd start cackling sickly. Talking to Ted was like mouthing words down a riverbank towards an Admiral observing through binoculars a half mile away...

Dirk, however, was lively – a freshman newbie obsessed with independent cinema & David Lynch in particular. His father was a Mormon preacher. He loved his punk rock and was learning keyboard & electronic music – especially industrial styled works.

Crenshaw and I felt the need to drastically "up the ante." Thus, we formed our band Third World Amerika by joining forces with Mackenzie (*now in Birth of a Tragedy*). The sound resembled a dirty garage amalgam of Prong/Sepultura/Spooky Kids...

We secured a 4 man line up with Crenshaw on Bass, Mackenzie on lead, myself on drums, and Ted on rhythm guitar. We desperately needed a vocalist so I convinced Robinson. When he hit that mic the first time he gave it his all, thrashing & screaming his mighty adolescent voice...

There were many factors leading to the Revolt of the Jocks. First, the obvious – our attitudes & actions. How could anyone blame us? We were surrounded by such hideous people.

Secondly, race riots had put the school on edge. It started with a fight in the parking lot – a handful of Arabs pulled a gun on some jocks. The kid that had pulled the handgun also tried an armed car-jacking later that day – Captain Brilliant chose an undercover squad car and died from a gunshot to the stomach! His friend with him was also shot in the face!

It went down at lunch – 8 fights broke out, a huge food fight ensued, one security guard got fired for kicking a Saudi in the head. We were on the news: "*Edsel Ford: Melting Pot or Boiling Point?*"

I had generally been cool with the Arabs – they respected me because I openly hated Christianity & would make fun of Jesus with them as well as America in general. I'd also stick up for the scrawny Arab kids that couldn't speak English the jocks would always pick on...

Crenshaw was suspended for calling a flighty English instructor a "*Filthy Cuntgopher.*" During his absence, some random kid asked what happened. I figured he'd get the sarcasm when I said: "*He got shot by Mexicans during a bunk drug deal in Del Ray... Fucking awful...*"

Well, it got around school rather quickly and then all these kids who hated him were emotionally fried. People I didn't know were coming up to me with a deep & sincere empathy for the loss of my good friend.

Ted caught up with me: *"Dammit Bartek – did you tell everyone Crenshaw's dead?!?"* I didn't mean to, but then I realized the situation – I replied: *"Just play along with it – this is too damned funny."*

The students were on the verge of forming a candlelight vigil when the principal called his mother to send his condolences...

When he came in the next day people were either hiding from his apparition or trying to hug him. When confronted by a mob of faceless overjoyed strangers he shouted, *"GET THE FUCK OUT OF MY WAY!! WHERE THE HELL IS BARTEK?!?"*

When he found me & fully understood the humor, we stood there pointing & laughing our asses off at everyone that mourned his death. It was one of the highest points of my teenage existence. *Moral of the story: there is nothing more glamorous than a high school death.*

The following Monday I had my first run-in with Dante. I was in the parking lot enjoying a cigarette when I noticed this semi-prep girl I was fooling around with trying to break into her car with a coat hanger.

Dante was attempting to use the macho leverage of helping the defenseless girl to better gain entrance to her panties. I approached & he gave me an animalstic *big-man-beat-up-smaller-man-for-fuckbox* typical jock look so I let 'em be & went on my merry way...

Dante was a foot fairy/football bencher that was a little slow from a car accident he got into a year before. He'd stolen a carton of Newport's and made his escape attempt via roller blades. The fool glided in front of a truck, got drilled & the gas station dropped all charges on the grounds of sympathy since he'd turned simpleton.

After a good year of putting up with us, Dante & his sidekick figured they'd lead the *"Anti-Freak"* campaign. Dante soon jumped Sid with carloads of jocks. Sid was on the ground covering his face while Hilfiger strom-troopers kicked him repeatedly.

The populous of Edsel began walking by Miriam (*seven months pregnant*), calling her a *"freak whore."* They spray painted "FUCK THE FREAKS" on Crenshaw's windshield and slashed all of his tires...

Dante and his sidekick were in the hallway, puffing out their chests attempting to act threatening. Crenshaw and I started laughing and Dante said, *"You best watch your backs."*

Crenshaw replied: *"I'm gonna rape your Dad."* Oh their faces.

In the parking lot there was a mob of 30 waiting for us. Dante threw Crenshaw into the fence, calling him "faggot." I did the same to Dante but he didn't register it. Crenshaw said, *"Look man, I don't want any shit – I can't be doing this anymore, I've got a kid on the way."* The security guards broke it up & we went to devise our plan...

We told 'em if they had any balls meet us at the park after school. The staff found out and ratted us out. I told the principal that Dante was just a "Joe Pesci" and that we weren't going to do anything. They cut us loose and we gathered our crew. I was so excited I'd been boxing all week.

Sid, Crenshaw & myself were ready to scrap; Ted & Dirk were coming out of obligation. Sepultura's *"Biotech is Godzilla"* was our battle-cry. We pulled up to find ourselves outnumbered 250 to 5. The entire school was patiently waiting to see our asses kicked.

Crenshaw and the sidekick started it off. He was this skinny hoodrat kid that had obviously never been in a fight. He pushed Crenshaw to the ground and started hitting him like a girl – and quickly broke his wrist & stumbled away crying.

Crenshaw could've mauled him but instead stood there surrounded by 100 kids screaming for violence with an intense look of disgust...

Dante ran up and plowed his fist directly in the back of Crenshaw's skull. Immediately Sid cracked him in the head – I lunged forward catching Dante with a right hook, busting the left side of his forehead.

We duked it out & he got me in a headlock. I was kicking his legs & biting his arm to get free. He dug his thumb into my eye so hard I thought it was going to pop. I was shouting at him to let go & fight like a man – surprisingly he did (*dumbass*).

I backed off to face him; my eye was watering from the pressure. Everyone thought I was crying & started laughing.

Dante shouted, "*Fucking FREAK.*"

I looked around & there were hundreds of kids - pointing, cackling, howling like riled chimpanzees. "*The freak's crying... Fuckin' Freak... Kill the freak!!!*"

I started to erratically question him: "*HOW AM I A FREAK YOU UGLY MOTHERFUCKER???*"

He insulted again & clocked me, spitting in my face. I punted him in the stomach hard as I could with my steel toe boot. Park went silent.

I grabbed his shirt and started pounding my fist into his face with full force, breaking his nose. We tumbled onto the ground & I stomped on his legs 5 times fast.

I grabbed his shirt and pulled him up to finish him off, punching him 4 more times & kneeing him in the stomach before I grappled him into a headlock, defenseless. I cocked my fist back and...

Giant jock spears me off him. Not surprising, I knew we weren't going to walk out of there with a clean win. I got up and realized my shirt was covered in blood, none of it mine.

Dante was hobbling away a broken mess as Miriam ran up in a pregnant rage and started slapping him crying. The air was filled with the shouting of "PIGS!" and everyone ran...

We took off in a hurry; all Crenshaw said was, *"That was the stupidest thing I have ever been involved with in all of my life."* I was hysterical, muttering, *"I got him didn't I? I showed that motherfucker didn't I?"* like an underdog hitting his first homerun.

Sid high-fived me laughing, and Crenshaw was depressed. We went back to my house where the rest of Third World Amerika was waiting & jammed the best set of our short-lived career...

The next day at school people I never met congratulated me. Dante was limping around with a black eye telling everyone how badly he kicked my ass, yet none bought it. Everyone turned on us...

By Summer, Third World Amerika played our first gig with Asphyxiation (*Simon on vox & Nez on drums*). We gave it our all & made as much noise & distortion as we could, thrashing around on stage warping tempos with slop perfectionism. The crowd dug it; I was amped, stoked & relieved.

We gained a positive buzz but needed to reorganize. Robinson didn't really believe in the message since he was now Born Again Christian; a weird, cultish version hosted by a "telepathic prophet" from Africa. One day he just walked off from rehearsal in frustration...

Crenshaw took over vocals & Byron now played bass; we dropped Ted & hired Dirk for keyboards. We were progressing & producing a harder edged, more industrial sound. But then...

I was offered a scholarship to live Downtown Chicago & attend Columbia College for the summer, as to study Film/Video/TV editing for free, at an accredited University many Hollywood professionals come from, with free room & board, for 6 weeks at age 17. Could I say no?

Had Vic not been hit with his usual luck, he would've accompanied us as well. The school sent an incorrect report to his house claiming he was failing all his classes when he had a Three Point Average! His parents forced him to drop out!

He now worked at a butcher shop, killing animals all day & losing his mind in the summer heat. *Poor Vic!*

I broke the scholarship news to Third World Amerika. Crenshaw was pissed 'cause it meant hiatus of his lifeblood. I wasn't backing down with it either – he & they had to deal. We put on our last show at Mackenzie's – a keg party for Fourth of July.

Sid dropped by, who'd freshly beaten the shit out of Dante – *he bit a chunk off his scalp with his bare teeth!*

We smoked 8 joints in a row & went on drunkenly shitfaced for a wonderfully noisy set for drunk teens. Next morning, we marched through the streets en route to breakfast, smashing every pint-sized American Flag along the way – the territorial pissings of a brighter tomorrow...

Miriam had her child, a baby girl named Dakota. Jack was kept off of the birth certificate so that he wouldn't be devastated by child support. He swore on his life he would financially support her with what little money he possessed & I left to Chicago in search of my roots...

A Death In The Family

Afghanistan... Easy target. Even before the bombs started dropping the GOP had remodeled itself in Bush's image with Reagan abandon... Those press conference monkey faces, micro-piece sharks dictating every sentence. That teleprompter swagger... I got the Nostradamus blues but where is Churchill or equivalent? This man is such a puppet you can literally see the strings being pulled. *Novus Ordo Seclorum....*

Afghanistan... They wouldn't give us our back alley oil deal. Powell even admitted we'd planned to invade last June on the timetable of now. Oh harken ye convenience of terrorism... Don't ask questions, just raise that flag. We never car bombed a mosque, never hijacked a plane. And we certainly never started taking Cipro a full month before the first reported anthrax outbreak, nor did we circulate high-level memo's informing top brass to stop flying commercial airlines this summer...

Afghanistan... Our mess, our militants; everything we swept under the rug. Just keep shifting the blame. Pay no mind to the strategic line forming down the Middle East... *Operation: Infinite Justice* – after public relations hell they simply changed it to *Operation: Enduring Freedom...* What's next, Iraq? No, no way. Hell no. *No one could ever be that stupid...*

I'm given the ultimatum – either quit the landscaping gig or be available 24-7 for snow removal. It is now December 2001 and due to my commitments to Real Detroit Weekly, Birth of a Tragedy & my convoluted masterwork, I have no choice but to exit gracefully, fully expecting another form of employment within days.

As per usual I end up driving up and down every major street within a fifty-mile radius putting in applications at every business in sight. Nothing, nada, zilch – *Taco Bell won't even hire me*. My resources have dwindled to $72 dollars & momma killed my cat 'cause it kept pissing everywhere in terror.....

Something has to give – I am an internationally renowned heavy metal journalist after all and this has to be worth something. It is to PIT Magazine, an international metal zine based in Colorado, and squirm my freelance way into the back door...

I am summoned to a band meeting by the Mackenzie brothers and told that I am *"too rock & roll"* for BOAT and that I should concentrate on my guitar playing which far exceeds my percussion talent. They are very professional in their assessment and dealt this blow of creative death in a friendly, businesslike manner.

Although I offer to work with them to correct said problem they decide to let me go anyway because they assume I'll be much happier jamming out in a heavier band. They tell me that although I may initially be upset by this situation everything will work out for the best and they will do everything in their power to get me situated in the right hands...

Sunday afternoon and I am hit. The phone rings, the answering machine clicks on. The caller hangs up leaving a trail of dial tone that resonates through the empty house, cold and gray from winter darkness.

Again & again it rings. I force myself from bed and put the receiver to my ear begrudgingly. The voice at the other end lays it all down – Lisa hung herself using a cat collar and her own body weight. They found her dangling inside the closet of a Southwest crack house...

Last I'd seen of her was at Ram's Horn a few weeks prior. She had just joined the Navy on a whim and was drinking coffee with one of her sisters in an obvious state of distress.

I talked to her for a moment or two but moved onto the next acquaintance after I realized that something was horribly wrong. I received a strong impression of death from her – perhaps a friend...

It was always an awkward scene running into each other considering our history. After our fallout in '99 I had only crossed paths with her about four times, each an occasion characterized by uneasiness. It was the same body but a different mind – a different look & charisma.

She didn't detest me nor did she have an authentic grudge – I had simply become a minor character with no real sense of gravity in her life. There was no way to turn back the clock because we were now completely different people. It was a mutual sadness both felt & observed, yet no true moment of reconciliation...

11pm, surrounded by the weeping, broken down remnants of Edsel. Most of the Old World are at Zoe's getting drunk, playing Atari 2600. It mirrors the essence of an IKEA support group.

It is calm, collected - ready to shatter at any given moment. Zoe, the die-hard unbreakable uber-political daydreamer of the ultimate punk rock triumph, lays broken, passed out on her bed, unable to fully coagulate that which is now forming, slipping in and out of the waking and comatose nightmare, drained vampirically.

Crenshaw is nowhere to be found & the first time in nearly 2 years I'm able to have a conversation with Dirk. He is scattered, unable to hold attention to any topic more than 30 seconds.

The night wears on and the cycle of acceptance continues it's ugly march forward. Skepticism is professed; the dirty phrase "*homicide.*" More waves, continued shock. Zoe passes out, another stares at the floor in catatonic distress after bawling beneath the plastic Christmas Tree. The Atari 2600 burns on until 9 am…

I'm the first to show up to the wake, besting Lisa's parents. I wait in my car observing the sparrows perfectly lined on electric cables tightly strung from an endless succession of wooden telephone poles.

Dirk walks up and offers me a hit from his flask. I decline and he swings open the passenger side door, plopping into shotgun. We speak of the profound imagery in *Blue Velvet* until the caravan arrives.

We're interrupted because some random kid still in shock locked his keys in his car and has requested us to blow out the passenger side window. I keep kicking the glass with my paratrooper boots to no effect.

Dirk finds a lead pole in the alley and vaults it at the window but all that accomplishes is a small chip in the glass. We give up, call a locksmith and saunter into the basement rest area alongside a handful of skinheads drinking black coffee… …

The funeral home is bursting with nervous tension. In the main room Lisa's coffin is wide open surrounded by delicate, professional bouquet arrangements.

Zoe is chatting with everyone, erratically obscuring her inevitable breakdown. Her nervousness, that curly mop of frizzled hair dyed Ronald McDonald red. She has on an ugly 70's polyester checkered shirt, a short red plaid skirt and blue tights complemented by army boots.

This was the first individual ever to die in her life and it just so happened to be her best friend. Dirk hits the flask again and we approach the damage. Lisa's face is sunk in. She looks Chinese. Her hand is stitched up from a shattered wrist on the downward fall. *Another jigsaw premonition of seemingly ancient origin...*

Human shrapnel detonates in the parking lot; nervous laughter, scattered emotions, train wreck thought patterns. The boyfriend's here; whigger entourage awaiting confrontation. Lisa's mother bolts outside screaming bloody murder: *"YOU KILLED MY BABY!!"* Repeat. *"MURDERER!!"* Repeat. *"FUCKING LEAVE!!"*

The stand off is vicious – one wrong move and a riot ensues. The line is drawn – twenty of them, 200 of us. The boyfriend backs down, jumps in his car. The skins throw rocks, wiggers grip their pistols in retreat. The boyfriend's mother tries to get into the car with him. He panics, blasts in reverse and runs over her leg. She pythons inside the Tempo, they scoot. Three squad cars shark the parking lot for the eve...

I slam black coffee in the rest area as a gentile knock focuses my attention. *"There you are."* Cassie stands in the doorway smiling, clothed in loud apparel, ambivalent to the darkness. We chat awhile - the fifth time in nearly two years... The scars still bleed. I question her emotional detachment towards the death of her friend. Says, *"After what you did to me, could you expect anything else?"*

4 days later & sitting next to Jamison, a packed chapel. Lisa is to be buried next to the Slag Plant, not far from Zug Island... I feel sick, I am sick; I didn't know the extent of abuse... Her father & uncle took turns raping her until she was 12... Mother knew & did nothing... Sisters knew, did nothing... The priest hands the funeral over to Lisa's father for a rapport of self-denial which the mother aids & abets... Sterling parents. Upstanding Christians. Outstanding pillars... *Every last one prays for homicide...*

ROOTS

The state I left Dearborn in was not pretty. Brandon was incarcerated over a bogus rape charge & Smitty/Vic were snorting coke. This acceleration galvanized when Z stumbled into the scheme of things...

Z had moved from Northern Michigan after he'd thrown a keg party & an underage drunk crashed into a wall, mentally retarding him. Z was sued by the parents, barely got out & moved to his sisters near us.

His ride was a rust-bucket '83 Rabbit with a stick shift. It'd constantly die in traffic & we'd have to hop out & push it to jump start from the clutch. His eyeball was cracked like a fractured, hard-boiled egg 'cause his ex-girlfriend had a bunch kids jump him *in his sleep*....

Z was built thick, about 5 foot 11, and limber in his movements as much as his eyes were googly.

First I met him, he had a piss-yellow shirt with the phrase "BEER" in puffy, iron-on letters – he whipped out a crack rock the size of his thumbnail, inspected it like a diamond collector, and called it *"the greatest iceberg"* he'd ever seen.

He had this Hunter S. Thompson drug-rampage vibe. Coincidentally, around this time *Fear & Loathing In Las Vegas* came out – Z never saw it, but Vic & Smitty both did. They basically let themselves be taken hostage by their self-created Raoul Duke.

We were in the early days of the drug houses; carloads would "mission" to different ghetto spots for ganja, coke, whatever. I was always paranoid; one of Smitty's prep buddies was carjacked at gunpoint doing it.

It was always this nervous thing – deeper & deeper into the unending maze-like corridors of Detroit's grim neighborhoods. Driving to a bud house was like a space flight to another galaxy, and ever dangerous.

If some suburban white kid knew where to go, then the cops did too – these blocks would get shut down fast, and worse places you'd have to seek out.

Late at night the boys went on an unsuccessful coke mission. Bored of driving, Z pulled into a deep ghetto housing project. Smitty figured he knew someone, but Z jumped & just to be batshit crazy & shocking, the lunatic hollers: *"HEY YOU FUCKIN' NI**ERS!!!"* loud as he could at the building!! As in demanding he be shot, or pulp beaten!

Not 'cause he was racist – the dude listened to rap constantly. But cause he was a fuckin' psycho who wanted to see how far he could possibly take it, how over the top & obnoxious & rude & insane you can push it to it's ultimate limit, like a living cartoon seeking absolute suicide. *A 17 year challenging a Cabrini Green of gangbangers to an all out brawl!!*

Vic & Smitty desperately try to start the car from the clutch, pushing it down the street on foot, overlooking their shoulders at the death-trap & adrenaline-fueled, maniac white boy. From out the complex charge a dozen bloodthirsty thugs – *"what ya say you stup' muh-fukka?!?"*

Z shoots a flare gun at them, like it's some massive over-the-top magnum – the fiery gun comet lands directly in their path, instantly lighting up the dead grass like a wall of fire! Z runs to the car right as they clutch-jumpstart the engine...

Smitty at the wheel, they speed off laughing. Soon after they got an 8-ball, then drove around shooting the windows out of liquor stores in the ghetto with Z's .22 caliber. These guys had some seriously crazy ideas for Devil's Night that year...

I didn't like this – they were taking shit too far for no reason at all. What was I to do? It takes me a long time to care about anyone, and here I was locked into a whole spectrum of people towards the end of high school, and all these plot lines – I felt like I had to ride it out: *"this era is what it is, just let it be – graduation , then who knows?"*

Would I ever consort with the likes of a Z again? Hell no. Point is, I was buried up to my neck in teenage lunatics who were all totally out of control & spiraling wildly.

No matter where I went, someone would hook into the immense waves of our age groups. Everyone knew each other somehow. All these dudes on Vic & Smitty's side from their high school – these preppy yet slacker/stoner kids absorbed Z into their ranks. He was entrenched everywhere, immediately.

\ The very existence of his Z's "wild man" syndrome pushed everyone to a Dial 11 with their personalities – their shit-talkin', wacky situation brewin', psycho-driving, road raging' Detroiter Attitude where everything is a ridiculous, rough & tough cartoon.

It was monkey-see, monkey-do with Z – everyone rowdier, trying to out-hardcore each other, turning to harder drugs, seedier atmospheres – it kept mixing with a larger pool of people, like circles of power emanating from this bizarre goof, utterly hidden from view.

He knew not the chaos he wrought – he seemed vastly ignorant of his own effects! As was his power, essentially. He was full throttle shoulder demon, doing' whatever was ear-whispered All these kids from Dearborn High – they wanted a Hunter S Thompson to show up – he gave 'em the whackadoo act they sought...

I couldn't abandon my friends, nor could I tarnish my reputation by looking like a flake. You know, at 17, that whole Detroit Male thing of being called a "pussy" cause you won't step up to some reckless, stupid behavior – well, you do dumb things. Like willingly get in a car with Z...

Although Z freaked me out, he was also damn funny & totally fearless. It was his nature to stare down death & make the fucker retreat in cowardice. But he was an asshole who dropped the n-bomb to be shocking & politically incorrect, even though he knew he did not really believe in it.

What pissed me off more were all the kids who looked the other way and didn't see it the way he meant it – his *"throw feces everywhere because they tell me I can't"* kid-like mental approach.

Most our days were spent ghetto cruising, Z refusing to let anyone else take the wheel after pounding 40's. If anyone hollered something at him, like a shit-talking pedestrian or driver – he'd jump out his car & chase them, ophysically threaten then in jammed traffic & getting out the car demanding they also get out and fist fight him – *always speeding, blasting music loud as possible, flipping off cops & inciting road rage...*

Most nights were in group bonfires with Smitty's crew, a woodland area of a forgotten Detroit park. Gunshot echoes would mingle with the ever-crackling blaze...

Z nearly killed Vic after sucking down a nitrous balloon while drunk, veering off & slamming into the wall of a Toys R' Us. They just backed up & drove off in the mangled wreck...

July 4th Z came over for BBQ with Smitty & Vic. We walked to this park filled with families playing baseball – Z whipped out a blunt.

I protested & Z grew perturbed, whipping out his butterfly knife & stabbing it in the picnic table hard as he could – crazy eyes, half-coked & long night of crack blaze: *"Yer' gonna smoke every - last - fuckin - bit."* Oh well. Thick clouds of reefer drifted to the diamond & suffocated the Little League dug-out.

After I left for Chicago, Z moved back from whence he came & vanished, luckily I guess, because he'd have sent half my friends to prison if he kept playing leader & compass bearer. Last I heard he'd joined the Navy to weasel out of an assault charge...

The night prior to my Chicago leave was a dip into "Saigon" – a crack infested gangster hood with "*one way in/one way out*" entrapment.

I'd been working with Sid & Sloppy for Crackfiend Bobby in a small-time BMX theft ring. We'd shuttle stolen bikes Downriver for pocket change & a hefty sack of bud in return...

Crackfiend Bobby has me drive him to Saigon then wanders inside a ramshackle, graphitic apartment. 30 minutes of paranoia brews nefarious – something is amiss, as it were...

A dilapidated '88 Buick rolls behind us slowly and in my rearview mirror a thug is cocking a handgun. He flips his door to get out and I blast off at 50 mph down streets covered in glass, booby trapped so you'll get a flat. The duelist chases Sid and I, with Sid wide eyed and laughing wanting to fight the guy with a crowbar. The unidentified thug follows us through a mile of darkest night, speeding like a heat-seeking shark on my tailbone...

We make it back to Crackfiend Bobby's thinkin' we have to tell his pregnant wife that he's been murdered by junkie gangstas. We huddle as football team, extracting our monologue.

Bobby runs up panting for breath, hands on knees, coughing out his lungs. "*What the fuck man*" he jabbers as he reaches into his pants, pulling out his torn underwear ripped in half from running so fast...

Once inside the Saigon house Crackfiend Bobby kicked the gun out of his cash-burned hookup's hand & lunged out the window, booking it like a champ all the way to safety. *Never work for an unprofessional...*

While I was in Chicago, Sid lapsed heavy into snow and was breaking into cars, mugging easy targets to support his habit. He wrapped a heavy chain around an ATM & dragged it away with a pick-up truck! He fled the state, never to be heard from again...

Chicago was a great experience – such solitude allowed me to revise my agenda. I felt myself withdrawing from the world in a vacuum sense; I was siphoning the junk pile of my subconscious & questioning future aims...

I began writing heavily, trying to discover what I was made of. Everything was a lightning rod towards discipline. I shaved my head & opted for earth tone clothing instead of flaming skulls & black wardrobe.

I felt stronger, yet uneasy – a shaky crossroad. High School would soon be finished, and more then ever I felt my own man. The need of co-dependence on anyone had come to a finale...

I recognized the vulgarity of my past. My fascistic treatment of Christians made me no better than the legitimate fascists I despised. I no longer considered myself a Satanist either – I'd evolved into a view of humanism wrapped in vague paganism, with a cold & calculated existentialism rendering everything analytical & distant...

Satanism held a wonderful gimmick, surely, but hokey as shit & rancidly egocentric. I still believe in most everything LaVey vomited, even if it was blatantly lifted from Ragnar Redbeard.

Anton's carny act is still worthy of standing ovation, yet what's more hardcore then out-hardcoring The Devil by claiming that you're too gosh-darn hardcore for him yourself?

Satan is my favorite character in the history of literature, for we are all black sheep and he is our lord. Yet the truth of the matter is the only real way to actually defeat Christianity is to disown all its mythological bearings; playing into their madness is for you to continue their game...

I returned from Chicago a changed man & headed to Mackenzie's – *Crenshaw had thrown him out of our band!* Mackenzie was fine with it & starting a black metal project.

I hunted down Crenshaw, whose hustler comfort spoke away the rockiness. He claimed everything had been going well. He was giving $30 out each paycheck to Miriam (*$20 life*), had diligently been working on a veritable galaxy of ground-breaking new music (*4 lazy riffs*), and was aggressively searching for a new guitarist (*random drunk guy*)...

As Crenshaw & I ate fast food in a parking lot Downriver, this redneck pulled up beside us with a lunatic grin – *Crenshaw's dad!* I watched them reconicle – he invited us over & we all bonded at his apartment, passed bong loads.

His pops' habitat reflected Crenshaw's bedroom – Boris Vajello art, showpiece swords, D&D, tarot cards & Classic Rock vinyl. He was a tatto artist & to be the needle-work initiator for many our virgin flesh...

Kaitlin moved back to Dearborn & Maurice was now in boot camp. We weren't really talking anymore, yet still I thought about her.

As for Seth's side of the fence, their group had deteriorated into shambles – heroin use was out of control & crack was quickly invading.

Mackenzie's new band had a gig that Dirk & I attended at Pharoah's. I read over the set & there was a song called "Beatle Crenshaw And The Carwash." I snagged the lyrics from the vocalist's folder & the ditty was a character assassination against one of my best friends – *and the vocalists cousin!* It was low, back-stabbing shite...

I demanded an explanation. Simon had written it & they were intent on playing it. In my charming, adolescent way I told 'em if they played the song I was gonna *"kick the living fuck out all of 'em."*

Simon ratted me out to Riverside Tony, who respectfully asked me to leave while shaking my hand. I got to my car & the headlight had been busted out! A giant gob of spit on the windshield! *It was fuckin' ON.*

Dirk & I rounded up the crew, as well as Vic who had nothing to do with anything & extremely offended & pissed at me for dragging him into it. We were all raging – Vic just sighed: *"I'm not going to jail for this bullshit – fight your own goddamn wars."*

We hit Pharoah's & Crenshaw runs inside – we're waiting on him to bait them into the open so we can hop out and attack. Inside his cousin, Mackenzie & Simon lie about the entire thing, kiss his ass like lambs.

Bright & early Crenshaw & I hung outside the carwash where Mackenzie worked – I sat on the hood of his car, chain-smoking. He hid inside all day – no one called the cops...

That weekend, Pharaoh's lost its license when the singer of SPINFIST flashed a 13 year olds' tits to the crowd. It was crawling with undercover cops just looking for an excuse.

Crack & heroin had become so omnipresent its reputation stretched into PTA groups. 14 year olds were having sex on the couches in plain view, gangs were forming, people were shooting up dope in the bathroom, smoking crack in the parking lot...

Smitty was slowly mutating into a meathead jock & Vic was locked into this butcher shop gig having perpetual nervous breakdown, slaughtering chickens all day.

He was still upset with me over the Pharaoh's thing, but our relationship was on the rocks mainly due to his pathological behavior mimicking that of a pregnant woman...

There are many things you need to know about Vic... First off, he wasn't always the stone-cold psycho. That was mostly behind the scenes, top-secret info. In public he had a nervous, silly demeanor. Twisted humor, always cracking punch lines few understood.

He was highly charismatic often stealing the show at parties with his unique storytelling abilities. The ladies dug him but he never had self-confidence in this arena and regularly sabotaged himself. Occasionally he'd hook up but it'd never last. He never had a real girlfriend.

From '94-'97 we were inseparable – we were to name our first sons after each other! I'd try to mimic his cool in social situations, always needing his approval in nearly all aspects of my life. So many girls I didn't go for 'cause he didn't like them, turn on people for the same reason...

One day in '97 he admitting it was the same deal on his end. I was his confident heroic buddy and we were just feeding off each other like leeches. This admission came after writing him a pissed off letter explaining I was sick of being treated as his subordinate sidekick and couldn't take his condescending, brutal attitude anymore.

After that, Vic felt like he wasn't important anymore and that's when he started winging towards Smitty...

Brandon was released from prison and we started hanging out with Cassum again because he was no longer held down by his father's strict discipline. Smitty was caught up in Dearborn High's semi-preppy circle – all those kids were coked out, drunken train-wrecks...

Gio had hit rock bottom. They had gone to his dealers' and were smoking dope in the garage. Gio was on acid and started getting weird, forgetting to breathe. The dealer began acting strange too and turned on his car with the garage door shut to try & get "*high*" off the fumes.

Vic, Smitty, and a few of the other guys got up to leave and Gio started freaking out, demanding they stay. After a vicious dialogue they left him with the carbon huffer.

Smitty is driving & Gio flies past them doing 70 mph. He slows down and rejoins their lead, but starts swinging his car around trying to hit Smitty's truck. It's bad trip central now. Gio speeds up again, loses control, flips his car three times before it smacks a telephone pole.

They jump out to see if he's still breathing and Gio climbs through his broken windshield. With both wrists broken he tries to pick up a slab of concrete hollering "*I'm so strooong!!*" but it slips & breaks his toe.

Smitty snaps, grabs Gio's shirt & starts punching his face – "*What*" THUMP "*The Fuck*" THUMP "*Is Wrong*" THUMP "*With You?!?*" Smitty dropped him & Gio cried on the ground until the cops came. After that he had a nervous breakdown, was on probation for years, grew a teenage beard & was only seen at night wandering the streets alone…

Even though I was briefly fucking an Asian cheerleader, it was the roughest summer to fall depression transition since 8th grade. I would now be graduating and everything would change dramatically…

Mechanical Animals came out and Manson drove the nail into his own coffin with the glam image & alienating androgynous homosexuality.

Manson fagged it up so hardcore he ruined himself to American youth – it was just too much & not the right time. The music was ok but the magick was gone, and no one would be caught dead defending him

again after robbing Bowie blind. From Antichrist to Space Liberace – America just couldn't deal with it...

I knew it was over for Marilyn Manson when Crenshaw & I were offered *free backstage passes* – and Crenshaw turned them down in spite! Without even asking me!

I sat there feebly with these tickets in hand, unable to locate a driver – not one person who owned 20 of Manson's t-shirts would pick me up! Millions tossed his albums in the trash, burned his shirts & posters, walked away from it like a cheap fad...

The Antichrist Superstar was dead. He had the world in his palm, and blew it harder than any rock persona ever had. All the other heavyweights that could've rescued my dying "Dark Age" subculture had disappeared & not one new album to regenerate a crucial lapse in enthusiasm & attention – and if an album did appear, it was crap.

Where was Trent Reznor? Skinny Puppy? Tool? Danzig? KMFDM? Pantera? Ministry? Type O? Megadeth? Anthrax? Metallica?

Everything 1990's was to be irreparably lost. 4 new rock stations popped up and all of them (*plus the existing channels*) followed the exact same lead of banal repetition – a full-scale takeover of the dreaded nu-metal & all it's meathead accessories: Korn, Limp Bizkit, Godsmack, Staind, Distrubed, Nickelback, Soulfly, Kid Rock & *Creeeed*....

I started writing heavily, pounding out short stories, essays, dream narratives, poetry & aphorisms for a project entitled *Atheism In A Foxhole (eventually The Silent Burning)*. The early work was an amalgam of Henry Rollins' point blank realism & the downtrodden Beat Generation. I had never identified with any literature as much as *The Portable Rollins*.

I began questioning the schematics of what we were doing, preaching new ideas which frustrated Crenshaw 'cause they were lessening his control freak charisma on the group. The frustration kept mounting...

In midst of this all I fell madly in love with Lisa, who came from nowhere. I'd known her in passing, but not well.

She was best friends with Zoe, a punk girl that, same as Lisa, came from a Hispanic background. Lisa was an unbelievably cute Mexican girl with button eyes whose family had escaped the gutter of Del Ray.

She grew up by Zug Island before transplanting to West Dearborn for a higher quality of life. She shined outwardly, brilliantly, although trailed by a morbid substratum, a vast sadness beyond the veil.

Open and loving, she was fixated on the ironic humor of existence. That is, to say, she *understood*. The first time we actually spoke she mentioned something about me being her friend which I had denied by labeling her an acquaintance. This really upset her.

From thereon I couldn't deny her – she'd slink into my personal space, always stopping me from trailing off. She was expert at keeping me in "The Now." She casually became a sentinel, never allowing me to be consumed by the madness she saw within me.

I never actually had anyone *want* to know me. She would spindle me with questions, but always accepting of everything, wanting more only because she liked me that much as a person. She said she once had a massive crush on me, although it was obvious it still lingered.

It took a few days for me to work up the nerve to make a subtle advance. I was ready though, I felt a shoe-in. I turned the corner and she ran up *holding Dirks hand*, who was my sophomore body double.

I hoped it would end soon enough, 'cause I had too much dignity to sell out my accomplice. Weeks went by, they grew closer and closer. She'd come over, sit on my bed talking for hours.

Her simple presence would clear my head of the ubiquitous confusion. She confided her "big brother" role in me, designated me her own guardian angel.

She let it all loose – her suicidal impulses, her parents physical and mental abuse. Beating her, locking her in the cellar, hints of molestation. She told me something fierce and awful, but I began laughing.

I didn't think she was serious – she had said it so direct and unemotionally. She was so hurt, but I thought perhaps she was still kidding – what I didn't understand is I was the first person she ever even tried to tell. She was turning to me to escape a situation of sexual abuse and psychological torture – and I just didn't believe her.

For this teenage brain of mine, it was another thing in & out the ear in a fuzzy mess of motion...

She was very interested in the punk scene and at her behest we went to see the GBH/Against All Authority show. Now in Detroit, Harpo's Concert Theatre is without a doubt the most hardcore venue in the Metro area, if not the entire Midwest. Located in one of the toughest ghettos in America, described by many as the "*House That Slayer Built*," Harpo's has become the epicenter of for the extreme metal movement.

On any given Saturday you'll find acts such as Goatwhore, Dark Funeral, Suffocation, Mortician tearing up the stage.

Harpo's is my favorite place to go for concerts – it's loud, it's crazy, it's drunk and the intensity wires itself like a ticking time bomb that explodes like C-4 under the abrasive drop D distortion grind. I just can't get that same sense of satisfaction anywhere else...

It was at this particular venue when I witnessed the largest display of human idiocy I have ever encountered. This was in '98 when Harpo's maintained a nasty rep for being a skinhead hangout.

Tonight was straight old-school – GBH & Against All Authority;. I was wearing a big fat Anti-Nazi patch on the leather of my jacket...

First band started & a dozen Nazi skins showed up & headed into The Pit, charging each other like bulls. After the set, Nazi skins swarm lnear our table, makingr acial comments...

Harpo's has a projector screen – Slayer's *Seasons in the Abyss* came on. Like moths obsessing over a porch light, the brutal epic drew all to the floor.One of them (*the leader I assume*) took control of the situation.

He was this giant fucker built like HHH, bald shining Aryan head accentuated by the sharp contrast of his blood red t-shirt with a huge fuckin' swastika.

Marilyn Manson's *The Dope Show* video came on next to a heavy stream of delightful comments such as "*Kill the Faggot*," "*Salad Tossin' Queer*" & "*Homo Nigger Fucker*" ...

Local band walks onstage – the vocalist grabs the mic: "*Fuck Marilyn Manson!!!*"The place explodes & Nazi skins beat the living shit out of each other in Aryan rage.

Bartenders & staff start abandoning ship – this is getting extremely out of hand. About 200 Nazi's are swarming The Pit. Every C.H.U.D. starts shouting: "*Zieg Heil, Zeig Heil, Zieg Heil!*" & working that Hitler chest pledge in unison. No shit, I was 30 feet from the 6th Reich.

They began circling everyone that wasn't a skin like bloodthirsty sharks in the upper levels & we barreled out of the place...

The next day I talked to a friend who stuck around to watch. The second AAA began their set, the Panzer division threw everything that wasn't attached to the floor at the black trumpet player.

They bolted for the tour bus & the Nazi's beat the living shit out of everyone, landing 4 people in the hospital...

That Monday, Gibson assigned a documentary project. I told him I wanted to make one on skinheads. I wanted to make a film about *real skinheads* doing *real skinhead things* and exploded on him, expressing my hatred for that entire scene, explaining point for point why he was delusional.

My relationship with Gibson faltered then. Things only worsened when Dirk, Lisa and a few others asked me to teach them how to edit on a Sunday afternoon. When we arrived Dumis was with a handful of rave junkies snorting coke in Gibson's office.

The next day I was blamed for the theft of a gold ring from his desk. He refused to believe me, took Dumis' side, and fucked me out of a $15 an hour job I was promised making training videos for the Ford Motor Company. I played out the remainder of the year expecting an apology that never came. Gibson never did another thing to help me...

February '99. Shortly after ramming Triple J's car all over the school parking lot with his Astro-Van, Crenshaw was expelled for threatening a teacher. There was also a brief scare involving a 15 year-old freshman that he possibly knocked up (*"miscarriaged" later that week*).

At the Rivergreen Projects Byron's mom was smoking crack and had turned to the needle. She contracted HIV & gave it to Marvin. It was a grim scene watching both on the couch in a darkened room fixated on a fuzzy snow channel in silent, vicious agony...

A week later she overdosed in her friends' car. All it took was one heavy drag off a bad fix to make her heart explode. The driver passed out in shock, slamming head-on into a streetlight. It was all over the news.

The funeral was packed with the entire host of 7:101 characters. I had never been stoned at such a function but Pegleg Pete insisted because it was the way death was approached in that group. Crackhead Ruthie was stricken with grief, coherent for once. She'd quit everything.

Byron's mom looked like a wax replica in her coffin. Her friends slipped joints into her sport coat; I gave her an amulet deflecting evil spirits. She was buried in a tie-dye headband & corduroy sport coat, a Joe Camel t-shirt & black denim Levi's. She was only 40 & Byron had no choice but to drop out of school & move to Ohio with his Dad...

We all began using drugs more heavily as I started my job at a Hindu-run donut shop. Crenshaw was discovered secretly shooting heroin again (*he was once a full-fledged junkie*). It hit him fast, that ancient wound...

By March 1999 the great acid frenzy began – some 500 sheets of gel-tabs entered Metro Detroit, for the first wide-reaching time. It was always near impossible to score acid – now every hoodlum in Michigan was now devouring the shit like candy in massive group freak-outs.

I was to turn 18 on April 4th & had to do something bold. My birthday was the night of Hash Bash (*a college town festival celebrating marijuana legalization*); I decided it was finally time to trip out, having held back all these years & devoured a mushroom & jelly sandwich...

It was myself, Crenshaw, Angelica (*his new girl*) & Billy (*this goon who'd finally won our respect*). We all piled into Billy's car (a Festiva named "*Pinkeye*")...

I gazed down the street & saw a white rabbit scamper across black asphalt. This was much too early for a hallucination, but no one else witnessed the Jefferson Airplane encounter. It was so cliché, no one would ever believe it happened. *How perfect!*

"You know, I hope you're more than ready for the hideous beast I might turn into kind sir." Crenshaw replied, *"It's just like Peter Pan – think happy thoughts & you'll fly high; meditate on evil and you'll plummet like a bowling ball off The Empire State..."*

Driving towards I-96 exit painless pinhole tear in back of brain raw pink meat and cosmic vibrations from feet bottoms manic energy coursed through veins swirled round head ascension freeway tip spontaneous immolation red stencil rays of Legacy Virus right eye shot harness powerful psychic force thick blanket rabid howls mutant quasi-goth teens embedding spirit of grander pale radiant moon everything right and true magnificent hallucinatory sparrow lands shoulder shadows form symbolism first time in miserably weary manic depressive neurotically schizoid life finally home in power of radical evolutionary neo-God uninhibited orgasm laughter sixteen thousand long dead soul exploring revolutionaries shooting 100 mph into uncharted abyss old Tim Leary hovering cosmos floating psychedelic hair rug golden eclipse above Nile zooming onward rubbery highway liquid beneath spaceship iron blissfully far from orthodox Angelica interrupt exotic disposition with hypnotic piercing gaze into deep crimson red camouflage vacuum...

"Your shirt... it's *beautiful*..." I looked at my apparel shades interchanging with one another like light reflecting from the shallowness of a pond engulfed in a moment of zen staring out windows of zooming highway eyes open for first time giant cross lit up sky Jesus hover above landscape pope space shuttle frowning drug addled inertia. *"Oh shit... it's Je-sus! The time of reckoning is at hand! Oh fuck, oh fuck, oh fuck..."*

Crenshaw began giggling like a schoolgirl in affectionate bliss, *"Fuckin'... lookin' like a scarecrow... BWA HA HA HA!!"* All emptiness forgotten detour incorrect exit & found selves smack-dab hilljack farmland. *"Help me... I can't stop talking like Richard Nixon."*

Maybe so, but I couldn't deny the overpowering feeling of jealousy that emerged regarding something I couldn't place my finger on. I knew that someone somewhere had to pay – I'd defenestrate the culprit through the Plexiglas window of a VFW hall & set it's lawn on fire...

I snapped out of the head-trip into an even deeper head-trip as we parked the car in front of some indeterminate business. Crenshaw was swinging on the vines hanging from the top interior of our space shuttle like a mutant Tarzan & it was time to run amuck on those weird disco streets. *"Sorry, there's no way I can voyage – my legs fell off."* *"If I leave him now he might eat his liver or something... I'll keep him sane..."*

Billy & I ran off into the night, frantically searching for the den of the hippie archetype. That damned rabbit had multiplied; dozens of them – moist, swarming like locusts beneath our feet.

"How did we end up in Seattle?" Downtown streets illuminated the greater pathway to a liquid tomorrow. I tried to read the signs but I'd been rendered dyslexic. Each letter, as I tried to concentrate, transmuted. Everyone looked like an undercover cop – plotting, awaiting their strike.

We approached an art exhibit. There was an attractive young beatnik chick in a black beret & even blacker turtleneck talking to a preppy guy that was hitting on her & pretending to be interested in her artwork to get in her polyester jeans. Gigantic pillars of intricately carved wood captivated the room. Forest faces winked then turned painful groans..."

We ran for the hills & ended up on top a parking structure. Gazing over the ledge of the world the sky melted down the Northern horizon – my head exploded, frantically shooting bits & pieces hundreds of miles in undetermined directions, slapping back together in one awe struck piece. Billy was eating his hand, staring into infinite concrete abyss. *"Do you think I can fly?"* I grabbed his coat & dragged him from the ledge...

The city had become a Fritz Lang nightmare. Were those people androids to a secretive German society?

It was past midnight & I was now 18; we approached Pinkeye & hit the freeway, burying the needle... An hour later we transferred to Crenshaw's Van. He whipped out a bowl & we drove near a bridge; Billy & Crenshaw jumped out to explore; Angelica now passed out in shotgun.

As I gazed into the black sky I was entranced viewing the branches of an oak tree sway to the overlooked majesty of the Michigan night. I was then attacked by the dismembered head of a buck: *"We were running through the woods & thought we were in 'Nam! Charlie was coming & Billy ran into that artificial nature!"* We had a new mascot!

Days later, I had band practice with Crenshaw, despite our lack of other members. I arrived 15 minutes late & he'd come & gone, picking up his equipment. He refused to speak with me. I didn't understand, 'cause there honestly isn't much a drummer & singer can accomplish by themselves.

He just needed an excuse to throw me out of the band. No big deal – I wasn't really into it anymore. Later, at the Donut Shop Crenshaw came in shooting off over-dramatic languag – I was fired & never speak to him again. And he stormed away in a fit of hysteria & childish bickering...

Bad Hit

April 16th, 1999. In eerie calm, outside the sliding glass doors, are 2 police officers frozen in eerie calm. The young one motions I come outside with a snakelike curling finger.

"So, uh, what's going on here?" he asks politely. To my right, flashing red & blue lights cut through the night. Donovan's car is blocked in by two patrol cars – he & Cassie observe through the back windshield in stark intensity. *"Well, nothing much officer – just gonna buy raisin bread."*

My tripped-out attempt at a "cover story" for exactly what I'm up to in this Walmart-like store doesn't fly with him. I'm screwed, and we both know it. *"Oh no, it's a little more than that isn't it?"*

The one interrogating me is about 25, 6"2", short black hair buzzed into a crew cut. The older one is 5"11", short brown hair accentuated by mullet & manly man's mustache. Authoritarian Cop-Speak drags me back to the nightmar: *"Oh we know all about it – just come clean man, don't make it hard on yourself."*

"Well, alright... you got me – we smoked some pot."

"Oh, I don't think so – you're too spaced for reefer." The mullet approaches & holds my chin up to get clear view of my eyes. *"Loooook at those pupils... I've never seen anything like this this, this, this, this, this...."*

I feel like a gerbil about to be mutilated for the chemical safety of artificial beauty products. *"Put 'em in the back."* Tony & I are led to & confined within a third patrol. Inside it looks like a Death Machine. The seats stiff & plastic, frontward view distorted by bulletproof glass...

"Ok, don't panic," I think to myself, *"There's no way that this is a hallucination. Ok, LSD consumption – that's a mandatory <u>10 years</u>... oh*

fuck oh fuck oh fuck... Ok, just concentrate on the backseat. It's not my enemy, it's not my friend – it just <u>is</u>... Zen don't fail me now!"

Tony erupts with nonsensical laughter. I relay: *"You know, maybe this isn't so bad after all. We get to see how law enforcement works on the inside – you know, just like in those projector films in 2nd grade."*

A frantic woman starts kicking Donovan's car maliciously – *"They did it! They tried to steal my fucking car!"* It all makes sense now...

Tony was hovering outside the spaceship like Nosferatu, deforming into a giraffe. *"Hey guys – I struck gold! There's all sorts of money in that car!"*

I get out of the submarine & confronted the leprechaun head on. *"In the car, the car! We just won the jackpot! We can buy a circus or a barbershop or a pyrate ship or..."* he trails off & I've no choice but to follow him, flaccid heels sinking into blackened whale blubber.

Tony takes me to a Chrysler & hops into the backseat, digging through some random human's belongings as if his toy box.

"Dammit, stop this nonsense! You're just going to get the fucking cops called on us!" In a gesture of gentlemanly respect we arrange the items into neat little piles & lock all the doors: *"There – <u>much better</u>. We broke in to make sure no one would ever break in. They'd appreciate us!"*

"Hey Bartek, we're going on a mystical voyage – you take care of Tony." Donovan & Cassie take their leave inside the mega-store, both tripping hard as we were, hobbling down a labyrinth corridor of hygiene products. *"Funny,"* I think, *"They look like lawn gnomes from this angle..."*

Tony's dart off, howling like an emu in heat towards the helium balloons modeled after Barney The Dinosaur. He dashes while I clumsily follow in still frames.

I catch up with psycho-boy knocking a shelf of argyle socks onto the floor; he runs into the toy section & flips on a pyramid of "Tickle Me" Elmo's – *an armada of furry red creatures erupt in elfish glee, like a Red Wave of Muppet Extremity!...*

Then to the produce section where the view stops me dead in my tracks as if I've walked over my own grave – a fragmented Polaroid snapshot of Déjà vu. I've dreamt of this scene before – Tony fondling the cantaloupes as if the were Dolly Parton's luscious breasts.

I lunge forward, forcing him to lock eyes with me. *"We must leave! Something very bad will happen! Don't ask me how I know this 'cause I'm way too fucked up to explain!"* He shrinks with a subtle: *"ok.."*

We make a split for the front door but it's shrunk into a triangular emergency exit. I push the steel bar & a noisy mechanical beeping erupts. *"Fuck! I think I just set off the fire alarm..."*

After desperately sprinting through the parking lot, Donovan's car is nowhere to be found. Fear overtakes us. *"Ok, there must be a legitimate reason – Tony, go sit on that bench a sec..."*

I search through the aisles for eternity & give in to the growling of my stomach. I grab a Snickers & Coke & walk up to the cashier – a pyramid of feathered blonde 80's perm, face breathing contortions.

"Hello, I'd like to purchase these items." A skeletal arm points to the cashier 30 feet away: *"Yoou haaave to goooo ovverrr therrre..."*

To relieve tension, I try to win her over with whimsical sentiment. *"Oh, I'm sorry,"* I say shakily, *"I must be reeeeee-taaaaar-dead,"* turning midway through the last syllable to face none other than a mean retarded employee giving me a mean retarded face... *Noooooo....*

I dart back to Tony, who's giggling, childish, staring at something strangely. "*Look Ryan,*" he says – pointing out the window as pleasant as John Steinbeck would be on a travel with Charley – "*Police.*"

The rookie comes back and opens the passenger door, speaking to me with glowing red satanic eyes. "*I hear you're on a little bit of geltabs.*"

Terrified, I reply: "*Yes… yes it's true.*"

"*So what are they man, something new on the street?*"

I give in and blow my cover, "*It's acid man – fucking acid!!!*"

Immediately he lets us out of the squad car in an altered state of niceness that only seems to come from female dental assistants: "*Hey, no problem kid, just go sit over there.*"

All of us are back together on the cement ledge, huddled next to a carefully manicured corporate garden. Hoping to enlighten the devastation I blurt: "*Oh well, many fine books have been written in prison.*"

Cassie is giggling like a schoolgirl without the faintest idea of what is happening. Donovon has turned quivering lump of flesh in catatonic distress.

Rookie approaches, points to Tony – "*this one.*" The mullet shoves him in the patrol car, locks the doors & they drive off with Tony's hand pressed gently against the glass like a puppy at the Humane Society that's begging you to take it home so it don't get gassed.

The rookie asks Donovan: "*What's you parents number?*" You can hear his mother flipping out on the other end as the cop instructs her to pick us up. He gives us a long-winded spiel about how lucky we are not to & if he ever finds us in "*his*" city again we're totally fucked.

The ride home is eternal, having transformed into scolded 6 year olds awaiting hardcore grounding; I'm let off in front of my house & cautiously walk up the steps to my front door.

The minivan lingers outside, making sure I get busted by infuriated parental units. I turn the key & bolt inside, flicking on the light to make it look like a dramatic disturbance.

I blast through the empty house to the back door, nearly ripping it off of its hinges before sprinting to the backyard gate. Leaning over the fence, I keep repeating to myself *"It's over. It's ok. No pigs. No fear. Just concentrate on Zen, think Zen... FUCK ZEN!! I need a cigarette!!!"*

I zip to the Mobil gas station with ninja stealth; back to the calm safety of my porch where I chain-smoke 5 in a row...

A venomous surge of rat poison blasts my brain & I start peaking – consumed in one fell swoop. I lift my head up & look into the street where I hallucinate an army of pigs in full riot gear smacking billy-clubs in the palm of their hands, just standing out their like a Roman legion. I rush inside & frantically lock the door...

A cackling laughter catches my attention as I turn ever so slowly to embrace the microwave mutating into an aborted fetus, scalpel lodged in its forehead. It starts crawling towards me snapping vampiric fangs, bloody placenta dragging a sloppy trail...

I run into the living room, shoving the front door closed with the full strength of my shoulder. A distinct *"Hey Buddy"* comes from behind as chainsaws rev in the basement. I flip around & Ed is swaying back & forth in the rocking chair with half his face torn off, blood flowing from the top of his head like an erupting volcano.

He tears open Artie with his bare hands & maggots come pouring out like a broken piñata. They inch towards me, each with the head of my smiling dead Grandmother.

The walls are covered in pulsating masses of mayflies fucking, reproducing. The carpet is a horde of flesh-starved South African fire ants gnawing away the pristine leather of my boots. The house begins to implode like the end of *Poltergeist*...

Inside my room the *Antichrist Superstar* Marilyn Manson is underneath my bed slowly disemboweling himself & Hewitt is decomposing in my computer chair.

In my closet the Elvis impersonating rapist from *Unsolved Mysteries* is masturbating, slicing off hunks of flesh with a rusty straight razor, sucking the blood out with puckered lips like a dehydrated leech...

I hide under my blanket for safety yet it has become Ed Gein styled designer quasi-silk of carefully knit skin. Thousands of cockroaches with the head of Osama bin Laden swarm the floor; I close my eyes but all I see are three headed dogs giving birth to reptilian aardvarks...

The room begins melting, a living mass of organic tissue. Outside the house is being torn apart by thousands of Nazi skinheads screaming *"WE KNOW YOU'RE IN THERE YOU FUCKING NIGGER!!!"*

They rip at the aluminum siding with the sonic roar of a jumbo jet, breaking windows & struggling for entryway; from the ceiling a Nazi midget skinhead in corpse-paint is lowering himself via spider webbing from his spine, slashing grizzly-like claws inches from my face. I wrap myself in bed-sheet human skin – *they all attack at once, fangs & claws ripping at flesh, insects laying eggs in my eyes sockets...*

** *black out* **

1999

...Imploding, exploding, compacting, grating, smashing, starving, bleeding, cracking, rusting, falling, claustrophobic in my own body... Thus was the condition of my mind after the worst trip in the history of mankind. *Was it all a dream? Had I slept?*

I slowly vacated my room & examined the empty house like Duane Johnson sans forehead sniper. I instinctively went to the stripmall & the corridor was hellish slow motion, the silence like a jumbo jet screaming through the hall & shoppers faces distorting...

Still half-tripping, I flew to Brandon's. Everything melting, tripping on & off in bad head chemical blasts... I went to Lisa – the moment I glimpsed her I had a *"someone trampling my grave"* rush... Babbling paranoia, I accomplished little. At Zoe's it was the same scene. I soon passed out on her bed for hours...

All it took was One Bad Hit to send me back to the winter of 1994, at the worst time it could re-emerge. Locked into a freaky perma-trip of sorts forcefully unlocking every substrata doorway within.

All that shit Grandma told me about when I was 5 – about telepathy & ghosts & soul rapport – *GAZOOM!!!* Had I gone insane? Was I totally fried? I'm picking up all these weird transmissions like a CB radio, hearing things before people are saying them...

Events I'd dreamt of for years were unfolding – nightmares constantly. The LSD had completely altered my mental operation, paradoxical pressures ensuring collapse. It was like staring into the sun; an alien perception of the world, sensations of subliminal clockwork...

I was thrust into this new, very scary, very bizarre world, like if you were raised in the Amazon untouched by civilization for 18 years, then

were discovered and shipped to America without any understanding –
integrated without any moral or religious belief. I'd arrived at a total
psychological orientation to life, an evolution I could not grasp. Every
crack in the ship exposed, sinking toward the bottom of the Antarctic...

Monday at school they told me it was a dirty geltab soaked with 25
blotter hits, and I wasn't alone in its mangled impact. Anyone who'd
gobbled this batch had a terrifying night, or otherwise freakish & dark....

Looking around, everything had changed – the entire nature of the
school system, the meaning of classmates, the experiences of adolescence,
children becoming mute robot automatons even more obviously in the
grasp of a prearranged mold they were cursed to act out.

Everything was a shoddy ship about to collapse with graduation.
All I could do was brace myself, neurotically. No more Smitty or
Crenshaw; no more Prozac Nation, East Side Crew or Old World.

Vic & Kaitlin were now like inseparable newly-weds& locked into
nose rubbing, blueberry muffin bakin', pop culture worship. Robinson was
now in a bizarre Jesus cult & I was still at war with Kelly. Outside
Cassum & Brandon, all long-term relationships had deceased...

The following afternoon (Tuesday) – still spaced out yet slowly regaining
control – the 1990's "Dark Era" abruptly died in unparalleled carnage.
April 20th, 1999 – Columbine High School.

There I was, a deer in headlights – the Poster Boy for this type of
loner & all the cops & adults who already loathed me beforehand now
wanted me vicariously punished for the actions of Neo-Nazi's I never met
who likely would've gunned me down too..

. Like a lightning bolt from the vacuum, it was the death knell of
that era – no one anywhere wanted to be associated with the Columbine

Kids, and all over America kids removed their KMFDM & Marilyn Manson t-shirts & trenchcoats & hung 'em up in the closet. Because a couple crazies, and the media wanting a scaegoat, the world that had bred me was essentially gone – *Industrialized RivetHead Nation, bye-bye...*

When I walked in my front door my mom was frightened of me & my uncle called me physically angry as if I knew them, as if I supported this. And as I watched the footage on CNN, the reporter talking about "*Marilyn Manson types*" ...

I was soon out of high school, but the following year would bring a nationwide alteration so every learning facility would be militarized like juvey – metal detectors, ID cards, armed security...

At school I was like Moses parting the Red Sea, students barreling out of my path. I was an icon of fear; unnerving yet glorious at the same time (*of course I did show up in a KMFDM shirt, camo pants & a black trench but that's beside the point*). The pigs were questioning everyone, directly gunning for me 'cause my big mouth happened to rant all kinds of revenge plots over the years, just talkin' hard-assed shit like all kids do...

At the police station my mom was nearly fired because of my taste in music & apparel. If Toby hadn't been in the picture she would have gotten the axe. I was now confirmed as the #2 suspect on the mad bomber demon kid list, beat out by none other than Crenshaw.

I tried to call Crenshaw to warn him but he absolutely refused to believe this was happening, he thought I was delusional – he told me I was insane and never call him again!

I literally had first-hand info from my own spy in the police station, basically – and he would not believe me! Me trying to tell him the truth was the thing that made him never want to speak with me again!

Cops were pushing around kids on the street to roll something on me, harassing oddballs everywhere. My phone-line was tapped because I could clearly hear people chatting underneath, weird clicks, surveillance vehicles parking outside my house and others around me. And to my horror I learned the identity of the local neo-Torquemada...

Robert King is a pig in every sense of the word.

He is a short, ornery pug with a Napoleon complex that's abused the badge for nearly a decade, racking up a wide variety of accusations and recriminations including harassment, police brutality & planting evidence. He drags kids from the streets & fabricates lies to beat them for kicks. The good cops loathe him & bad cops exalt him...

My first encounter with King was during a routine traffic stop alongside Crenshaw, Dirk and a few others. King and his partner pulled us over claiming that Crenshaw hadn't used his blinker during a turn.

They dragged us from the van and tore apart the interior desperately searching for drugs or any visible form of paraphernalia. They found nothing and carried on with individual searches in which I swear King made a grunt of hideous satisfaction while molesting my scrotum.

They began digging through our record collections harassing our musical tastes: *"So you kids like Manson huh? What are you - fags or something? Oh yah, Rage Against the Machine. You hate the popo, the pigs, the fuzz?"* They demanded to know what our street names were, where we tagged and what we were pushing.

We hadn't ever heard the term "tag" before so they got really angry when we asked what they meant. King was holding onto his Maglite like he was going to clock me.

They put our names on the *"Disenchanted Youth List"* – a journal the cops passed around filled with notes on all the juvenile delinquents. That was back in '98, but now King's absolute legitimate mission was to take me down that summer, bragging about it to his fellow pigs...

And then The Curse of Edsel Ford strikes again.

See, Edsel was damned – a scorched earth replica of it's former glory. Back in the 60's it was among the finest public educational facilities in the nation, funded directly through the Ford Corporation. The staff were exceedingly left wing – the ceiling of each classroom that of glass to embrace the natural sky. Lava lamps & alternative lighting sources fueled each demonstration, classes were held outdoors...

30 years had passed and a gray cloud grew overhead. The beautiful glass roofs were replaced with grainy fiberglass, the inviting light exchanged for harsh fluorescent dimness, cushioned seats for uncomfortable plastic, progressive teachers laid off or transferred...

A massively high mortality rate ensued whether it be car wrecks, freak accidents, homicide, suicide, sexually transmitted diseases or worse. The pretty girls had big scars, misshapen appendages – every team lost terribly for nearly 2 decades.

Well, the curse returned Senior Pride '99. Actually, it was the second Senior Pride that year, since the curse forced it re-scheduled...

Flashback to February '99. It's Senior Pride Day & at lunch I arrive – but kids are crying everywhere, cops are parked outside...

Turns out that morning – as all kids were walking into school 10 minutes before the bell – this Arabic girl rear ends a parked car & her brother flies through the window like a torpedo. He face-dives into the concrete. She runs up in a white headdress attempting CPR even though he no longer has a jaw. Her head-dress was slathered in blood...

Turns out the kid was a bencher on the football team (*who were losing horribly; their record was 14 losses, 2 wins*) & all the jocks shave their heads in support, training like mad to defeat their blood rival that weekend – Dearborn High. Kids are wearing t-shirts that read "For Waseem," which by now is the triumphant war cry.

The big game comes around and Edsel is pathetically destroyed 36 to 3. Dirk was working his McDonalds shift when a group of jocks came in bawling their eyes out, cheerleaders cradling them in comfort...

Senior Pride Day is rescheduled. It's now deep into the great acid frenzy of '99 & after we get our class photo taken, Cassie & I skip out. En route to my house she downs 3 gel-tabs. We're there 5 minutes before kid's daytime programming starts taking it's toll – Teletubbies have her gripping the couch cushion like a jet flight in the eye of a Class 5 hurricane...

We walk to the gas station where it's revealed *yet another freshman* has been slaughtered in a freak accident. I panic 'cause I think it's this skater Cassie has a crush on so I drive her to Zoe's where we can hopefully isolate her from said news until she comes down, but Zoe & 6 others are on the same shit she is and a fantastic Warhol mess ensues.

Tony is already tripping on 3 gels when he & I down 60 grams each of hallucinogenic Morning Glory seeds...

Turns out it wasn't the skater kid but rather some jock on the hockey team who got aced by this kid that got his license two days earlier – full load of kids in the back of his pick up truck and was speeding along at 50 mph down a residential side street thinking he was invincible.

So the wheel pops or hits a wrong curve and flips over – kids fly through the air and the truck lands on top of the 15-year-old's head. The others survived with minor injuries. Tripping balls Cassie, Tony and I head on down to the scene of the accident...

Sobbing teens are spread all over in group huddles refusing to leave the area. Cassie is bugging out thinking she's surrounded when a reporter grabs her, shoves a camera in her face and starts interviewing her for grim sympathy sound-bytes. Her pupils are black holes & she's wearing a KMFDM shirt & a nametag sticker reading "ACIDFREAK."

She stands there not knowing what to do, broadcast live, all Detroit watching. In a flash she convinces herself the newsman is a zombie & books in the opposite direction, camera zooming the lens after her. They back up then turn to me, Plan B.

I flip on my sunglasses Hollywood-like and mouth off a ridiculously over-the-top anti-liquor *"he was such a good kid"* rant. I'd no idea what he even looked like...

Back at Zoe's kids are crying, bouncing off the walls. Someone has posted newspaper cutouts of all the Columbine victims on this upside down, half burned American flag.

Soon as Tony & I reach my house I can tell the Morning Glories are right under me (*you know their in effect as soon as the worms writhe through the arteries*). We chow down another 30 grams each & go to Brandon's – at this point I'm cuckoo, thinking pigs are everywhere. I wanna get my hands on a chainsaw so we can run around cutting down telephone polls. Instead we end up seeing *The Mummy. That fuckin' face coming out of the sand duuuuude...*

So you can see where this is going. I'm out my mind having constant nightmares about Anti-Matter devouring reality and a -14 Calvin quasi-nuke device that will freeze all energy to a standstill, destroying the very essence of the human soul vanquishing any hope of life after death...

I feel like a lab rat in a maze of razors – everywhere I go holds the possibility of police brutality, lingering bad blood feuds, aggressive wiggers, jocks searching for Littleton pseudo-revenge, crust punk & heroin goth junkies of the Old World lusting for long neglected vengeance.

I stop watching TV in a full-out media sXe boycott and keep learning more about bin Laden who I am positive will unleash a Ukrainian black market suitcase nuke in the middle of New York on Y2K and I must prepare, gather my soldiers and lead them into the *"Promised Land."*

I am fully engulfed by the prospects of the Millennial computer bug and absolutely positive it is going to occur, researching all sorts of household chemicals and exotic drugs that are not illegal in America because they've never been abused.

I'm attempting to hunt down *Yage* and this weird Amazonian plant that you burn in a fire, put a blanket over your head and inhale lungfuls of smoke because it enables you to talk to the dead.

I'm also working on finding a strong peyote hook up and a concrete method of extracting DXM from Robitussin. My room is beginning to fill with old chemistry sets stolen from school, garage sales, my cousins' basement...

Lost, confused, hunted by police, I finally gave in and sent her a letter through an intermediary demanding an emergency public relations meeting. What else was I to do? Who else to reformulate the master plan with but Kelly, the "Queen" of the Prozac Nation?

We met up at The City Club. It was difficult - I couldn't look her in the eyes. She was calm, razor sharp - a beacon of clarity with humongous, freshly composed devilish angel wings tattooed on her back... or at least she was in the beginning.

She started getting drunk and just unraveled. Her sister (*the closest person to her*) had died a few weeks after I stopped talking to her in an unexplained phenomenon. While sleeping she was victimized by "infant death syndrome," a rare anomaly heart attack at age of 33.

This was, for obvious secretive reasons, a terrifying shocker that melded with the nightmare lunacy. Kelly was a walking schism. She kept going on with whackadoo rhetoric I've no interest in repeating. In short, the last person I felt I could turn to was now a living train wreck...

To top it all off my girlfriend Patricia was insane. I met this quiet girl at WDHS and kidnapped her, forcing the female to go on weird, compulsive exploits. She was a dead soul, mentally aced from childhood molestation – desperately childlike, covered in deep red scars from self-mutilation.

Her room was stacked with piles of Ayn Rand – walls covered in magazine clippings of Tori Amos and fetus ultra-sounds...

The last day of high school I was completely on edge & unprepared for graduation. When the bell rang I grabbed Patricia, shoplifted whiskey from the party store, and we went to Simon's to party with Cassum, Nez, Ricky, etc.

Hysteria abounds because these crazy fucks never have to deal with report cards, permanent records, asinine jocks or shady teachers ever again. I'm in the first 15 minutes of post-dope smoking and locked into the initial fuzzy blast when I realize Patricia is nowhere to be found.

I hear some mumbling from the washroom and she's lying on the shower floor banging the back of her head into the steel wall hard as she can telling me I have to kill her because she's such a "terrible human." She downed a 5th of vodka in 1 slam & I had to carry her out over my shoulder, drive back to West Dearborn & dump her on her couch.

After that, in my weakest of psychedelic states, I continued dating her because I feared her suicide. It was a sick, unwanted dependence that I eventually just refused to continue whatsoever, and completely bailed...

Cassum knew of everything going on & extended friendship. We started hanging out with all of the guys mentioned in *"The Locals"* – Nez, Teeth, Simon, Johnny, Ricky – and was seen as a rogue...

Most of those guys were at war with Smitty's group and especially the entire Crenshaw/Edsel reality at large. There was a near riot at Johnny's when Smitty and the preps showed up 30 against 5, trying to battle their way through the corridor to Johnny's backyard – Johnny & Dre swinging baseball bats – chains, lead pipes & fists.

Cassum & The Boys were on edge 'cause they also accidentally stumbled onto the bad batch of gellies as well as the psychological repercussions Columbine now presented + paranoia of the Y2K computer bug alongside Cassum's similar worry of the bin Laden prospect...

Their bad trip happened at Irish's house (*I had yet to meet him at that point*). A dozen kids were tripping balls and it was this Bonnie girl's first psychedelic experience.

Cassum and Irish were clam-baking with a few randoms and she started flipping out, demanding to know where her boyfriend was, not having the slightest clue of what the hell was happening. Her annoyance drove them to violence and Cassum, Irish and this Mexican kid went into his garage, trashing everything in a frenzy.

The neighborhood had become a Zug Island parallel universe, machines and soulless industrialization far as the eye could see. Irish jumped onto the garage beam and flung himself upwards, busting out a window and cutting his foot when tearing up the sneaker.

He and the Mexican kid dismantled his boxing bag with their fists and bare teeth, wanting nothing more than to kill Bonnie because all of the repressed rage built up their entire lives was now pouring out.

The Mexican kid grabbed a butcher knife and lunged for her. They had to tackle and hold him down for twenty minutes foaming at the mouth like a mad dog until he calmed down. It was catastrophic, fucking up the minds of everyone involved...

At graduation I was limber from lithium and Southern Comfort, stumbling around the ceremony "accidentally" spilling soda on cheerleaders' pantyhose. I felt as if I was in *Logan's Run* – hitting the correct age, jewel glowing, sent to the gladiator death pits.

At the opening of these ceremonies, everyone claps for each student as they walking up to snag their diploma. Usually this applaud goes on until the M's before people are tired and it becomes as docile as a golf audience. I was the 8th student up because of my alphabetical disposition, and the previously roaring, energetic crowd came to a dead stop. You could hear crickets.

When I snagged my diploma not a single clap was heard from any of my class, nor the parents of the other students. The only few who applauded was one single girl I'd known since 3rd grade plus my aunt and mother in the bleachers. I was now liberated to derange the world through psychotropic oblivion...

After all I had been through in their institutions – the aggression, violence and despair of a low-rent prison – I felt like a 'Nam vet unable to readjust. Bred on violence, secure in violence, but now it was like, *"Hey, none of that matters anymore. Join the army or go to college or become a docile worker bee. If you resist we'll put you in prison or an asylum or grind you into desperate poverty..."*

"...accept the preordained fate drilled into you by our useless teachers and flaccid role models. This degree we brainwashed you to work so hard for is really just another piece of meaningless paper to wipe your ass with. Fuck you chump, get the hell out of our parking lot..."

Perhaps, but a mutant such as I don't croak so easy. Sorry babe, my heart is in Rosa Rio under the Argentine sky. The Old World was dead and anything was possible. But first it was time to party...

Intoxicated with Daisy who has by now recovered from crack cocaine... a drunken cohort and I saunter the streets, stealing mail on our way to purchase burritos from 7-11. We smoke a joint, heat the Mexican entrée's & I wander into the night beans on face, spaghetti strainer on head in search of an American flag to do a striptease with...

Midway through a dark, unknown neighborhood sirens flash and this cop jumps out. I toss the strainer off immediately to not look as insane and he thinks I'm bleeding because I have this Anti-Flag bumper sticker on my left forearm...

He throws me in the back of the squad-car because someone broke into a house and thinks I am the culprit. He is worked up and manic, unable to tell just how drunk I really am. I keep explaining to him the burritos, how good they were and how he should try them some day. He takes me to the B&E house and I am not identified as the intruder…

Feeding this random kid Valium during his first acid trip. He keeps screaming in the back seat of my Escort because he thinks the Mothman is on top of the roof, clawing through steel. I keep beating on the roof as we drive, screaming as he screams back in return. My head elongates into an eel-like shape & the seat-belts are poisonous snakes writhing across his chest…

Going to my first rave party in search of LSD with Brandon and Kluck (*first time we hung out*). I get some acid wrapped in tin foil and accidentally ingest it. Driving down I-94, crushing white rabbits beneath my wheels, we end up at some weird house party where a Marine who's gone AWOL is shitfaced in a diaper and paratrooper boots crying on the basement floor in front of a stand-up old-school arcade game of *Gauntlet II*. I attack a boxing bag viciously, ripping the stuffing out of it with my bare teeth. Brandon tells me I'd have no problem making it in prison...

Tony wide eyed and flipping out on acid swinging a hammer through a massive cloud of pot smoke trying to kill a moth in a 104 degree locked garage filled with 12 petrified kids tripping balls…

With every paycheck accompanying Cassum to purchase intricately crafted bongs, picking up our "Y2K defense" katanas, blueprinting our scheme to turn Simon's house into a post-nuclear warfare *Steel Dawn* styled fortress…

The great acid frenzy continues, high school acquaintances and enemies found all hours of the night in chemical schizophrenia stupors…

In River Rouge a stray ghetto dog walks up and as I go to pet it I find it's covered in infectious scabs. It starts shaking, half barking strange noises and a five-inch tapeworm crawls out of its asshole, edging its way towards my shoe...

Driving around 3 am with Brandon and car full of kids stalking a man on roller blades fully decked out in zebra windbreakers with headlights off, cruising behind him jamming the Jaws theme song...

One of our pot dealers is shot five times by a rival dealer and receives over 273 stitches and a crucifix disposition...

Tony running through Harry's Army Surplus on acid hollering anti-Semitic remarks wearing a staple-hemmed American flag as superhero cape...

During a house party Kelly convinces herself there is a starving kitten locked in her garage. We follow her home and after her delusion is proven false we devour lithium and smoke pot out of a makeshift Faygo three-liter bong and stare into the night sky which has now become an organic painting...

Cassie crying in my automobile on three hits of blue geltabs as I force her to listen to Nifelheim...

Pushing out a full-length screenplay entitled *Urban Dojo II: Suburban Decay* in which I was to star as Billy Jack Jr. alongside a nomadic disco warrior coined "The Gilla Fighter" only to have my co-director bail when we're ready to film...

Disembodied memory of a dirty loft, strobe light flashing, running in circles with a half dozen cackling crust punks thrashing everything in sight with baseball bats, machetes, harpoon guns as "Do The Bartman" jams through the ancient PA system...

Trailed by a '57 pink Cadillac at 4 am, Christine is enraged in *Maximum Overdrive* fury...

Throwing Columbian coffee beans at Billy, telling him to go fuck himself and piss off forever for talking trash on Cassie and maintaining allegiance to Crenshaw...

Cassie thinking the Chinese restaurant is the Queen Elizabeth swaying in black waters, pouring crumbled fortune cookies in a bowl of soy sauce and eating it like Crispex...

Forcing Brandon to wake up and buy me the pellet gun I never got for Christmas, going deep into backwoods trails only to find the fresh trail of a mutant-alligator-fish-deer-dog monster in the swamp (long story)...

Ending my involvement with Patricia by chucking raw sunscreen globs at her porch as a smell/taste form of revenge...

Yemenis Edsel kid coming into my work telling me how different I was than the others and that Allah will protect me because the Jihad is coming and I should leave America because bin Laden will be bringing down the hammer on New Years Eve and to stay far away from tall buildings and skyscrapers in particular...

Going to Belle Isle with Smitty and a few others, the field trip beauty of my youth turned ghetto drug-land - ice cream man selling crack, Negro children barreling down the now rusted quarter slide; stared down by Cryps for sporting blue camo...

At MI Central Depot the infamous ghost train roars overhead in broad daylight, it's full speed steam scream piercing our ears...

In the back seat of my car during a raging house party drunk and cradling an intoxicated sobbing girl I just met and had sex with explain how she "needs to escape Detroit at once," begging me to move to Utah with her even though we've both forgotten each other's names...

Waking in Morning Glory head stupor taking a piss, looking over at the hair net in the shower drain with a telekinetic impulse. It shoots six feet in the air and lands in the middle of the tub...

Tony exiting his involvement after chasing him around my house at 2 am, katana blade raised in hand prepared to slice off his head...

Mid-July, consuming a two gallon jug of Vitamin D while playing basketball, giant streams of white liquid projectile across the court...

Driving a screaming 15 year-old I just met down this street of pothole craters at 60 mph blasting Mortician until my suspension system cracks & the engine shuts itself off thinking it just got macked by a semi...

Chugging Morning Glory microwave slop with Vic, running amuck in the Hyatt Regency as green hair protrudes from his arms. Beast creature Vic claws at doors eating plastic flowers nearly getting the police called on us...

Vic's sister took a Y2K class that was shut down by black suited government agents...

Teeth and I smoking a bowl in his upstairs bedroom at night paranoid his father will come home and he'll get kicked out. We see lights pull into the driveway from below, nothing is there. We hear the front door open and shut, his dog starts going crazy. We hear footsteps up the stairs then it stops. We hear two more steps and the bedroom door gets beat three times from the other side with Joe Louis right hooks like the post-"Spawn" nightmare. I kick open the door – no one is in the house...

It is now late July and I am utterly fried, consumed by the twisted realities of the Donut Culture; at all angles breakfast propaganda fills my vision. The wallpaper is little logo symbols, in flawless unending columns.

I hide in the back room contemplating Nine Inch Nails' *The Fragile*, banking it's September release as the last possible hope of re-instilling The Prozac Nation and the only time where it all made sense.

The last remainders from The Old World besides Cassum and Brandon were Lisa and Dirk but they hate me now. I intensified the Crenshaw war not only by turning on Billy, but bringing to light a scam scenario that I misunderstood.

Towards the end of '98 Crenshaw & Billy purchased a rather costly keyboard for Dirk ($1000). When we met up they were laughing about how badly they ripped him, mentioning the Roland was only $800.

Dirk was rather livid to say the least. I called Guitar center and the manager checked the computer logs. I had Crenshaw by the balls. I was shaking with anticipation as I ran up to Dirk and explained everything. He simply replied, *"Yah, the 'board was only $800. They bought FX modules for it which jacked up the price. Crenshaw gave me the receipt yesterday."*

They had gaffled a mere $15 for gas and Burger King. Dirk shook me off like a psychotic vagrant begging for change and I sunk into a patio chair looking about Lisa's birthday party.

Everyone was either giving me dirty looks or refusing to acknowledge my presence. I was no longer welcome. I got up in a nervous twitch & walked off without saying goodbye…

I had to quit the donut job – it was driving me nuts. I put in my notice & found a replacement worker – Smitty's little brother. A week later, he jacked $60 out the register & walked off the job with an electric gram scale. *He left the store unlocked & open to the public!*

It was hours before the manager caught wind. The owner called me panicking and said he's have no choice but to file charges unless I was able to get this equipment back from said scoundrel.

I showed up at Smitty's cursing up a storm and returned with it late at night. I was stoned and they were touched. Babu opened the swinging door and said, *"You are employee all the time,"* allowing me to pick up free donuts for the rest of my life. I reemerged into the night with a mob of smiling Hindu's behind me, all seemingly waving in slow motion...

It was at this time that we all discovered the magical wonders of the infamous "House Of Beer."

The H.O.B. was an exact replica of the frat from *Animal House.* The security force wore t-shirts proclaiming, *"Where stupidity and alcoholism are righteously promoted and encouraged."*

All night long there were ruthless boxing matches, strip poker, fun with arson, bumping polka, nudist colonies, fireworks, explosives, a five-keg minimum and a general sense of brutal decadence.

It was at the H.O.B. where I bumped into Irish for the first time whilst he downed a handful of iridescent pills with a 151 Bacardi chaser (*he and Kluck were having a consumption duel involving Depicote, Aderol, Mobutrin, Zoloft, Prozac, Lithium, Ritalin, etc.*).

Through an inapt narco-analysis I discovered he was the self-destructive product of a broken home. Just as I, he was an intelligent kid forced into adulthood during his early teenage years.

His father was a firefighter who had ruthlessly disciplined him through childhood – years of abuse had produced this walking time bomb. Only now had he began to strike back and was entangled inside a web of threats that included mental hospitalization, rehab, boot camp and much, much worse. Within a short period he had become my right hand man...

The bender continued to no end. I realized I had blown over fourteen hundred dollars with absolutely no fiscal responsibilities whatsoever. To top it all off Daisy, whom I was about 2 weeks into officially dating in a weird little moment, was raped.

This incident did not impact me the way it should have, because I was so out of it that it was just another thing floating there like a lucid dream unable to materialize in my brain fully.

It happened while at *"The Loft"* – a creepy band rehearsal complex with tiny rooms and no windows. She was wandering around intoxicated, dragged into one of the rooms, bound, gagged and worked over by some sick fuck blasting death metal to drown out her screams.

She refused to ever go back pretending it never happened, ditched the punk thing and went raver. After that there was nothing left between us. Besides, I can barely go for more than a few hours without Sepsism, Nifelheim or Machetazo...

My conception of time had gone out the window alongside the possible chance of a Jessi Spano no-doze intervention. Late August it all came crashing to a standstill. Nez and I were alone in Simon's garage, pissed because everything was dry. Nez looked into the sky that was growing dark and said, *"Gettin' cold."*

For some reason it was an earthshaking moment of clarity. I snapped out of the manic head-trip and jumped in my car, hightailing it back to the Hyatt Regency where the frenzy truly began. I retraced my steps; flashbacks of Donovan, Vic turning into a wild beast.

I drove to my house with lightning thoughts of her. I lunged for the phone to confess what I could never before. I was ready to express my love of her, pouring out like a volcanic eruption...

The voice on the other end told me Kelly just moved to Seattle on a whim. No address, no phone, no email. I'd only missed her by a few hours. I hung up in catatonic distress and looked around my room.

Hundreds of dollars crumpled into meaningless little balls all over the carpet. Holes punched in the walls, stacks of drug addled notes lacking any coherent logic. An empty house & shattered relationship between mother and son. An address book filled with numbers of people who no longer wanted anything to do with me.

A tapped phone line picking up weird clicks. Brandon either dead or in jail (see *Onyx*). The shattered, vandalized fragments of a life of self-destruction strewn about at every angle. The perma-trip from hell that refused to end...

I was now living in a hallucination with no escape from the decay. After Grandma died I only saw dead people and felt as if I was the last living soul on Earth.

But now I was the corpse and all that remained were the living. And I broke down crying, confronting a God whom I knew was non-existent and long since vowed to destroy, pathetically babbling to be taken back to a time before everything...

It was the cornerstone origin of the worst depression I was to ever face. I had no sense of purpose, no refuge but drugs; no friends but a vast system of cluckers far worse than I. *The Fragile* had no effect on anything, bombing harder than any release in the history of the Billboard Charts.

Three things were to hold me together that fall. First was the structure and sense of purpose provided by Spartan Trucking, a job

Cassum offered me as a stock room rat/parts driver. The second was my quest to right the wrongs of the past. I had to save Cassum, Nez, Simon, Teeth, Ricky, Johnny and all the rest.

But the main focus was Irish, who unlike the rest showcased a greatly positivist hope and willpower for a better world. He reminded me so much of myself in those formative years that it was like traveling back in time to ensure my current self never existed. Third, the soft, innocent voice on the other side of the line...

That would be Natasha, a beautiful young girl that edged her way into my life through an inadvertent encounter in February '99. It was right before Val died from that nasty fix. While shopping a random girl asked her for my phone number. She started calling me on occasion and I was her only real link to the outside world.

She was from Mexican town – on a green card in fact – but was closely disciplined to maintain a house life, taking care of the younger siblings. She went to school directly across the street from Clark Park and was the only freak in that side of town.

She wasn't really that weird, she just liked *Hackers* a lot and wanted to be a skater. But in Mexican Town that was some hardcore strangeness – that and the fact that she was a natural born witch.

She'd stay up all night on the phone with me – this quiet, mysterious, beautiful thing – trying to escape the grimness of Detroit anyway possible and telling me her wondrous dreams for the future.

Every once and awhile we'd meet up in person but only on the rare days when she'd be over her aunt's house Downriver. In my darkest storms she would always be there – this gentile voice that might have well been from another planet. And I just listened...

It was now September and a dangerous trend took hold; the East Side Crew began invading the rave underground as a means to gain easier access to more hardcore drugs.

The group collectively discovered the sweet tooth fallacy of ecstasy. Grandiloquent tales of the MDMA baptism were building a hyped momentum that spilled into other circles, cliques, internet chat rooms, web pages, fanzines, high schools, elementary playgrounds...

The acid boom was replaced by the pill and it wasn't long before the positive emotional aspects of the drug wore thin. By mid-December Irish was going to extremes. Cassum &Nez were rolling 3 days a week, Johnny & Ricky twice. Then K, coke, nitrous, crystal...

Directly before this great decline an Alamo took place with myself, Irish, Nez, Simon &Cassum. We were in Simon's garage – literally about to fist-fight on a mob of 40 Arabs in the street over whatever beef Simon had kicked up with them. No joke – dead serious.

Simon's dad stumbled out – said he'd kill as many of them as possible, even if he had to go down with them. They backed off, he went on a 'Nam *"You're a bunch of pussies/I killed over a dozen men with my bare hands"* rant. After that there was a war brewing right under the surface of the neighborhood that never materialized.

Opie & Scooby became two of our rave buddies. Opie was this wiry red haired kid covered in tats. Scooby a quiet, black belt trained ninja dealer of many varieties calling his goods *"Scooby snacks"*...

The rolling fiascos got increasingly out of hand in September. Auto wrecks nearly killed a handful of our friends – like when a buddy of ours jacked up on E rammed some poor lady at a 100 mph.

The lady's car ping-ponged the side of the freeway four times – all the windows shattered, the thing looked like an accordion and she was taken to the hospital on a stretcher. The left side of Irish's face was black and blue from the airbag – no one else had a scratch even though he was the only one wearing his seat-belt.

Cassum & Irish began driving around 9 hours at a time huffing the cheapest starter fluid with the highest concentration of ether they could get their hands on, nearly crashing a good 30 times.

Cassum almost died on the floor of this party after snorting way too much crystal meth alongside a rather intense speed-ball combination. The party got raided and some random kids had to drag him off the floor. They almost died a good 7 times because he kept passing out at the wheel.

Cassum got arrested later that week when the cops flicked him for a broken taillight. They found all of the fancy bongs we'd purchased in his trunk. Irish was now dating Samantha, the better half of The Twins. They were nothing but trouble. She got him to smoke crack out of a light bulb, making him the first of our group to venture that avenue...

It's now mid-October and driving non-stop for 10 hours a day in the worst, shit-ass areas of Detroit has freed up some lost baggage.

I'm about to get off shift and I decide to impulsively hunt down my long lost half-brothers. I figure out where my aunt lives through an old postcard & just show up...

We drank Faygo and talked about what a piece of shit my dad is. Apparently he, "*still sees me all the time.*" I also find out the time he disappeared was also the time my Grandma (his side) died of a heart attack. No one ever notified me. If they did my mother refused to tell me.

My estranged uncle gives what little information he had on my ex-stepmother's whereabouts as well as some info on a cousin I've never met. My pop's brother was so abusive she changed her name.

So I hunt her down at this apartment complex and she pretends to know nothing about this person I'm looking for. I don't tell her who I am and instead walk away since she obviously wants no part of it...

The next day at work I'm not far from Zug Island when I see this prostitute get stabbed in the stomach. The image sends me into a dark temporary trance, replaying itself over and over cinematically in my head.

It overpowered the callousness triggering years of repressed anger, manifesting itself as an uncontrollable urge to brutalize my father with a crowbar. Literally, dead serious, I was going to put him in the hospital.

Moments before I was to punch out and hunt him down I received a 911 page from Irish, begging me to stash him somewhere. He said the police were coming to drag him away because he flushed his Lithium, Depacote and Welbutrin down the toilet (*keeping the Aderol to snort later*), destroyed his waterbed, stereo, punched holes in the walls and ripped the door from it's hinges in a fit of rage.

His parents were trying to give him a pharmaceutical lobotomy because he disagreed with their perceptions of reality. This began five weeks ago after he told his mother that he felt the government was dishonest and there were many hidden conspiracies at play.

They took him to a psychologist that asked if he liked school and how many cigarettes he smoked each day. He said no and two packs and was either given the choice of reprogramming his chemistry with drugs 100 times worse than the ones he was on or spend 6 months in rehab.

He chose the medication which in turn slowly remolded him into a soulless robot. He went to a party where he consumed a hit of blotter, 4 pills, 1 gel & 2 drops of liquid within 6 hours & got nothing in return 'cause the meds even though Espa wigged out from the exact same shit.

I ran to my car & buried the needle, arriving at his house 15 minutes later to find a squad car patrolling the street, searchlight grazing the local park. I quickly drove to Espa's and he sprinted out. We blasted out of there and went to my house to get something to eat.

Less than ten minutes passed when I received a knock at the door. It was King. *"Hand him over and I'll leave quietly."* Irish put up no fight. My mom was in the kitchen the entire time, clueless as to what had just happened. When I told her the only thing she asked was if his Mother loved him or not...

I returned to Espa's to find a gathering of sobbing teens speaking of Irish in postmortem dialogue. I flipped out with the surge of another jigsaw premonition and began shouting *"He's not fucking dead!"* at the distraught gathering, barreling down the stairs and driving across town where a similar scene was taking place.

As I pulled up to Teeth's I nearly hit his dog who was running freely in the streets. I hopped out and heard mad laughter almost drowned entirely out by the intense refrain of *"Were In This Together Now"* emanating from the upstairs window. Cassum was rolling around on the grass having a psychotic episode.

Inside Nez was venting his frustration by beating the shit out of the walls and furniture. Teeth had locked himself in his bedroom, frantically smoking a bowl in a drastic attempt to purge the intensity.

Once we all ran into each other the kinetic energy in the house turned on us and we were at each other's throats. We nearly killed each other in a fit of maddening despair...

Turns out this whole thing was spurned from King's vendetta against me. Irish's dad was a friend of his and as soon as he heard Irish was getting into trouble King got involved.

When he found out I was his friend that's when the TNT exploded. The cocksucker couldn't get to me so he had to dismantle my life piece by piece and "*save*" this poor kid by locking him up in a loony bin and pumping him full of drugs until he worshiped Rush Limbaugh...

In a fuzzy reverie that following Monday – having tripped hard on shrooms that weekend at Cassie's dorm – I was driving the Spartan parts van and received a $150 ticket that gave an automatic two points if convicted.

While I was parked behind this school bus unloading children a cop was waiting behind me. For some incoherent, drug addled reason I thought he wanted to get by so I slammed on the gas at 50 mph. I just flew by this bus, and looked into the rear-view mirror to view his happy face.

He blinked and shook his head, not sure if this was actually happening. I continued to drive, realizing what I'd just done, then snapped into reality land as he chased me down in disbelief.

Shit, what do I tell this guy? Well, the only thing that would possibly make any sense – I thought the kiddies were unloaded and it was safe to pass. It might have been a bullshit excuse but at least it made some kind of believable tapestry from the nonsense...

Irish was released that Friday after bouncing between 3 psyche wards. In honor of his release Cassum, Irish, Jessica (*Irish's girl*) & I drove to

Chicago for no logical reason except peace of mind. Cassum had been up 3 days straight on an MDMA binge...

Johnny and Susan (*of The Twins*) were already in Naperville visiting J's mom so we had a base of operation soon as we got out there...

We began by filling our bellies with 50 cent apple pies from McDonald's. The mop lady was giving Jessica crude looks because she had no shoes on (*she never wore shoes*).

I pleaded with her the importance of sneakers on a mission such as this but she insisted on going barefoot the entire way. *"How are you going to give me shit about my feet when you're wearing that stupid fucking referee uniform?"* She was right. I looked like an escaped mental patient ready to call the shots in a little league game.

There was always a slight grudge between her and I. Years ago she had attempted to have Smitty beaten down by Johnny, Dre and few of the others. I never knew why until she explained that Smitty tried to fuck her when passed out drunk...

We had $75, two packs of Zig Zags, a gram of marijuana, a 24r pack of Labaat Blue & a razor sharp Katana (*the almighty Horned Dragon*) in case we had an unsightly run in with a pack of mutant ruffians...

The first 3 hours were a commotion of dialogue; our storms calmed as we progressed into the desolation of Western Michigan, gray skies thickening to a dark blanket of night.

As we neared the outskirts we viewed a rather unique sight; a Wendy's franchise inside a behemoth viaduct, windows ajar to view the maddening rush of traffic. The melding of concrete and grizzled lard to symbolize the unholy rotten womb of Dave Thomas.

A buddy of mine had been a golf caddy for the Wendy's patriarch years ago: *"I lugged around that decrepit bastards clubs in the blistering heat for hours on end. When it was all said and done I had peeling skin and all the fucker did was toss me a quarter. He actually told me I'd never amount to anything. One day I'll have my fucking revenge"* ...

"Are you sure there's an M-55?" Jessica gave me querulous attitude, insisting she was correct. Her sloppy momentum caused us to miss our exit, traveling fifty miles out of the way. We were hopelessly lost in the middle of hill-jack farmland.

We pulled into something of an interstate oasis. Irish hopped out and sprinted for the restroom. I turned to Jessica, *"Come darling... chop-chop,"* while opening my arm to lead her inside like a proper gentleman. The interior was modeled after a semi-truck cab, *Smokey and the Bandit* written all over it. Cassum and I spotted a Burt Reynolds shrine, autographed black and white glossy the crowning triumph...

I took control of the wheel, jetting onward into the starry night and realized the power steering fluid was empty. I was steering a battering ram at 70 mph cursing the little control I had over the steel juggernaut. Cassum roared with laughter, *"That's the way I like it"* ...

We arrived in Naperville (*statistically the safest city in the United States*) with a great euphoric surge. The dreary interval of strip-mall after Wal-Mart after strip-mall after Wal-Mart gave the emptiness in the truckers' eyes took new meaning.

We had stumbled onto the punch line of the most ludicrous joke of them all. The bulk of our great society is nothing more than a glowing neon empire – a lavish assault of advertising, consumerism and iridescent light winding about the blackened arteries of the mainland...

Soon as we parked outside Johnny's I melted from the driver seat onto the freezing ground & lay gazing at stars. The home was expansive, reeking of white upper class suburbanism...

I drove towards Downtown Chicago via Freeway; to the Belmont district, where were dismal & unpopulated. Our first stop was a store called *The Alley* – every rock t-shirt, bondage accessory, leather coat, patch, pipe & bong in the past 15 years...

Cassum had the ultimatum of returning by 9am to drive his Father's car to Ypsilanti so we shot back onto the main drag promising we would make the trip again soon enough as we all had an appropriate amount of money, and better yet, a non-spontaneous plan...

We returned to Johnny's to meet his mother's boyfriend who was slightly drunk. He was wearing a cowboy hat & rambling fascination with Stevie Ray Vaughn.

He dragged Cassum & I into the kitchen to dig his chili pepper & salsa collection. None of us really wanted any of it but he force-fed us the hottest gut churning peppers he had to offer.

I swiftly snuck away, leaving Cassum to his almighty wrath. He pleaded in desperation, "*No man, I'm full... I just want a burrito... Please, just one burrito... Soft... Tender... Filling...*" The man simply would not have it. "*No sir-ree... No pussies in this here house.*" Cassum joined us back downstairs looking raped...

We warmed the car and refilled the trunk with illicit substances and battle weapons. We gave Johnny some beer and Susan hugged us for good luck on our backtracking voyage.

The ride home was relatively smooth except for the hectic piecing together of carpet shake to form a pinner at the prime moment of 4:20 am (*hardcore traditionalists you know*).

I put on Beethoven's' soothing masterpiece "*Moonlight Sonata*" to aid the exhilarating peace. Jessica kept bitching about the "*shitty music*" so

I jacked the stereo up as loud as it could possibly go and shouted *"Hey Betsy... SHUT THE FUCK UP!"*

From then on it was golden silence. Jessica and Cassum had both fallen asleep. Irish sat quietly in back, eyes hypnotically fixed on the purity of the road. I went on for about three and a half hours before nearly passing out at the wheel. Cassum took the chore, prattling on & having a mild nervous breakdown, punching himself in the face to stay awake...

I came to as the gas gauge rose from it's infinitesimal readings. We were back in East Dearborn but I refused to let the adventure end without necessary drama.

We went to the park and played on the swings. Jessica was lying on the merry go 'round, exhausted and slightly hallucinating. I hopped on and spun it wildly: *"I claim this park in the name of France!"*

She stumbled away sullen and writhing in nauseous dizzying agony, cursing hellified obscenities. *"You are the craziest mother fucker I have ever met and you should be committed to an asylum and left there to rot for the rest of your miserable Godforsaken life!"*

A startled old woman watering her lawn threatened to call 911 and I retorted by calling the elderly hag a *"filthy cunt-gopher."*

We jumped into the Taurus, gunning onward towards freedom. I was dropped off and staggered into my house like a redwood crashing towards the forest floor. I slept for a good 15 hours into the next day; we drove over 800 miles that night...

Back at home with constant newscasts of bin Laden's intended New Years Eve plans for world destruction and months of newspaper clippings I'd paranoia-amassed showing the obvious trail of his and inter-related terror groups actions, Cassum was just as flared up over our the massive amount of suspicious activity now taking place.

With the worldwide fear of Y2K & my own jigsaw premonitions – Cassum & I decided to flee Up North for New Years & stay away from any major city, convinced things might be going down in the ugliest way.

No one believed us. Still, when the deadline for the escape pod drew near, our paranoia infected Irish & Simon, and they agreed to join.

Simon's girlfriend Espa convinced her entire family that the right thing to do was also follow our lead Up North to their cabin as well.

We made the reservations to stay at a small motel not far from them, and on Wednesday, December 22nd I received a 911 page from Natasha. We were together now officially, although I rarely was able to see her in person. She was the glue holding me together.

The only time I ever went to her house was the day before when her brother told me to stop by. I was only able to talk to her for a few minutes on the front porch because she had chores to finish.

Soon as I left the father tried to kill her because I was white. The piece of shit strangled her, she wrestled loose and called the authorities.

They arrested him, threatened to put all of the kids in foster care, and the mother attempted to slit her wrists from the exceptionally volatile situation I knew nothing about.

He had been sexually molesting her for years and I was the first guy to ever come into her life, disrupting his sick operation.

I spoke to her all night over the phone in shock. She was leaving for Texas in the morning to stay with her grandparents. I fell asleep to the distant voice saying it loved me & I was the only good thing about its life. I awoke to the dial tone and fell back asleep, dreaming of nothing but the purple fingerprints on her neck…

MILLENNIUM

12.28.99

Hospodi Pimulodi is imaginarily carved deep into the faux-oak tabletop; delicate patterns in the grain bend & twirl beneath crumpled cellophane wrappers, spent half & half containers, disorganized stacks of loose-leaf.

Each sheet contains the scrambled notes necessary to our survival. I catch Cassum's face jump a beat, teeth mashing a pearl like protean substance. I shake off the hallucination in a nervous twitch and he belts out yet another fictional reality. *"I talked to this guy that always comes into our work today. He's a coast guard over at the Ambassador Bridge."*

"So why does he come into our work? It's not like u-boats utilize the same mechanics as a rig."

"Man, you'd be surprised at the schematics of this automotive shit. Look, this guy comes in all the time for fan belts and I always bullshit with him. He told me they were doing a routine patrol of the bridge and they found a shit load of C-4 attached to the supporting legs. Terrorist motherfuckers were gonna take it out on New Year's. Serious shit is going down man. They didn't tell the news because they don't want to start mass panic. The whole fucking city is going to go up in flames."

Irish and I exchange the *"completely full of shit"* glance, but there is such a degree of urgency & sincerity in his words that I can't dismiss it so easily. Anne looks horrified, Simon is nervously smoking a cigarette. It's hard to tell with Cassum nowadays. He's so far out on the ledge with drugs that he honestly believes his delusions…

I take a deep breath and ingress, examining the situation disembodied. It looks like a canvas by Parson on absinthe. The 5 of us hard-boiled intense, chain-smoking, plotting the Armageddon strategy guide at Ram's Horn.

There's Cassum, an 18 year old Caucasian/Arabic half-breed perpetually strung out from a psychotropic drug binge since the tender age of 12. His eyes are bloodshot and desperate, black hair a rambunctious mess, five o' clock shadow a permanent fixture. He's wearing the olive green WWII Marine trench coat I gave him for Christmas.

Simon's a skinny 16 year old with bright blue hair and thin lips, the bags under his eyes permanently etched into his skin like congruent scars. Irish is next to him in an Adidas t-shirt analyzing the situation – you can smell his cologne from across the table.

His latest in a string of girlfriends is tightly gripping his hand beneath the table. She's a cute high school sophomore – a definitive Korn Kid with parachute pants, candy bracelets, glitter & a pewter necklace glimmering in the fluorescent light.

I'm the most drained of the lot – a burned out neurotic caricature sketched by an insomnia-riddled Tim Burton. I'm only 18 and most think I'm in my mid 20's. My hair is a sporadic amalgam of blonde, gray & red.

Eyes a once wild beacon of energy, they've turned abysmal conduits into a desolate soul. The bags below them are just as black from sleep deprivation as my cashmere trench coat…

I snap back into reality with Cassum's incessant rambling: "*I still plan on bringing a suitcase full of drugs. If the worlds going down then so is my equilibrium,*" Cassum shifts into drug-freak mode and starts naming off all the possible narcotics he can get in the next 3 days. I lose my audience to his weird charisma. Fuck it. Slip away…

We are only 72 hours from the catalyst that will procure the fall of civilization. On every street corner, in every cathedral, church and confession booth – every prison cell, cubicle, restroom, subway, high school - humanity shares the same held breath.

We now approach the terrifying conclusion of a million forlorn prophecies – the fate of science and technology – the evidence that we have finally outgrown ourselves, divorced ourselves from nature; condemned, automated and enslaved our lives to the machine...

In 3 days the clock will strike midnight and the world will fall under a systematic blanket of night. Six billion sheep running headfirst into mass hysteria, unleashing all their immolation head desires...

Martial law will take hold as the governments of the world move their pawns into position. Armies waging war in the name of ideology, fossil fuels, resources; zealots sparking Jihad of all divinities. We stand at the very threshold – *the death of the illusion, only 72 hours away...*

The Christmas bell jingles as the entrance swings open, shattering my head-sick elation. I turn and lock eyes with Crenshaw, face obscured beneath the brim of his pitch-black cowboy hat. He's trailed by the whole bloody lot of them – Lisa, Dirk, Ted, Billy, Zoe, Angelica, Tony...

The waitress leads them to the smoking section ten feet away. I grab a fork out of primal reflex and prepare for a full-blown riot. Cassum and Simon begin crooning *"YAH YAH I'm the one that you wanted - YAH YAH I'm your Superbeast!"* Cassum has been waiting 2 years to fight Crenshaw; I see the itch in his bloodshot eyes & intervene: *"Don't do it – there's way too much on the line."*

He relaxes and slants into the booth discouraged like a child scorned by an overbearing father figure. *"But anyone of these GOTH*

FAGGOTS could have thrown that brick through your car window. Please let me kill them. Want to kill them. Very important. Must do now." It seems likely but I'm not ready to single anyone out just yet. To me, paranoia is as vital to survival as blood.

Everyone at our table is in attack mode. Anne is exchanging menacing looks with Lisa. Irish looks chemically unstable. Even Simon, who avoids physical confrontation, is prepared to scrap.

I let out a sigh in lieu of the hostility and Billy hollers out my name; his smile resembles a middle finger. They're all observing me for a reaction. Crenshaw is unmoved, silently anchored in the corner. The shadows seem to flock to him like sparrows during a seasonal change.

"Yes William?"

"So Bartek... what are your plans for Y2K?" In turn, I deliver a polish knee slapper. *"Detroit's fucked – buy a gun."* They begin laughing a profound naivety. To think it has come to this. At one point I was a spiritual leader; now I've degraded into a bathroom poetic.

They're getting kicks from my blatantly obvious neurosis, except for Dirk. He seems disenfranchised, ashamed. Idiocy continues to flow from Billy's mouth like a ruptured sewer main. *"Is that so? I'm just gonna get shitface drunk & pass out in a bathtub somewhere."*

I pause for a moment and examine the drizzling rain flickering underneath the streetlight aureate. *"You know... Someone fucked with my car a couple of days ago... Have you heard anything?"*

He's laughing on the inside. I can hear it fill the viscera with swollen pus. *"No, that's fucked up. What did they do?"*

"Took out the side window with a brick."

"Nope, haven't heard anything. What are you gonna do to the guy when you catch him?"

I can barely restrain myself. I begin shaking and turn around to pierce the vortex of his soul with my intensity. *"Break his fuckin' legs."* He cowardly backs off & ignores me for the remainder...

Rage is building and nothing but physical confrontation will come of it. I flag down the waitress. She hands me the bill and we head up to the cashier. Not a sound from the others. I want so desperately to be followed out to the parking lot.

We head into the rain and Cassum throws me his keys as he & Irish scratch up Crenshaw's van. How long will these children play these games? I embrace the cold impassively as the rain loosens the gel from my hair. Blonde spider legs drip fluidly, clinging to my brow.

I observe the soft distortion in the driver side glass. I'm staring at a stranger. An anti-drug commercial from my childhood circles my train of thought; *"No one says I want to be a junkie when I grow up"* ...

What the hell have I become? Outside I'm a concrete mask of willpower and determination; inside the static is overwhelming – pulsating, festering, imploding. It's malignant, spreading itself like a cancer throughout the very fabric of my soul. It's replaced me...

Only 72 more hours and this will all be over. All the madness, the obsession – all the spoils of a life of self-destruction. In 72 hours my cycle shall render completion.

In 72 hours my friends will break down the door to find my final artistic rendering splattered on white wall canvas.

In 72 hours I'll put that Remington underneath my chin and another random suicide will enter the annals of American history.

In 72 hours I'll be dead...

12.29.99

"I'm not coming back." The words echo around Kelly's head for a good thirty seconds until she fully realizes what I'm communicating. *"Look me in the eyes and tell me that."*

I can't, I feel like such a fucking asshole laying this terrible goddamned thing on her head. It's not the thing one wants to hear after spending 6 hours on a flight. *"I think you're bluffing."*

I whip my head up in shameful intensity. *"I'm not coming back. I... I just wanted to say goodbye."* It's all the proof she needs to see that this isn't some sort of cinematic moment I'm trying to live out.

"Why...?" I see something breaking inside of her and it's tearing me up. I can't stand myself right now. I'm destroying one of the last people that still authentically cares. I don't want this, I don't want to hurt her. I just want to scream forever.

"I have nothing left."

"For Christ's sake Ryan you're only 18 years old! You're just starting you're life..."

The imagery hits me like a freight-train and something begins to swell. *"That son of a bitch... tried to kill her because I was white... all I see when I close my eyes are the fingerprints on her neck..."*

"Why don't you come with me? We can start over." Always the heroine; her best quality. She creates, I destroy. We are unstoppable...

It's the next day and I'm back at Ram's Horn – I keep looking for Crenshaw but a trucker is in his place. *"You see Kelly, after this is done, after I pull the trigger, everyone will come together again. They'll look at my corpse and say that was the one we thought would make it. That was the smart one. They'll look at their lives and the direction their headed and... it will change them."*

"They'll leave the drugs behind. They'll crawl out of the gutter. They'll go back to school. They'll get their shit together. They'll make amends and everything will be as it was. Just like Damian. I don't have the will to keep going on. I can fix it - I can fix everything... I'm prepared to pay that price. It's all I have left." She stares at me blankly.

"Kelly... you don't know what it's like to be in my head. My life's a fucking nightmare. I live inside a constant hallucination. It's not my fault. Nature turned on me... I tried to tell people before and they just thought I was making it all up for attention. Nobody knows the shit I've been through. The fact that I've done an obscene amount of drugs does not help the situation any... "

"I'm not even sure what's real anymore. I don't remember the past, I fear the future. I look around and have no recollection of how I got here or how I became this way. I look at my mother, my friends. Are they really the way I remember them? Was she the demon I recall? Is this all the truth or are these gross distortions? Is this actually happening?"

"I can't hide it any longer. The static in my head is so loud it fucking drowns out everything... It's like I'm just below the surface and the undertow is dragging me down in slow motion and I can't break the skin. There's nowhere I can run to because it's all in my head and I'm so very, very confused... I'm sorry Kelly, so very sorry... I'm not coming back. I just wanted to say goodbye..."

"Are these people your friends or just more of your projects?" That's one hell of a statement. She always sees through my agendas.

"At first... but I've become them. I am them. They're my friends and they're all I've got. But I can't let them fall. I hate to abandon them but this will fix everything... Where are you going for New Years?"

"The City Club people have everything set up in case something does happen. We'll be guarded. You should come with me."

"Fuck that, there's no way I'm getting stuck in the middle of Detroit. It'll be a fucking war zone."

She drifts away for a moment and then comes back with sharp lightning. *"I think its all bullshit – I think they just want to make some quick bucks off panicky survivalists."*

"It's going to happen. It has to happen. I've been waiting my entire life for this. It's our only chance at freedom."

"What do you mean?"

"As the clock strikes midnight across the time zones, slowly by slowly the grid will fall. Police will run to their families and abandon the streets, military will go AWOL, radio and television will cease. For a brief moment the human race will realize how dependent they've become on these things. The true colors will show. The entire race will be fully conscious for the first time... There'll be no illusions, no laugh track, no ads. And when the power comes back on – if we don't destroy ourselves first – we'll never, ever forget. They won't ever be able to control us again – never. We'll win. It's going to happen. Just 2 days Kelly – 2 days."

"Something like that has to happen... but not this."

"It needs to. It has to. It's going to."

"It's all bullshit Ryan..."

"No, it can't be. It's all part of the dream... the same dream. Ever since I was a kid. I know it's coming, something horrible. It doesn't make sense though... In the dream it's hot, really hot, not winter... Some huge metropolis with lots of skyscrapers. New York, L.A., Dallas... There's some huge explosion, maybe a suitcase nuke. The sound of something huge crashing, like a giant missile into a mountain, but it doesn't explode like a

missile... I know this sounds crazy, it doesn't make sense. It should be clear blue skies but it's gray from soot and black smoke like a volcanic eruption. And there are millions of people screaming, panicking, running through the streets. Papers flying everywhere...

"I'm kneeling in the street & it's snowing ash – snowing fucking ash in the middle of Summer. And there's a blood red moon with an Islamic Star inside of it, everything's red... It doesn't add up. It doesn't make sense but I know it's real. I'm not crazy, it has to be. Ever since I saw the first picture of bin Laden I knew it was him... going to be him."

"And whatever it is that happens, it's going to kick start WWIII. Everything is going to change. I know bin Laden is going to start it, they keep busting his operatives. And the FEDS know he'll strike on New Years when the power goes down..."

Kelly just stares blankly at my generic, fear-induced delusion: *"And what if I try to stop you?"*

"You can't."

"..."

<u>12.30.99</u>

I wake to the screaming alarm clock and hit the snooze button 4 times instead of the usual 3 trying so desperately to reenter the tranquil semi-comatose peace of REM but I know I have to get moving because there is little time to spare if I am going to reach the time clock at 7:59 am so I rush into the bathroom half awake and take a power shower and shoot out the front door slamming on the gas hightailing it to work blaring Front Line Assembly at 70 mph flying over the Miller Road sky hump only to have my vision diseased by the South Dearborn city of industry pulling into Spartan where I run inside and punch in three minutes late and dart to the shipping and receiving area where I toss myself into an uncomfortable plastic chair and enjoy my third Marlboro of the day...

I complete my morning deliveries, cruising through skeleton neighborhoods on the outer reaches of Zug Island. Flipping through the pages of USA today, the country is on edge with Al Qaeda surfacing.

One article: *"'We are looking at potential targets within our city,' said police chief Ed Winchester of Fresno, CA. to the Fresno Bee Newspaper after it was revealed that about 125 lbs of dynamite & C4, as well as 75 lbs of gunpowder were stolen sometime between Sunday & Monday form a police bomb squad bunker."*

I'm in the darkness again, cradling Natasha. I feel her breath on my neck, heart gently beating against mine. She is blissfully asleep subconsciously knowing that nothing bad will happen because I'm there to protect her. Holy light radiates from her soft skin...

The darkness breaths; animate, shifting. She begins to twitch because of a nightmare. She turns her head and the purple fingerprints on her neck bleed profusely. Hideous laughter bursts from all directions; the piercing screams of a million enslaved souls...

She is torn from my arms, slowly dragged away into the center of the abyss. I am frozen, concrete, gazing into her blood red eyes. With tooth and nail resistance she claws, snapping her fangs. She is mutating, becoming them. Her face blurs and returns to normalcy as she completes the transformation. She is crying, praying to God to save her. She looks into my eyes one final time before they drag her into the void and screams, *"WHAT THE FUCK HAVE YOU DONE TO ME!!!"*

My fist slams into the dashboard as I snap back into reality. It's time to punch out & start the mission. Cassum tells me we're all going to Simon's later tonight. We're gonna pass out on his floor & wake at 4:30 am to watch the New Zealand click-over then bolt onto the freeway to best the mad rush of traffic.

I punch my timecard, hop back into my ride and repeat the high-octane speed back home. I toss as much as food possible into my old high school backpack caked in band insignia, inverted crosses and Alec Empire rhetoric. I attack the war zone of my bedroom floor gathering together the remaining writings to be included in my briefcase, throwing trinkets and apparel around in a whirlwind frenzy.

I change into a clean pair of gray polyester work-pants, the black sweater I used as a security blanket during middle school, pull my leather fingerless biker gloves on and slick my hair back like Steven Segal, flipping my black cashmere trench over my shoulder.

Halfway out the front door I realize that I almost forgot it – I scan the floor like a pelican gliding over the Gulf of Mexico & snatch Natasha's red bandanna, all I have left to remind me of her. I turn to leave and my mother stands in her bedroom doorway telling me to wear my seat-belt. I hug her goodbye & instruct her to stay with Toby...

12.31.99

The alarm sounds at 4:55 am and I flick on the tv while everyone is still passed out on the floor. Kiwi women dance in celebration of the new millennium as New Zealand authorities prepare the countdown.

The 10 second mark clicks by while my cohorts groggily peer through one eye – nothing but fireworks. I mumble something about satellite conditions and time zones and we all go back to sleep for a good hour. By the time we leave at 7am the world is still fully functional...

Six hours to Grayling & 3 packs of Marlboro Reds later, the trip has been a multitude of revision, examining the exploits of '99 with surgical precision.

Cassum rolls face in shotgun, hiding beneath his winter jacket from the blue dot hovering in the sky as we enter the "city limits" – a maze of dirt roads in midst of undeveloped terrain.

We approach a steep hill that will no doubt shoot us downwards with maddening velocity, frozen solid with ice an inch thick. We spin out and get stuck in a pothole of solidified H2O. I try revving the car back and forth but it's useless. I let Simon take the wheel and the rest of us push.

As we thunder into town it resembles a small New England village from a highly atmospheric Lovecraftian saga. Buildings are old & there is a slight fog thickening the air.

We check into our motel and the others run into the bathroom to clam-bake. I relax on the bed, passing out immediately. The next few hours I break in and out of consciousness...

"Ryan... Wake up... It's *beautiful*," Cassum says, still rolling: "*Look – World Peace.*" Nelson Mandela is reading a carefully prepared speech on human unity. Not a violent cry on the earth, only panoramic zen...

The room is a cloud of dope when there is a knock at the door. Everyone panics because we are convinced the rednecks have caught us and we'll either have to deal with the yokel sheriff or be thrown into the freezing dead of night.

I cautiously crack open the door hoping not to let any aroma pour out. *"Mr. Bartek? For you."* I close the door and stand in awe. They ask what's wrong & I read the note. Cassum's jaw drops; Simon is petrified...

"Hi Ryan."

"How the fuck did you do that?"

"I have my ways... Look, I can't allow you to do this. We've both been through way too much together to let it end like this. This is stupid. We need you, I need you... everyone needs you."

"It's really cold up here..."

"Ryan, if it really is that bad you can come with me. We can escape together. Seattle is beautiful, it's not at all like Detroit. All of the hate and mental death and garbage they put us through – it's not here."

"I'm not bluffing..."

"I don't believe that you are. You've proven it. Doing this isn't going to fix anything. It's just going to make it worse. You're going to drive all of these people over the edge."

"I'm just so fucking confused..."

"We're all confused Ryan. We all have the same problems. We all share the same fears. You're not as alone as you think you are. I don't know everything you've been through, but I know what we've been through. I know what you're feeling... I've been there too."

"The dreams won't stop. The voices won't stop..."

"You don't owe anything to anyone. Everywhere you look there are roads that lead anywhere you want to go. You don't have to do this. You can start over. You're a full-grown man. The world is yours."

"..."

"I care about you more than I could ever express. Please don't do this. Walk away for me. Walk away with me. We can start over. Please."

"...Are there still grunge bands in Seattle?"

"Yes, plenty of them. And lots of good industrial too."

"...Does it rain as much as everyone says?"

"Not any more than it does here. And the people are smarter and the coffee tastes way better."

"...How's the pot?"

"Really, really, really fucking good..."

20 seconds to 2000. We're watching the ball drop in anticipation of a suicide bomber. If bin Laden pulls a dark horse at least there will be some kind of justification for all of this humiliating paranoia.

Espa crashes through the door drunk with a 2000 party top hat on (*yet another jigsaw*). The sky explodes with confetti as the biggest party on the face of the planet bursts into world peace hysteria. Cassum tells me if I don't drive them to the after-party he'll, "*Steal my fucking car.*"

En route I lose myself to Noise Unit's "Neuron" which has become the anthem of this particular trip, although my shitty K-Mart "Rampage" audio system keeps skipping and turning itself off. The irony of it all – the only thing Y2K affects is my car stereo...

The fireplace casts our flickering shadows against the walls. Transfixed on the glowing embers I rise and nonchalantly stroll into the back room when they aren't paying any attention.

The world grows silent as I stare at the Remington hanging on the wall. I open the dresser drawer and discover the bullets. Nothing can stop me. Not Kelly. Not Cassie. Not Cassum, Irish, Simon or any of the rest...

And *It* returns – waiting, watching, observing... Breathing down my neck again, charismatically reenacting our first encounter. I examine the trigger, flashes of Natasha. I think of everything I have done, all I've destroyed. I reach for the stock and it all comes to me in one giant flash, like a reel of film breaking in the projector. *It all floods back...*

I instinctively punch the side of the face as hard as I can. I keep swinging and busting my jaw and forehead and drop to the floor tugging a patch of hair, unable to cry or feel anything except stubborn refusal.

In the living room everyone is laughing, loving life. They have no idea, whimsically ignorant. I go under immediately and dream of the blackened core of Zug Island. Gears clanging, steel melting, human flesh ripped to shreds by its inner workings. *For I have become the machine...*

1.01.00

I wake up dry heaving over the toilet unsure of how we've gotten back to the motel. Thoughts of suicide are replaced with thoughts of Kelly and I want nothing more than to blast all the way to her but we've already paid off another days rent in advance and no one wants to leave except me.

The diner is packed and everyone stares at us funny as we pig out & rack up a $34 dollar bill, a cathartic day-starter. The ride back is hindered when we get stuck in yet another ice pothole. A rusted old truck with chains on the tires pulls up and a gruff hill-jack that resembles Ed Gein hops out with a shovel. He speaks in singular word bursts and instructs me to toss a pile of dirt under the tire.

At the motel everyone starts bitching about drugs. I tell them to fuck off 'cause I want to go to sleep but they're fresh out and if I don't take Irish to the store to steal some booze it's going to get real ugly...

25 minutes later they're doing shots of whiskey, huffing WD-40 from an American flag bandanna and I'm hiding in the darkness of the closet mumbling, *"Get me a ticket for an aero-plane/Ain't got time to take a fast train/Lonely days are gone/I'm-a-comin' home/Cause my baby just-a-wrote me a letter."* Cassum attempts to lure me outside by playing *"A Warm Place"* 'cause it's widely known as one of my favorite songs. It doesn't work and he sits outside the door, trying to coax me back.

"I want to go home."

"You will. Tomorrow. Everything is ok. The world didn't blow up; Nostradamus was wrong."

"That isn't my home."

"What is Ryan?"

"10 years ago."

Espa and her sister burst through the door and a great ruckus ensues. Everyone cheers because they have pot. Irish falls over giggling because of the ether. I don't want to leave my post-death womb but Espa rips open the door and forces me to reemerge.

She pulls a faded green bible out of the nightstand and begins reading a random passage that states: *"But now having been set free from sin, and having become slaves of God, you have your fruit to holiness, and the end, eternal life."* Everyone laughs and mocks God, except for Irish who is an unrepentant Christian…

Espa grabs a light blue writing utensil out of her purse and starts scribbling in the appendix of the propaganda: *"I believe that all that has been written in this worthless piece of trash book is a crock of bullshit. There never was a God… Never will be a God… NEVER. It was all a lie. This lie was created in order to keep people sane. To keep people thinking* *that there may be something better. Something after death. A place where only good people go. There is <u>NOT</u>. When you die you die. That's all."*

"Why the fuck should you follow these rules? The 10 Commandments... Who made those rules? If God does exist - he was probably a judgmental piece of shit. So why would you do what someone else says in order to be "A Better Person" when the only way to be the best person you can is to be yourself. Not follow what others say. But to lead your own life. The way you want. If you want to believe in a God... At least believe in yourself first. <u>FUCK THIS BIBLE</u>." Oh Espa, my beautiful one – what a fine woman you will one day become...

<u>1.02.00</u>

We depart before noon and the ride home is merciless. Not only does my transmission begin to slip but we get caught in a monster traffic jam, road clogged with NRA types disgruntled they didn't get their apocalypse.

I drop both Simon and Cassum off, and once Irish & I are alone I tell him I went to Grayling to shoot myself.

He looks horrified and tells me not to worry or obsess over it because, *"No matter what they say or what they might have us believe – whether it be tomorrow or 5 years from now, Jihad will explode. And nothing any government does will stop it. And when that day comes I'll be by your side – I fucking promise."*

We shake hands, he empties his belongings from the trunk & I blast off towards Kelly's for sweet salvation...

I'm going to spill it all out – everything I've ever felt for her, everything I've ever wanted to say but never had the strength. It all floods, all on the tip of my tongue as I knock on her front door. Her mother slowly answers: *she left for Seattle one hour ago...*

PURGATORY

I knew I had to escape – a man on the run unable to remember how or why this situation was formulated except for fuzzy, mangled fragments which would quickly dissipate soon thereafter...

Seattle was the greatest opportunity I had so I began funneling all income into my moth-fluttered savings. January was tumultuous daydream – *lethargy, depression, a self-medicated torrent of miasmic despair...*

Espa & Simon split up after bad noise, causing an ugly rift between the East/West Dearborn cliques. I remained friends with her ambivalent to the grudge, honing our late night phone conversations of stargazing suburban boredom. Night after night she'd lay her ambitions of running to New York to extract a world infamous hair stylist career...

Both Kluck & Huxley (*this loudmouth hippy kid on the peripheries of our group*) were imprisoned for assault. Incited by a scantless hoe to kick the shit out of the captain of her high school football team, they took on both the jocko & his pops with a Louisville Slugger.

For the next year Kluck kept bouncing in and out of different cells & rehabs, whereas Huxley got the blunt end for swinging the bat personally. If he fucked up the wraith of God would come down upon him.

And fuck up Huxley did, majorly. First he was placed in a halfway house where he refused to drop his rampant cockiness. Disobedience landed him a few weeks in county, then he was dropped to a tether.

His mother soon found $20 worth of shrooms stashed in a sock and took it upon herself to snitch on him. As the cops were en route he ripped off the tether & bolted into the streets.

They picked him up the next day and he faced 6 months in county. Instead of jail he was offered boot camp in which he characteristically went AWOL. Picked up after a few weeks he was sent to the big prison we all know quite well in these parts – Jackson State Penitentiary. One year of hard time for the skinny hippy kid in tye-dye…

The drug appetites continued to explode & a creeping paranoia slithered in since we were constantly hearing about individuals dropping dead from bad pills, rough blow & dirty acid. The long-term effects were setting in panoramically – everyone cursed by perma-trails, hallucinations…

After Natasha faded away, I started doing push-ups & sit-ups, reading Nietzsche & Kerouac, hammering out a surge of poetry for *The Silent Burning*. I wrote a letter to Kaitlin apologizing, but never heard back. I wrote to Kelly, made up with Cassie; called a handful attempting amends. *Simply pissing out the ashes…*

In early February a fight broke out between Simon's parents. Within 20 seconds the entire family were going at it, so catastrophic you could hear it down the block.

Simon was slamming his head into the wall threatening to kill himself; he tried to call 911 and his dad attacked him with a steak knife… We both ran before the police came.

The poor kid was such a mess I figured I would take him to the movies & halfway through *American Beauty* I received a 911 emergency page from Irish. I figured he would go to someone else with whatever he needed so I concentrated on the situation at hand.

The next day at work Cassum explained what had transpired. Irish's parents had King & a half dozen white-coats drag him off to this isolated boot camp/rehab center in upstate New York. He was to be incarcerated until 18 without the privilege to receive or write letters (*even to his parents*), make outside phone calls or even return home for the holidays. He was guaranteed to be in a sort of solitary confinement for the next 3 years. His parents threw out all of his personal belongings, repainted his room, swept him under the rug.

I sprayed down my work van seething in grim reality. As I stood in the cleaning bay among all the dirt, oil & grime, high from the monoxide fumes, I held back tears and punched the wall repeatedly. Knuckles bloody and raw, I cursed myself for letting it end like this...

Yet that was that – my best friend wholly erased & sure to be poked, prodded, rearranged by psychiatric fiends of mental cleanliness & re-education... No happy ending. That was the last we heard from him...

And from this void I caved in, joining my comrades amid the hardcore purgatory of Detroit's underground rave scene.

The first party I attended was at *"The Whorehouse,"* a venue deep in an abandoned factory section of East Detroit. It was a former bordello; all the windows were boarded up and sound proof so it appeared desolate from the outside...

Sweaty bodies were pressed wall to wall in a swathing mass of ecstasy. It reminded me of 30's Berlin cabaret, Athens at the height of the empire – a hedonism so extreme & godless it could suffocate the heavens.

The rave scene was the last refuge of romanticism within the age of extremism – liquid acid flowed like the Mississippi; at every turn assaulted by razor-sharp con-men pawning nitrous, mescaline, pills, coke, k, crystal, Valium, Demerol, Vicadin, the weird, dreaded pink stuff...

Three hours in standing by the front door a party kid shed his disguise and admitted he was an undercover cop.

The security guard blasted his fist into the narc's face, cracking it against the cement brick wall. The cop dropped & they dragged him into this room in pure reflex mechanism.

I turn my head and another security is halfway through an upwards leap, swinging a baseball bat which shatters a black-light tube across the tiling. *"PARTIES FUCKIN' OVER!!!"*

Everyone barrels out as a fleet of sirens approach. In the parking lot Cassum realizes he's locked his keys in the car and Johnny spontaneously kicks out the same windshield Cassum had just replaced.

We lunge in and blast off through frostbitten streets, nearly dying on the freeway a half dozen times because Cassum is so fucked up he's struggling to stay awake at the wheel. He's been up for 5 days, on 4 tabs of X, weaving through lanes at 90 mph with Johnny pouring shard wound plasma all over the upholstery…

Monday at Spartan, Cassum is leaning against his cellophane-wrapped window hot-boxing a Camel Light. He was just busted for embezzling nearly $10 grand.

His scam – selling auto parts & pocketing the money, just flatly erasing cylinder blocks, calipers, suspensions from the data systems until a random customer brought in a faulty component on warranty.

He was fired on the spot, taking his last gander of a made future in the auto industry. He'd started working there as a high school freshman. By graduation, he had $8,000 saved.

Now his bank account was empty as the chambers of Tutankhamen. No charges had been filed though, as to avoid tarnishing his fathers' credibility. It felt terrible watching Cassum's pops utterly humiliated at the counter…

Cassum always made a big deal about what a piece of shit his dad was, but from my experience, he was one of the nicest, most professional people I'd ever worked with.

Always these stories about being attacked with baseball bats, breaking dishes over each others heads. You just could never tell with Cassum what was real...

With Cassum gone the bosses began watching my every move, suspecting I was in on it. Innocent of course, with nothing to fear except detective-like stares, I continued preparing the Seattle escape. *Weekend after weekend, abandoned buildings in rapid-fire progression ...*

Two things brought heat on the rave scene like no other – the tragedy of S.O.S. & the casualty at WHITE where a 19 year old girl was accidentally shot in the face during a bunk drug deal.

It was splattered all over the news and incited an outcry for the authorities to do something drastic. That's when the waves of undercover officers began filtering in and those damn Action 10 Problem Solvers recognized a ratings spike...

Save Our Scene (S.O.S) was a free event with obvious intentions, a last ditch attempt to move beyond the bad ju-ju of WHITE. At least 3,000 participated, the majority of which were zonked on the pure liquid acid flowing heavy that night.

S.O.S. was held at The Theatre, a massive old-school concert hall so deep in the ghetto it was only used as a methadone clinic during the day. Just this dilapidated, rotting slab of concrete...

S.O.S. was a personal milestone – the first night I snorted both Special K & cocaine. I'd been in a small, freezing room with no door that had probably been a storage spot years ago, huffing balloons & squatting on the floor in *wah-wah-wah* medical grade laughing gas high.

I think I dropped maybe a $100 on the gas by the time Kluck came up, who was shortly released from county (*the assaulting the jock & his dad thing*).

He was glad to be back where it mattered, gripping five balloons, morbidly explaining how he'd witnessed an 18 year old convicted of "baby raping" get his face kicked in to where his eyeball was literally hanging out of socket & his teeth were scattered over the floor...

Through the haze of a *wah-wah-wah* hole one of Johnny's boys came up and shoved a key under my nose. "*Here man, Special K. You said you wanted it.*" I took a bump and felt strangely tripped out, then he busted out a folded up flyer from his pocket and cut me up 3 lines.

I hoofed them down and leaned back against the wall, where I could see the dance floor throbbing with strobe. I went into the K-Trance – that weird, worm-hole pull – and the DJ's shadow that was projected onto the ceiling from flood lights... I *became* it.

I *was* the shadow. I *was* spinning the music. I was every one of those partykids hopping around & tweaking & rolling. Then Johnny's pal threw another key under my nose, and said: "*You'll like this a lot more if you got some energy in ya.*"

I took a few bumps of cocaine for the first time and got right up, shaking off the residual balloon. I was determined to find Teeth, who had a fat bag of Special K as well...

I found him in a wide-eyed stare, kind of lurching along like Montgomery Burns. I slid in the group he was with and we went off in search of sweat-beading adventure.

Special K is a disassociate tranquilizer with acid-like effects, so I was quite peachy keen, even though walls were contorting as we broke into the lower levels of the building. We kept hauling down endless descending staircases, growing subterranean...

Six floors underground led us to an internal river, basement levels flooded with black water that had been sitting for years. We turned the corner and discovered a final corridor of mirrors which we traveled by Zippo's & miniature flashlights.

The floor was covered in mold three-inches thick that clung to our shoe souls like rubber cement quagmire. This was the actor's area, old dressing rooms filled with stage props, costumes & gas-masks...

Teeth and I snorted more K off an old wooden desk and went about flipping on old meat-hook elevator styled light switches that we really shouldn't have in a vain attempt of luminescence.

By now a dozen others have wandered to those depths as well, swash-buckling with fake swords & plastic guns from the costume arsenal.

We headed back up to the main room and began smelling an overpowering stench of burning plastic. Ravers were rushing by in a panic, hollering the place was on fire. I started laughing then noticed a rising smoke billowing from vents connecting the lower levels we'd just exited.

Even though drugged, I was convinced immediate escape was necessary. Teeth refused to leave our friends behind though, and I followed him back upstairs to make it snappy.

We push our way through a fear-strickin mob and get back into the main room where no one is to be found. The steel door is slammed shut and we're instantly bolted in from the crazed promoters.

We look back at the scene. The music cuts, smoke is pouring through the vents, and a good 800 people instantly realize they are trapped inside a pure brick room with no windows – and all of them are sky-high on acid, K & X absolutely convinced they are going to burn alive. This must have been what it was like on the Titanic.

Panic ensues, vicious fistfights break out, terror-driven psychotics attempt to claw through the walls in animal escape mechanisms. A dozen strongmen beat on the steel door, kicking the hell out of it. Little candy-girls cry & hold each other fearfully; the religious pray exit...

And then there's me – laughing harder then I ever have, absolutely twisted from drugs & absolutely convinced I'm going to burn alive, never having been so happy.

The walls are still breathing from the Special K, that badass, hard rocking noise end of Helter Skelter is jamming in my head, and I realize that it's all my fault because this is an electrical fire ignited by toying with all those old-school meat-hook light switches that haven't been touched in decades. Who could ask for a more catastrophic, epic demise?

The strongmen break through and everyone piles down the staircase like *The Towering Inferno*, stomping over the fallen. Everyone running, booking like terrorized gazelles, piling into the night.

Once I hit the exit cops are everywhere, tackling & arresting anyone they can, beating the shit out of kids with nightsticks & the butts of their guns. I dodge a few and keep chugging towards the parking lot.

I look back & fire trucks are glowing the night, spraying huge streams of water at the top of the building. At my car Cassum & a randoms are waiting. We jet off, and I'm still oogled from K...

The road is liquid tar, spilling like rapid. I'm cocked in the front seat, hunched over the wheel, straining my eyes on the realities of the freeway. We get off on 26 mile, way out in the boonies, trying to make it to Simon's cousin's house where the after-party was supposed to be. I'm having trouble driving straight, rolling onto the side of the road through gravel when we're flicked by State Troopers.

Everyone shits their pants because not only are we obviously tweaked up on a gazillion drugs and have a full car load with previous drug arrests on their records in mean hill-jack territory with no coherent alibi, we have nearly a sheet of acid, a jar of pills, an 8-ball of coke, a sack of crystal meth, an ounce of weed & an unregistered harpoon gun.

The cop walks up and I miraculously pull this half-cocked story out my ass about how we just saw our buddy's band play at a VFW hall and we're going over his cousins to hang out and are just kind of lost. Super Trooper buys it, politely gives us directions, and sends us away.

I still cannot believe I'm not in prison, let alone not burning 2000 or so people alive. Anytime I'm sitting home alone on a freezing Saturday night with nothing to do – no matter how vile of a scenario involving a girl might be, no matter how piss-poor broke & starved I am I never, ever complain. I just repeat three simple letters over & over – *S.O.S...*

That night I had a powerful dream involving a venue we were running. It's during the week and we're setting up for a party. I just picked up a pizza and am heading through the front door alone. I hear muffled screams, loud thuds. I walk into the open party room and a faceless man has all of my friends tied up in bed sheets, bound with rope. He's hacking them up with an axe, stabbing them with a hunting knife, floor a sea of crimson...

I finally quit my job at Spartan. It turned quite ugly when I ran someone over in front of the store with all of the bosses watching – like all the corporate overlords, no less. I was blasting the solo from *"Free Bird"* and wasn't paying attention when I nailed this drunk on his bike.

He was threatening to sue and causing quite an ugly scene but luckily Cassum's dad talked him down. I can't believe they didn't fire me. They just kind of let me float off without any struggle two days later, since I'd told them I was moving to Seattle in advance...

While I kept telling myself this would happen, with my newly found liberation I instead decided to gobble a handful of shrooms with the exact same group of individuals from the post-S.O.S. ordeal after this party in Cass Corridor. It was a monstrous occasion at the same after-party spot.

That night was the most fucked up I've ever been in my life. 20 kids are there all rolling on X, and I'm rushing back & forth between these two rooms where slabs of K & crystal meth are laid out and I'm just snorting everything in sight.

Luckily the meth *wasn't real*, which I'd no real understanding of. That would've been *really, really* bad...

I was so hopped up, tripping so hard I was trying to get everyone to fight me. I kept pushing people yet no one would come at me. I just kept laughing, jovial in my violence.

They were all sort of pressed against the wall as I was running around the house screaming *"AREN'T YOU PROUD OF YOU BABY BOY MOMMA?? AREN'T YOU FUCKING PROUD!?!"*

I locked myself in a bathroom fully decked out in Tommy Hilfiger. Everything had that red & white logo – *the towels, the toilet seat, the shower curtain.* For 3 hours I paced in circles pulling out my hair, talking to hallucinations. Kaitlin in the bathtub with slit wrists; Vic tap-dancing on the ceiling. *Natasha's severed head floating in the toilet...*

The entire crew was outside the door, listening in. By the time I wound down the sun was rising and I'd convinced myself I was the

Antichrist. I was attempting to set these construction workers across the street on fire with psychic mind energy. It was the most fun I ever had.

Next Friday was Hash Bash where I tripped on shrooms alongside Ricky & Teeth. I kept thinking I was in Paris... Cassie popped from nowhere when I was peaking and I ran from her convinced she was an evil leprechaun...

The following day I got a call from Cassum telling me I had to go to the Red Roof Inn because they were throwing a surprise party for me. I was delighted and expected a nice little "Happy Birthday" cheer...

Instead they were apathetic, tripping from Robitussin and barely acknowledging my presence after blowing all the cake & streamer money on pot. A dozen of us were smoking blunts when Kluck got the bright idea to steal a Playstation from Toys R' Us, drive around Detroit until they could find a crack house & trade it in for a few rocks.

Miraculously they pulled it off – and my surprise 19th birthday party became a surprise crack party. I left in disgust, heartbroken. After I was gone, Kluck was fiending so badly he accepted a dare to score the leftovers by running around the motel naked 3 times in a row while screaming bloody murder, totally out of his head.

Devastated, but not all that surprised, I went to a rave the next night only to have a panic attack and high tail it back to the same motel where two buddies were doing whip-it's.

And of all the chaos that ensued the night before, only now did the cops decide to show up, giving us a stern lecture on the naughtiness of whiskey & balloons...

So much time had elapsed since Y2K that Kelly wasn't keen on the idea of me running to Seattle with her anymore. Of course she never said this, but

I could tell in her voice. She was living with her new boyfriend and that would just cause unwelcome friction.

Natasha popped up in a string of phone calls but I'd stopped talking to her after awhile because it was nothing but draining.

It seemed like it was only a matter of time before people started dropping dead. The East Side Crew were becoming some of the absolute worst train-wrecks in the entire rave scene, fraternizing with all the dregs. Everywhere I turned there were free lines & human zombies...

Getting pulled over with Espa, who was dying in my front seat after snorting three grams of K. I told the cop she was my girl and ate bad nachos; I sat with her as she cried in my bathtub unable to move, and pale as a ghost. I was shaking her to stay conscious. She kept repeating. "*I'm already dead, I'm already dead*"...

Kluck fucking the cement wall of a party, five nitrous balloons in hand, drooling all over his shirt... Running over a white rabbit, having a religious burial ceremony for it in the middle of a park at night while tangoing with "Bob The Singing Infomercial Bass"... *Accidentally driving into Saigon & chased out by handgun brandishing 11 year old crack dealers on bicycles...* Riding a giant, prosthetic fish at a nocturnal barbecue... *Dre and the Twins hot-wire a Buick on speed, joyride for a few miles and crash it into a front porch...* Kluck eats 15 hits of blotter and hides in a dryer thinking it's an Iron Maiden, and cowering inside of it as cops loudly beat the living shit out of Maxwell on his front lawn... *Cassum and Kluck show up at my house at 9 am with a mound of K after being chased through Southland Mall by security guards...* Carl attempts to rob a gas station with a random sporting ski masks but they abruptly retreat after the register attendant shouts over the loudspeaker the pigs are en route... *In the ghetto trapped between a garbage truck & a Faygo semi. This little black girl sitting on a rusted car hood starts making tribal "kill the white man" hooting sounds and an army of Cryps come barreling out their homes. I immediately reverse & fling over someone's lawn doing 60 mph...* At a rave pursued by pasty-faced clowns forming animal balloons into big, blow up cock statues; in one corridor an entire cheer-leading team in school spirit get ups are rubbing each other with Vic's, making out, getting heavy... *Simon on five pills sees a pile of vomit, vomits in the vomit, sits in the vomit, gets back up to look at the vomit, vomits in it again and lays back down into the vomit nearly choking on his own vomit fifteen minutes later...* Clipping my toenails on the front porch a black man pulls up and calls me a nigger. I holler, *"WHITE TRASH!"* and chase his car down the street... *Smitty accused of a third rape & this time I believe it...* Feeding acid to the candy-flipping Susan, finding out 10 minutes later she was pregnant... *Laying in an overflowed toilet bathroom lake in a K-hole the heroin addict drooling on himself sitting next to me shits his pants...* "Maurice was impotent... you didn't know that?" ... *Getting stoned with Black Panthers, debating Malcolm X philosophy...* Mother angrily explaining the house is for sale & she's marrying Toby... *Dragging my television into the back yard & acing it with a Louisville. The neighbor comes outside asking what I'm doing. "Expressing my teen angst," I reply. He tells me the poisonous mist will give me cancer & I start doing a tumors victory dance...* Wandering endless corridors of abandoned buildings, convinced I'm in hell... *All our bud-spot dealers are systematically murdering each other in competition...* At Ricky's house everyone is tweaking out, having piled on the K and LSD, when all 20 present simultaneously witness a gremlin ripping through the space/time continuum, emerging through the wall & growling with razor sharp teeth.

They all shit their pants in terror and run screaming into the night... *"In the dream I end my life with the taste of gun powder & the stench of sex. I find myself upon a grand cliff. Below is an ocean of countless mangled suicides. They gesture inanimately, for we are all as one...*

I met Maxwell in 1999; the biggest drug freak of us all beyond comparison. He should've been dead 12,000 times – *he'd been snorting coke & eating acid since 5th grade!* He'd done LSD 1000+ times & barely made sense – extremely homicidal under the influence of hallucinogens.

It was his idea to invade the abandoned train station in Mexican town. He used to camp out there in his mid-teens when he'd get booted from his house & knew it like the back of his hand. Nearly a dozen of us followed him in there one day, tagging everything in sight.

We split into two groups – Espa, Kluck & the bulk one way; Cassum, Maxwell, Teeth & myself the other.

We had an 8-ball & were supercharged, going ape-shit with baseball bats & destroying everything in sight. All the built up rage barreled out of us – we totaled 4 floors, destroying everything in sight. We headed to the top of the building to take a panoramic look around Detroit.

As we passed the joint we heard the hum of helicopter blades – a news chopper was filming us! From a bullhorn below: *"Come out now and you will not be harmed!"* There were 12 squad cars parked around the building with K9 units! *We were surrounded by an army of pigs!*

From the other end of the building we hear Kluck laughing & he pushes a couch through the window 12 stories up. They had no idea the cops were there! We just hid on the top floor until dark, sneaking through secret the rail tunnel like ninja...

The Detroit Electronic Music Festival (DEMF) was marvelous – a true affirmation that the freaks now owned this city. DEMF was also the last time we were all together as a unit.

A million able bodies poured into Hart Plaza from across the world. Unlike other subcultures I'd been through this seemed more real than any other, because it wasn't restricted.

No one cared what you wore or what you looked like or if you danced or sat on the sidelines. The music was a pulse of inertia, a projector of motion. The music was only secondary; the vibe was the mainline...

This feeling was universal, pan-freak – dead warehouses across the globe, lighting up the human contagion of a bold new world.

We were all on the same team for once – this self-sustaining, self-perpetuating zeitgeist rolling into the mainstream consciousness. How long before every street in America resembled a Neo-Hashbury?

During DEMF most were up 3 days – most youth was, in all Metro Detroit. Those who'd never tasted the rave culture were enfranchised.

I walked up to Cassum, who in ecstasy reverie had resolved to form his own production company MKULTRA & throw events ASAP...

Nez was next to him, ghostly & spooked. All day he'd been sitting on a ledge next to a kid with a hoodie over his face. Nez was just rolling & bullshitting with people. When he finally leaned over to ask the kid if he could bum a smoke, the 17 year old's corpse thudded over...

GUTTER EXPATRIATE

It was late July & things had never been worse. Aggressive tendencies had sparked thefts, fights, bunk drug deals. Johnny beat the piss out of some guy Espa was seeing for no real reason.

He wailed the guy through Carl's window while Susan hung on the steps screaming, "*KICK HIS FUCKIN' ASS!! MAKE HIM BLEED!!!*", her arms fully covered in candy & sporting a pink PLUR t-shirt...

The excesses were unspeakable in every regard. It had actually come to the point where we were placing bets on who'd croak first. Cassum had best odds, but least payout...

All it took was one phone call from Brandon – that king among men – and the plans were drawn & finalized. After vanishing from the ghost house he ended up in Troy, a suburb in the northern outskirts. He was working as a security guard at City Club, hanging with Vikings, lodging in a trailer park with a clandestine creature known only as "Onyx."

In grappling to explain Onyx, Brandon simply stated "*he knows everything about everything.*" Onyx was a sewer rat enthusiast and carried two on his shoulders at all times, something of an urban priest. One of his acquaintances – another rat collector from the neighborhood – lived a few blocks away with his pregnant girlfriend & an embittered roomie choking to death from credit card debt.

So to make ends meet Brandon rented the couch, nabbed a local line cook job, and when Ratman II & Preggers split, I was immediately brought into the equation.

Troy was distant enough where I would be separated and finally finish my book. I was determined to cut my teeth attempting a new colony from scratch – cellular proselytization, as it were. If I could penetrate an alien habitat and start a franchise on a minor level, I could surely do so in any major city. Isolation was my best chance to get my head straight.

Without hesitation I barreled out of the Pardee Street once and for all, zooming past those echoes of cold humiliation – past Danny's garage of elaborate gun replicas, past the Morrison stronghold of Bronco worship; past those original twins, their raped Barbie's & the feline serial killer's neatly manicured lawn...

And as I roared past these monuments of degradation I flipped on the radio to a random station, cranking it loud as possible. And no shit, what came on? *"Fools Rush In..."*

I finally gave in and ate ecstasy for the first time. Amazed that you hear this, considering. I'd just simply refused to end up like the others, who were hooked & rolling an average of 4 days a week, 5 pills a time...

My first was a double-stacked White Fish. Earlier that day I was reading *Watchmen*. When a party kid found me squatting depressed & contemplative in a corner, my roll slowly kicking in, he asked *"What's wrong my friend?"* I turned and said in the most empathetic of all voices, *"They're gonna kill Rorschach..."* Then a big ole grin came a-raging...

I exploded with joy, telling everyone that they were my brothers, consumed by the neo-hippie coma of ecstasy. It was the most beautiful thing I'd ever experienced. I saw the entire rave scene in a whole new light – it was no longer a death trap but a glorious revival of humanity.

Not only the rave scene, but the overall contingency of our unanimous accomplishment – all the characters who've populated my life, the itinerary of our adventures. I was up until 8 am, arms outstretched in the pouring rain... *And then the big comedown...*

The next few days I wrote non-stop. The wall had fallen and I learned to let a lot of my hate go. The bi-polar hell of ecstasy gave way and I went cold turkey (*minus pot*), pushing out the greatest surge of writing in my literary career. I'd never felt so hardcore.

On the downside the after-effects of the pill shook loose a great deal of repressed information. I was remembering things I really didn't feel all so keen on pondering...

I'd secured employment as a line cook at a quaint restaurant down the street, doing remedial chores like pizzas and calzones. I attended another underground rave where I rolled on X for my second time. I'd been flirting endlessly with this girl all night, and as we were both deep into the MDMA soul-communion an army of pigs rolled up in full SWAT gear.

Paddywagons, guns drawn, all of them severely vicious & ready to bust heads. Huge cop runs up on a 15 year-old kid hitting a balloon. Kid's smiling in nitrous stupor, and this pig decks him hard as he could in the back of the skull & 2 other pigs stomp on this twig on the ground.

They herded us inside & wrote out 800 "*loitering in the vicinity of narcotics*" tickets. The entire rave were Indian style, kind of laughing at the jamboree. It felt like a high school gymnasium prep-rally, the cops as mean tough-guy coaches.

They took out Polaroid cameras & had the strangest dressed party-kids stand in front of the mob, calling them "*faggot pieces of shit*" as they snapped stills like fashion designers. We all just kept laughing...

We'd been arrested "on paper," and the girl & I went for blueberry pancakes. By the time I got home around 1pm I got a call from the restaurant, because I'd been scheduled for 9am. I rushed in still rolling, did a mountain of dishes...

I was still hopped up by the time I got off work; the pill had likely been cut with meth. Still awake, nearly 24 hours in, I drove all the way to her campus in Lansing, a 2 hour drive.

We stayed up the next 4 days straight, babbling non-stop in a strange, e-bond mini-fling. We never had sex, or even made a move, but fell madly in love for a brief moment, and took me home to meet her mom. I never really saw her again...

I started hanging out with this Slayer fanatic named Jay from work who began dragging me around to seedy Canadian strip clubs in Windsor. He had this band called Return To Dust that was kind of a mix between Machine Head, Living Sacrifice & Pantera...

This leads us to the late night Denny's coffee sessions where I'm nicknamed *"The Revolution"* – it as Troy's version of The Zone.

I walked right up to table filled with Northern Suburb punkers and declared, *"I'm the trouble you've all been waiting for."* They were bored as hell, and they were all really, really into *Fight Club*. Ho hum...

It was one of those rare moments where time slows down, and 3 short months feels a decade. I bought 20 black gravel notebooks and shot them to the crowd.

Thus begat a living autobiographical novel collective that soon trans-morphed into a parking lot brawl connection. A good dozen freaks on any given Saturday, pummeling each other with fists...

We had a nice crew going. Linda, the poetic ex-dominatrix waitress. The confused UAW-punker in a shotgun marriage of pre-programmed Christian morality; the lanky, sarcastic deep fry cook endlessly talking shit on Fred Durst; the basement dwelling gamers; the delusional *"Necromancer;"* the self-styled *"Mexican drug dealer"* of

Norwegian heritage running around naked at the drop of a hat; the male Goth idol on heavy probation for embezzling $10,000 from Borders...

Jay had never been in a fight and was overjoyed when I nearly broke his nose. He was laughing, smiling, bug-eyed with blood dripping down his nose.

The fights eventually spilled into my apartment complex. Brandon tackled a gamer through the plaster drywall. It was just another gaping dent though, since Brandon was increasingly out of hand, going berserk and punching holes in the wall in violent rages.

Smitty, Vic & Cassum soon came out to visit, the first all 5 of us hung out in 4 years. We got drunk & played Death Hockey in the basement, checking each other into the washer/dryers.

Smitty and Vic were different though, still locked into that high school mindset. We'd grown up in ways that hadn't hit them, and Vic was still terrified of disobeying his father at age 20. He made me drive him all the way to Dearborn at 5am because he had to cut the lawn that day...

In the rave underground people were now booting up vials of Special K as if heroin. One of the girls The East Side Crew began hanging with had actually done this and keeled over on the floor of a party...

Cassum & Stoney threw their first rave called "H2O" in the basement of a family restaurant in the suburban boonies. It was packed upstairs and downstairs on a Saturday night.

All these party-kids were stumbling inside the dining room rolling face and pressing their hands against the spinning pie columns like children at a Christmas store on December 23rd. Brandon and I worked security that night, and had to deal with undercover cops in shiny party get-ups & white cowboy hats. They were so obvious...

For that raid at the school bus depot I got six months non-reporting probation. If I was to remain down-low until May all charges would be dropped. I was ordered by a judge to go to an HIV education class for some reason, and hung around downtown Detroit with a bunch of scabies hookers who kept twitching from meth hangovers. *Man did they smell...*

I was set to continue my life in Troy since the lease was soon up, but everything came crashing down when I discovered Jay was fucking around with my girlfriend. No, they didn't actually have sex, but I was tipped off that they made out in her car the night before.

She was a tall blonde and had her head straight, she was good for me. But I was kind of awkward and I think she assumed I wasn't much interested, therefore creating that possible Jay rebound.

I flipped & at the restaurant I grabbed him by his neck & threw him against a fridge, threatening him with a knife. I was shouting in a total rage – if he ever looked at me again I'd *"slit his fuckin' throat."* So charming, I know.

Jay waddled back to the line in shock and I approached Zippy, the slow dish washer. *"Do you know how to cook pizzas? No? Well tonight you learn buddy."* I sent Zippy to my post and stole the dish pit. I can't believe they didn't call the cops...

My lease was up in a week; I felt unable to continue the charade. Pathetically, I decided to move back into the Pardee Street house I grew up in, as to determine the next step of life. The house was now up for sale.

On Christmas Eve Cassum was thrown out of his house. The night prior some hoodrat chick he sold fake K to showed up at 3am with some big fuckers threatening his father.

Cassum was a wreck, bouncing around a bunch of different homes and my apartment, trying to get me to move in with him. I didn't even want to touch it. His presence meant a walking felony and he was one of the worst addicts of them all. He smelled terrible – never washed his clothes, shaved or brushed his teeth anymore.

On New Years Eve a ton of us were at the bridge spot outside Mexican Town, this hidden semi-truck depot where massive raves were thrown. It was K central that night, we were all ripped. Afterwards I ended up with my Viking friend in this trailer park and we each snorted $200 worth of K in 4 minutes.

It was a no-gravity walk-around, immune to the effects of the 0 degree chill that night. I tossed the rest of my belongings into the Viking's car and we exited Troy for good...

Everywhere I turned it was as if some supernatural force was trying to kill me. Falling down the stairs, nearly cracking my head open after slipping on the ice, a half dozen near fatal car accidents.

Simon, Teeth and I spun out on I-94 one January night. I can't believe we made it out alive...

We were en route to a Value Village in Taylor when I felt control of the vehicle slip from under me. We were just skidding on this massive stretch of black ice.

Slowly the car began to turn at 60 mph – like a full 360. As we're revolving ever so slowly through the front windshield we see the herd of semi trucks which moments ago were right behind us. I'm gripping the wheel calmly saying "*fuck fuck fuck fuck*" with both Teeth and Simon absolutely stilted.

The car keeps revolving – by the time we're facing the correct way again we slide onto the snow bank of the road, which perfectly teeters us out with a slow thup-thup-thup of the tires.

Soon as the car stops dead five 18 wheelers fly past us, two of which are blaring their horns. We kind of just sit there for a moment, then I burst out laughing.

To make matters stranger, later on that same night I'd picked up another friend of mine and we went on a search for pot. As we were coming back down that same freeway, on the same stretch but facing the opposite direction on the adjacent eastbound road, the car in front of us slid a 360, flipped three times, and rolled over into the bank of snow.

No cars stopped to help, and it happened so fast my friend didn't even notice. When I ran up to the sideways car which was billowing smoke from beneath the hood and sure to explode at any moment, the driver crawled out the busted windshield.

"Fuck dude..." he said trailing off, looking around wobbly, obviously hammered, kind of looking at the car with hand on hip and other hand stroking his chin in contemplation. I asked if he was alright.

He said *"Hold on a minute,"* then climbed up the car using the axle as his ladder, dropped through the passenger door, and popped right back out like a gopher holding a glass of rum & coke with a little umbrella.

I offered a ride & if he wanted to call the authorities: *"Nah, fuck it, car was stolen anyway – can you take me to my girls house?"* So I did for a blunt in return, which he heartily fulfilled in the ghetto. He bopped out of this grim looking house clutching a massive Philly & bid us adieu...

I quit K after someone cooked a vial of the weird, dreaded weird pink stuff, like this ultra-K. I knocked back 4 massively thick 6 inch lines and made my way down the basement staircase, which was like thick gooey mud.

Daisy was downstairs crying in a chair, talking Jesus, and this druggie was trying to soothe her by spouting bible excerpts. I started telling her god was dead, and she started sobbing harder, and then the dealer started chanting and mumbling meditative sayings.

I looked at Daisy and her neck extended like a giraffe. I turned and saw my creepy old playroom from childhood and felt myself in there at age 7, then the walls started rumbling.

I made it upstairs and I wanted to fight people. I grabed a knife and started luring the house, but the K was so heavy it grounded me into a k-hole on the floor.

Christ was struggling to emerge from the wood pattern of my doorway and I slithered through the carpet thinking I was a South African python. When my snake-body made it to the front door it swung open and Espa was miraculously looming over me. But her hair was like Medusa's, like this awful *Killer Klown From Outer Space*.

When I woke the next morning I puked so hard a blood vessel popped in my eye. I was sick as hell for the next two days...

Nez and Kluck had a minor bout of insanity when tripping on shrooms. Both of them became claustrophobic in their own bodies and while peaking drove around frantically in search of a bridge to drive off. Kluck was slipping intensely, ever since he'd started snorting heroin...

As a form of rent I helped repaint the house and cleaned out the basement, moving all of the remaining belongings to Toby's. It was an odyssey of self-discovery tossing out forgotten elementary homework, trash picked toys, junkyard shards. Midst the clean-sweep I came across quite the discovery; a dusty, well-hidden box that contained three items that were to change everything I thought about my mother.

The first was a manuscript she wrote at about my age, a book of poetry and fragmented prose with racist and bi-polar overtones. Second, a file from the time my father had disappeared filled with warrants & child support claims. Had she sent him to prison and covered it up?

Then came the worst of all – a creepy gray folder with a white label that simply read *"Ryan Bartek."* Yes, a folder identical to what Vic claimed he'd seen the driver of The Gray Van hand to Cassum's father.

Its contents were of a good 150 "missing" school assignments from 6th grade until graduation. Anytime I drew anything on a paper or wrote a strange answer the teachers had kept it and passed it along to my mother. I wasn't paranoid after all – *they really were out to get me….*

I went over the new house to deliver some belongings and my mother was on the staircase in her nightgown, evoking some dramatic, cinematic moment. *"Toby wants to talk to you."*

Upstairs Toby's at his computer desk browsing through his Internet history. I had gone to the web pages of independent book publishers like Soft Skull, Feral House & AK Press and he was mortified, shocked, and acting like a stern parent from the Eisenhower 50's. He wanted me to *explain myself.*

He told me independent publishing of a subversive bent is *"un-American"* and that they were losing me to *"the wrong crowd."* He was shocked by this thing called "punk rock," which he'd never heard of. He told me I was *"like a nigger"* for voting for Al Gore. He was threatening a 10 pm curfew, like I was a teenage. I had to split, ASAP...

The Pardee house was sold late March & Cassum was imprisoned for 30 days over a floating drug warrant. He was in rough shape – so far gone no one wanted to deal with him. He'd been snorting heroin & breaking into cars just to stay warm in the dead of winter.

Brandon also had poor luck, being sentenced to 30 days in Oakland County for probation violation. Out of options I moved into Vic's basement which Smitty had been occupying.

Smitty had gone into the Navy, and I was the only old-school contact Vic had. He was reaching out for someone to talk to, since Kaitlin had left him and he'd been slam-drunk for 40 days straight.

It was good to catch up, but kind of an awkward set-up, since Vic had become totally blue collar and weight-lifting macho, despite obsessively listening to Prince. Still, I felt it could fly, since the house was up for sale & parents were already in Ohio. All I needed was 3 months.

I got a job as a substitute high school janitor and decided to go back to college for an English class. It was a ripe attempt of normalcy but the transition was rugged. I was in a massively fragile state, neurotic to the point where I refused to communicate outside those I already knew.

I'd hide in the basement typing furiously; spend my evening's chain-smoking, slamming black coffee, studying literature, and writing nonstop at low-rent family diners. I had become yet another detached ghost persona of the donut culture.

On the opposite end this created a bad problem. First with the jock creeps who now used Vic for his house to party in, and Vic's younger brother, who I once looked at as extended family but had warped into this art-rock, tight-pants, Velvet Underground is the end-all-be-all of music, Marxist reading, hate-everyone creep.

I had serious beef with him. I was friends with this nerdy video kid that Vic's brother was terrorizing, dumping porn on his front lawn, chucking motor oil on his car. We were outside one night – he & his sidekick came by trying to make trouble.

I threw a wood chip at their car playfully mocking them & they made a big stink. They swung the corner & drove by at raging speed, chucking a Budweiser long-neck at me which shattered on my leg. They hit the gas & bolted. Later they started coming around my house trying to fuck with *my* car, and I'd always chase them off.

Next I saw him was at his own house, and moving in we had a sort-of truce that I upheld but he'd no intention of fulfilling.

I went back to school – after the first writing assignment, the teacher pulled me aside curious how I did it. He offered me the honors program, taking me directly to The Dean. They tried to convince me to take out loans, but it would take 8 years to get a journalism degree...

The next week I handed in my second assignment and the English Professor told me there was nothing he could teach me. He gave me an A+, & said I didn't have to show up for finals. Serious.

Natasha showed back up and we started dating again but it was perpetually hollow. Anytime she'd see Vic's dad she'd speak to him in Spanish, and he'd laugh...

I didn't understand how Natasha could live with her father again, let alone her mother. She told me, "*Oh everything is fine now. He buys me whatever I want anytime I want, and tells me I'm his little princess.*"

It was deranged, insane – I couldn't handle it. We were in my car parked beneath a streetlight in the ghetto.

All of those images flooded to me, and when she started talking about Jesus, I snapped and told her if he ever did some back I'd "*nail him right back to that fucking cross.*" She faded abruptly...

The janitor gig was more like paid detention, post-graduation. But if hired full time I'd make $16 w/ full health & dental. Plus I'd be a city employee & therefore would have free community college in Dearborn (*thanks Henry Ford – one of the few good thing you did*).

The downside was all the schools were vigorously haunted. At Edsel I saw a girl in 50's apparel walk through a wall...

The situation at Vic's was rapidly deteriorating. He wasn't at all the Vic I remembered. His nickname was now "*The Duke*" and he'd become increasingly macho, homophobic, close-minded, drunk & elitist.

The house was infested with preps & jocks that used him for a place to get hammered. He read men's magazines to know how to be a man, drove by pedestrians saying cruel things & lifted weights angrily.

I was Captain Cool about everything – never caused a problem. But I wasn't like them – I was a freak. I'd stumbled right back into high school where Vic was captain of the football team.

Seriously? My once best friend, whom said he'd name his first born son after me? The Trenchcaot Mafia legend that had every KMFDM ever released & fought jocks tooth & nail??

I had hope the real Vic would return, not this caricature. But that whole crew – I was too radical, too political, too strange. They'd spend all night praising artists, yet mock the only active artist among them? And they all referred to the rave scene as: "*faggot shit.*"

Vic's brother went in my computer & rewrote my book, talking shit, viciously ripping me – went in my photo albums & punched holes through photos! *How low!*

Vic raised rent, talking shit behind my back. That weekend – hoping to clear the air & salvage what was left of our inter-personal relationship – I brought him to the 2nd Annual Detroit Electronic Music Festival; the Rave Party so legendary it would forever be written about as a Woodstock-level CounterCulture Breakthrough. With endless waves of extremely hot women his age, just dancing all over the place on ecstasy, everywhere, wanting to party for days – Vic literally *walks off*!!

In a macho tizzy, Vic declares how faggy everything is, how the DEMF is just filled with faggots, he didn't wanna buy their faggy concession food, didn't want their faggy soda pop. He talks like a Westboro Baptist Church member & likens it to a Gay Pride Parade!

He was *literally offended* to be there. – the greatest Rave Party happening on Earth! And he just left & went home without saying goodbye – *to go drink alone, lift weights & listen to Prince!*

I wasn't getting much work from the janitor job & was nearly hired as a Detroit Taxi in a pathetic fast cash attempt. I began calling RepoMen services – would they train me?

I could've moved in with Maxwell, but his apartment had become the last great drug stronghold. He'd gone completely insane, had 10 warrants out for his arrest & was sure to be raided any day.

\   His teeth were falling out, his nostrils rotted from coke, K & meth – and he'd just literally escaped from the insane asylum the cops forced him into, hanging onto his lease as long as he could before eviction…

Maxwell was institutionalized shortly after he set himself on fire. That wasn't the reason why, and it wasn't some Buddhist protest thing either. It just kind of happened, and it was legendary.

See, Maxwell was at a rave party on 10 pills & vanished with a jar of Vic's Vapor Rub. 7 hours later, they found him in his boxers eating Vic's out of the jar like peanut butter. He'd rubbed it all over his body.

The glossy-coated one was handed an unlit smoke – he flicked a Bic lighter & the fumes from the Vapor Rub caught fire!! He was a human torch, flailing about & stop/drop/roll. *Miraculously no serious burns!*

Later that week Maxwell's drug buddies (*plus Kluck & Cassum*) were over his apartment. Someone prank-called to start shit with him, a "random informer" snitching that his girlfriend was cheating on him.

Maxwell went fuckin' crazy because the guy was *in the living room!* This unsuspecting guy, who had nothing to do with anything, then gets chased around the complex with a butcher knife *in broad daylight!*

Kluck & Cassum ran & came back hours later – the cops were still there and the drug buddies were trying to pin it *all on them! Saying they were the ones feeding Maxwell coke!* Maxwell went to the psyche ward.

He escaped though – and went right back to the apartment! Where after 3 years of tumultuous hell relationship his girlfriend finally dumped him. He locked himself in the bathroom & refused to come out for hours. When he emerged he'd written all over the walls, the floor, ceiling, toilet & mirror in lipstick: "*I LOVE YOU/FUCKING WHORE/HOW COULD YOU DESTROY THIS/I'M GONNA GUT YOUR FAMILY/CUT OUT YOUR UTERUS/FUCKING COCKSUCKING CUNT/ETC.ETC.ETC...*"

He snorted 10 more lines of coke & blasted his fist through the TV. He kicked holes in the walls, tore out the cupboards, picked up this 6-foot nitrous tank and chucked it through the window.

He was confined to straight-jacket – but then he *escaped again!!* Backtracking again to the apartment – *to slit his wrists!* He was caught bleeding to death & was again locked back up – *only to escape again!*

And here he was, AWOL from the asylum, convinced federal agents planted video cameras in the pine trees outside, asking me to come & live with him so I could help get his head straight…

MAELSTROM

"The lowest depth to which people can sink before God is defined by the word 'journalist.' If I were a father and had a daughter who was seduced, I should not despair over her. I would have hope for her salvation. But if I had a son who became a journalist, and continued to be one for five years, I would give him up..." - Old Soren K, One Last Time

February 2002; slowly emerging from despondent coma. Surviving the heart of winter has always been one of my greatest accomplishments. Every year it worsens, as does the mania of mid-summer...

Where to run? My stripper friend's? I fear that reality after last week. One of her associates ran a drug house – we were outside this "snowy headquarters" hanging with some of her boys. Out of nowhere, a sneeze in the tree – from up in the branches, camouflaged by foliage.

So all these bad dudes come out of the house – everyone on X, K & yay-o. We surround the tree & there's this surveillance cop up there, like a ninja cop dressed like a black-ops Navy Seal.

The guy is clinging onto the branch for dear life, pretending he doesn't exist. He's setting up video feed which is totally illegal, and he obviously can't call for backup.

This pig is at our mercy. So we're like *"let's do it – let's fuck him out of his pension."* We all start laughing, we're so happy. *"Hey pig, fuck you pig! Oink oink motherfucker!!"* We're, like, throwing pine-combs at him n' shit, telling him we're gonna kill his children. I pull out a bag of skittles & start pelting him with every color of the rainbow.

We just decimate this guy for 20 minutes straight, and he's breathing heavy and totally panicked, 'cause he thinks we're gonna shoot him or something. Soon everyone loses interest and go back inside to pack up and export whatever they are hiding, participating the inevitable raid...

I stay outside, saying all these awful things to him. I'm dancing around the tree backwards chanting '*sausage links, sausage links.*" But then I realize "*fuck, this is like a crime on multi-international levels.*" I'm gonna do 10 years if caught!

So I start backing off slowly and tell the guy, "*Hey asshole – good luck trying to read my license plate, you bitch!!*" I cackle all the way to my car and drive in reverse the entire block-length so he can't read my plate & quickly jet off onto the freeway, Scot-free...

In Troy all of the Denny's crew have formed a commune above a Nextel store. Ironically it suited this exact purpose during the 60's; the walls still hand painted in ancient hippie glee.

It is cavernous & filthy, equally crusty as Maxwell's. In the middle of the coffee table lay a great triumph – *the dismembered cover of Klucks first burned bible...*

10 live there as well as 3 cats & 2 dogs. Stuffing juts from the garbage curb davenports, fluff drifting like artificial snow. Nights are ritualistically spent hammering booze with up to 25 people jamming acoustics or otherwise discussing ideology...

Realizing the building is commercially zoned, we plot the rise of our DIY guerrilla periodical "*Fuck Detroit Weekly.*" Linda & I are to be the editors while she isn't busy fictionalizing us all in her magnum opus *Cold Turkey Apocalypse.*

The cover of our first publication is to feature Charles Manson, GG Allin, George Bush, Varg Vikernes, bin Laden, Saddam Hussein & the Pope line-dancing in euphoric drag.

Stoner Joe is to scribe an article allowing readership to detail the stupidest ways they've been rolled by the fuzz. Krooner, who plays guitar in a noise-core band called Phallus, will be our advertising rep. It's his mission to study the grants open to public for such a business venture.

Jay doesn't really believe in the paper and is instead working on his band Return To Dust, which I am producing the debut album of. Their new drummer is a very strange black dude. Despite a 4.0 GPA in Detroit public schools, until last night he'd never heard of Communism.

The drummer's worldview is loosely held together by logic thin as dental floss strings, and he is utterly suicidal. He attempted to overdose recently from a stomach of pills, but instead ate his fathers entire year-long supply of Viagra, causing an extremely painful 3 day non-stop erection.

We made him play a live show like that too! He showed up, flipping that he tried to die but ended up with blue balls instead! They said *"fuck your self-waxing bullshit"* and they had him duct tape his boner to his inner thigh! No stopping the extreme metal double-pedal kick-drum!

As for Kluck, following his wild confrontation with Onyx, we hung more frequently, began drifting back towards heavy metal as a basis for life. We were mutually returning to our Beavis & Buttheady roots, realizing we didn't care about the next rave party anymore and wanted to know when Cannibal Corpse or Dying Fetus was gonna Harpo's.

The stories that started coming out of him were wacky. When Kluck was 11 years old, his mother had a priest try to exorcise the demons that made him listen to Metallica!

The priest came to Kluck's house where in his bedroom the clergyman spoke Latin rites! To his CD collection! He sprinkled holy water all over the bedspread while young Kluck was tucked underneath, terrorized! *The holy man blessed his Megadeth t-shirts!*

A week later, Kluck called begging to be picked up from Maxwell's – he sold fake acid and was surrounded by 20 dudes all ready to jump him! I pulled up as 4 were shoving him around; they all waved & laughed as I approached.

Kluck ran up to me, his savior, and I kicked him hard as I could in the stomach with a steel toe. I grabbed his shaved skull and threw him against my car: "*Get in motherfucker!*"

The thugs were laughing; I held up my bleeding hand, fresh from a recent wound: "*This asshole called & interrupted me chopping up a steak – the motherfucker is* mine!" I made him get in the car, and sped us away.

Kluck looked terrified, unsure what was going on, like I justr kidnapped him: "*Why the fuck did you kick me?*" I replied "*Because you stupid fuckin' asshole – if I didn't they all woulda beat the shit out of you! It was a diversion, you fuckin' brainiac!*"

I should probably have just left him there. He burned a bunch of our friends, yet I saved him. From that moment on, he kind of attached himself to me, seeking a bortherly figure, a source of reason, for better or worse.

I think, perhaps, at that moment I rescued him from an entire lifestyle – and all the people he inevitably burned bridges with, or any bad blood feud with may have gotten him in serious trouble.

But I went and stopped him getting jumped by a dozen guys, we just kind of drove off listening to Iron Maiden. And for a long while, that's where we stayed. Just metal guys going to metal shows, collecting records, hanging with gothy chicks & punks & metalheads &...

Onyx & Brandon demand I show up to "The Con." Unlike comic conventions, this is the adult-only version where an assortment of basement dwellers coagulate their own reality – Vikings, goths, satanists, D&D folk, blacksmiths, rennies, occultists & alchemists. They rent every room of a hotel for 3 days of inexplicable dork debauchery...

Onyx has drank so much whiskey he can barely stand. Either can Brandon, who has passed out a solid rock at the pool side. Onyx still finds the ability to get naked and wrap a plastic bag around his genitals so he can go swimming. He terrifies so many by his slimness that the pool area is now totally empty, save for unconscious Brandon & myself.

A Viking and I drink booze out of his horn and leave Onyx alone, who is obnoxiously nudging Brandon trying to awaken him. I tell Onyx this is a terrible decision, 'cause Brandon incoherently starts swinging when forced awake from drunken slumber...

5 minutes later I return from a party room and see Brandon kicking what I think is a duffel-bag hard as he can on the floor with steel-toe army boots, swearing in a violent rage – and FUCK – *it's Onyx' head!!*

I jump the wall and tackle Brandon who stumbles. then, like a tranquilized elephant, he comfily, drunkenly sleepwalks himself back to unconsciousness, curling into a fetal position beneath a table.

Onyx is limp, unconscious – face destroyed & covered in welts, bleeding everywhere & not breathing. *Absolute Panic!* I force Brandon up, get him to my car, then run back inside hoping Onyx isn't dead. Mangled, he now sits upright, crying like a docile lamb...

3 hours later, Onyx is dandy as if a miracle, if horribly puffy – and all was forgiven. Brandon gave him 2 black eyes, and still they were playing Dungeons & Dragons...

Later that week Aunt Tommy deflates like a balloon, leaving behind a stack of *X-Men* comics, a collection of Barbie's, and a number of autobiographies penned by prominent American women.

Brandon is finally at peace after securing his own bedroom for the first time in 3 years, playing *Perfect Dark* religiously & ritualistically plotting Armageddon...

Finally get a job after months of trying – Smart Transit. It's a UAW run public bus facility that is 99% black, therefore allowing me no possible chance of advancement. I work exclusively with gun-toting g-thugs in sub-zero climate, drenched in suds from 6pm-2:30am.

My job is to vacuum the interiors & clean all the blood, shit, piss & cum from the seats – refueling, pumping oil/trans fluid, scrubbing the exterior before automatic wash. Every night used condoms on the back of the bus, 'cause Detroit hookers work mobile in cahoots with bus drivers...

The depot is located in a ghetto prairie behind Saigon from the Crackfiend Bobby days. However, there is possibility of a transfer to the Oakland County depot a mile from *Fuck Detroit Weekly's* HQ...

March 2002. Tortured circles with Zelda; seedy affairs with Linda. Natasha returns briefly but there is no connection. Finally get to interview Marilyn Manson but he soon hangs up on me after grilling him on GG Allin...

Birth of a Tragedy move to New Mexico but break up in 2 weeks. Mackenzie comes out the closet & they reform as a synth-pop cyber-punk act named Vertigo Venus, headlining gay bars & pride fests...

Ricky's screwed with Lupus & Johnny/Susan finally broke up after The Twins inherited their dead grandma's fortune. Johnny moved to

Illinois & Susan allowed her aunt to adopt the child. The Twins now own a house together, working heavily as to attend community college…

Huxley eventually turned himself in. He was on the run in winter, breaking into cars to stay warm. One night he decided enough was enough. He ordered breakfast at Denny's, called the cops, and continued eating until they arrived, tipping the waitress excessively before ducking into the back of the patrol car. Huxley's now serving a 5 year sentence in Jackson.

Cassie is working on an art degree & editing her own zine called *The Politricks of Troll Poaching… Zoe is living with one of the guys from Downtown Brown, convinced Lisa is visiting her through dreams…* Tony is an unrepentant Juggalo, Joker Card decals stretched across on his Chrysler's rear window… *Miriam is a hard-working single mom attending community college…* Skinhead Mary married a cop & went super christian; *Helen The Pimp found her way into art school…*

Dirk is now writing screenplays, plotting his rise to the independent film-making. Says Crenshaw has another kid with Angelica and they live in a trailer park… *Ted is saving up to move to Australia where he can be a factory rat in peace…* Jack turned on Billy & now he pays college tuition by masturbating for gay men on internet webcam…

Kaitlin & I hung out for the first time in years. We got tanked and watched *Dawn of the Dead*, competing on the most dialogue from memory. She hates Vic too. After the house went up for sale, "The Duke" was dropped by the preps like a bad habit. He now lives in self-willed isolation, already a bitter old man wasting away & brooding darkly.

Smitty was dishonorably discharged for lying about his criminal record, though he was last seen deeply in love with a woman he considers marrying… *Caylin is playing bass & screaming in yet another hardcore punk band...* Kelly's in Seattle working on a journalism degree... *Maurice is now clean, attending college Up North...*

Robinson is in California at community college, watching the ocean crash upon the shoreline alone 'cause *"Everyone on the West Coast is a complete scumbag."* The parents ditched Jesus & got a divorce, scattering the kids in weird realities...

Carl drained nearly every dollar earned from his lawsuit on strip clubs & phone sex hot-lines & smokes grass all day...

Nez is slowly getting his life together & skinny whiteboy Teeth has found a nice black girl that is all-about pro wrestling too...

Simon is now manager at a bagel shop, obsessively collecting European metal, horror movies & GG Allin memorabilia...

Espa was driving & spotted Irish pumping gas...

Scooby dies when a cell phone airhead carelessly jutted out her driveway; he nailed her on a Suzuki crotch-rocket at 90mph...

Salem is a young married father struggling to form his own political party. He's entered hacker folklore by being the first indicted by a new federal computer crime law after vandalizing the Dearborn Public Schools website – luckily, the case was dropped by technicality...

Walking down the street I lock eyes with the driver of a van and we do a simultaneous double-take – *my father just keeps on driving...*

ROCK BOTTOM

"*I'm back with The Family.*" Cassum lurches a smile as skyscrapers whiz above our heads, shadows casting giant tombstones that plague the landscape. The gray blur of sun-bleached freeway, the lightning fast grain altered to vinyl grooves & the George Acosta that accompanies it ("*Fire ... Wire*"); *people & machines like workaholic Doozers in unison...*

Vic didn't have the guts to kick me out – had his dad push me into the street after shamelessly trying to thieve $300 in rent. If the brothers didn't break or steal half my belongings, I simply tossed them.

Now I'm at "The Box," the new HQ of MKULTRA – a basement full of impoverished, broke-ass, drug-addict party-kids in Detroit, right on the Dearborn border.

Two small rooms; one with a couch & TV, the other a kitchen overflowing with pizza crusts & spaghetti encrusted dishes. 5 of us down there, all at Rock Bottom & struggling to make The Big Score; a former Navy officer from Florida, our resident DJ, Cassum, myself & a reformed Neo-Nazi that discovered love was stronger than hate by eating ecstasy...

Sun descending, out of The City & halfway to The Styx – a remote farm where the pills flow like the Tigris. It disgusts me, the way Cassum operates – jumping in & out of cars all day, moving mountains without ever telling anyone what's in their car, then every cent goes up his nose.

He pulls this stunt constantly, playing not only with his own life but all other parties present. If we got pulled over & searched we'd all be looking at multiple non-negotiable felonies. And here I am, stuck on a mission without being explained the ride I was ignorantly volunteering.

Cassum's style – this sloppy suicide mission far too complex, scattered & insane to actually believe until irreversible proof is offered –

even the likely FEDS surveying him can't differentiate his pathological lies from the truth. Perhaps that's our great Catch 22 when the hammer strikes.

Cassum leaves the motor running and casually slips inside the lo-pro residence. Sitting in shotgun, it all feels like some sick dream, every sliver a lucid interval. My bad disease that warps everything, exaggerates & distorts... 1994 was 7 years ago and still I'm lost in a world of ghosts.

For 20 years I've done everything in my power to try and live a "normal life," or at least my version of the life everyone else seemed to materialize effortlessly. No matter how hard I've tried, something was always raped from me. It's like God, fate, destiny, whatever – *nothing but razor-sharp vendetta,* right at my personal bullseye.

Hope? No, I'm through with it. *Future?* Shit, I was created for revenge and truth be told, I just don't care anymore. All that's left is the gutter & no one is gettin' out alive – we're all going to prison or gonna get shot or we're all gonna overdose one by one.

Fuck it – revenge. Pied Piper with a nifty techno beat. Cassum & I, locked into a blaze of glory bitter end. The only 2 left from The Old World – a blood pact until the end of time. Our underground would destroy them; *a new age Gomorrah in the belly of the beast...*

Swarming, maniac masses ripe for revolution via LSD Stalags – a global orgy preventing the youth from a single shred of thought equating in the illusion. Who really needs a Spahn Ranch when you have 30 dead warehouses under your belt? Detroit's soul is on life support, and we will snuff it with a pillow.

And in the end, all I need is The Big Score – just one perfect no-holds-barred party to bank & book a flight to Puerto Rico, Amsterdam, Tokyo, the Bahamas – *anywhere the fuck but here...*

As fanciful a solution that was to the problem, no likewise amount of goodwill could transform the current state of the underground. No matter where you headed, what venue encountered, the rave scene was haggard.

This subculture was no longer the stuff of urban legend deftly discovered through a secretive & intricate web of phone numbers, last minute websites, hush-hush fliers & information points. Horror story yellow journalism was now rampant in every major news syndicate.

The word "RAVE" has become a feared term for every soccer mom in America. Sure, bad motherfuckers were sporadically out there, but this thing was about peace & love.

Disinformation was a national epidemic after bad pills killed the children of politicians. Congress reacted by signing a bill designating all parties to be legally treated as crack houses with severe felonies for anyone orchestrating them.

Patriot Act-like powers were handed to all federal agencies to ace this rising tide and a full year of police raids had left a desolate, fractured mess of things. Only a handful of production companies remained & attendance was dwindling.

Most party-kids were sick of the bullshit and started going to legit clubs to avoid legal hassle. The scene now consisted of the hardcore addicts/dealers, old-schoolers regularly tipped off before raids & newbies who really didn't know any better...

The media presence died down a bit after the "*Action 10 Problem Solvers*" stepped into some nasty territory. They'd go about "solving" problems the cops couldn't fix by plastering segments over news broadcasts.

They were vultures that would bust guys on working on unemployment, go after pot dealers selling bags, expose deep ghetto liquor stores selling booze after 2am for cheap-shot ratings.

Action 10 "bandwagons" and attacks the underground. They televise their raids of peon after-party spots where 12 kids will be sucking on a nitrous tank at 4am.

In Action 10's untouchable glee they decided to go after the big dogs – XTM, who were allegedly straight-up mobsters. No one fucked around at their venues – if they did they were warned once. No second warnings were offered.

So Action 10 sneaks an undercover reporter into one of XTM's parties and she's quickly busted wearing a wire/video cam. They march her out to the Action 10 van at gunpoint & demand everyone get out.

All 5 of the crew are crying, pleading for their lives on their knees with their hands over their heads. XTM busts out their van windows with crowbars, slash the tires, pop the hood & cut up wires; they smash all the audio/visual equipment they can find.

They grabbed the driver & shoved a pistol in his mouth – and *yes,* allegedly, they made him suck it like a cock. This blubbering heap deep-throats, gags & vomits.

XTM then hijack their wallets and made it clear that if the Action 10 Problem Solvers ever came fucking around again at one of their parties – *or any party in Detroit, for that matter* – they'd kill their entire families. Thus ended the media assault, and thus enters an even larger array of undercover FEDS & snitches all gunning for XTM…

Cassum stands tense & energetic from freshly blown cocaine, barking orders into a walkie-talkie. He's got a half-smoked cigar clenched between his teeth, blue checkered dress shirt opened 5 buttons from the neck in muggy July heat. We are practicing our cut & run drill to vanish the nitrous in case police roll through.

Cassum has promised little trouble, claiming Sanchez's unseen partner is related to a cop from the nearest police station, therefore granting immunity. I'm still distraught from an episode with a 5 month pregnant & toothless woman that was sobbing, openly begging for crack money as I sat in the drive-thru of a ghetto McDonalds. Cassum recognizes and crams the ganja-packed blunt in his mouth, takes a deep drag & hands it over.

"*You'll find everything in working order,*" he says as the smoke billows from his mouth. "*I need a good man like you.*" Effective immediately, I relieve the current commander of security from his duties. I now have full control of floor operations from here on out. What I say goes and all the big, nasty motherfuckers we have pay-rolled answer to me.

This is ours. We fought for this, and no one is going to take it. This deathtrap outpost sandwiched between ghetto prairies & dead factories – mangled steel & broken glass at every turn like a tornado ripped junkyard, fenced in by giant sheets of gang-sprayed metal & barbed wire, stray packs of feral dogs wander the streets foaming with rabies, every rare house still standing an arson shell in near empty fields of towering grass...

In *The Box* we were like one happy family; at the venue we broke our backs clearing mountains of scrap & power washing the walls. Constant unnerving jolts would hit as every fragment mirrored the nightmare I once had, the monstrous jigsaw watching my friends butchered by the faceless assassin. I began dissecting Sanchez' every move...

The first party was a minor success; we broke even with some extra loot but Sanchez wouldn't pay us more than $20 each, saying he had to pay off the owner and it'd all come next week.

We continued our routine hard and by the next party XTM reps showed up looking for Sanchez because they had beef with him over past ordeals – and *our* party made *theirs* tank. They were visibly pissed.

They kept asking for Sanchez but I was told not to let them in and that "*he wasn't there.*" So I played it by ear and did my job. They also did theirs, waiting in the parking lot all night. They had a nice "chat" and Sanchez was warned not to fuck up again...

A bombed out stripper named Jade slipped into our ranks – everyone thought she was a spy sent by XTM, but also thought it funny. If so, the best way to fool XTM was by using her to send false information.

Paulie became Cassum's right hand man (*the ex-Neo Nazi*). He was a world class acid-monster on lengthy probation for assaulting a police officer. Paulie's the only guy I know that could show up to a party broke & shoe-less, yet walk out candy-bulging & a cool $1500.

Following the latest burn by Sanchez, I stopped by Maxwell's where he confided many details about our mutual non-friend. Sanchez was notorious for wandering into rave cliques and exploiting them.

He was such a scumbag he got his own dad hooked on heroin just so he could pick up another client to sell shit to. It was rumored that he had a dozen hits on his head – and allegedly a deep-cover serious snitch.

Sanchez was in his late 20's but looked 34 'cause he'd been living on the streets since he was 15, blowing down crystal, K, heroin, crack, X & snow for years on end.

I warned Cassum and by the time we inked a deal to throw this half punk/half rave show I was inciting a full-blown mutiny. The next two weeks we busted our balls – and were guaranteed 9 grand out of the occasion, distributed evenly...

Black Friday was the last of the great acid freak-outs. I played psychedelic referee once again, conducting the session while jumping in & out of different costumes and characters. The Box crew were present as well as Kluck, Daisy, Ricky & Zelda, all who devoured an entire vial of acid...

1 hour later our DJ'd turned rubber, Jade was cowering under a blanket, Daisy attempting to molest Ricky, Zelda kept running from me, Paulie babbling about aliens, Kluck trying to pull the skin off his face, Cassum rocking back & forth on the back porch laughing, laughing...

Everyone is pressed against the garage door. Paulie's romantic interest is ranting like Ed Gein at the peak of skin stitching & Zelda is trying not to fall into the sky, crying for us to hold her down so she doesn't float into the galaxy. Paulie's fling, who is jabbering like a retard concubine, abruptly pulls down her pants in front of everyone, grabs her clit like a dick and starts pissing upright, babbling incoherently. All jaws drop in hallucinogenic terror – *and no one was ever the same again...*

After blowing down 2 vials of K, Paulie & Cassum climb into a Capri which mutates into a high class Belgian limousine; Cassum is arrested for chucking a brick at someone's head and cornered by pigs with ecstasy. He's out the next day with shifty eyes & nonsense excuses...

Mutiny is official the day of the punk party. We snatch the venue from Sanchez after our bodybuilder associate throws him against the wall by his neck. Sanchez scuttles off but the party is a total bust. When we attempt to collect, the promoters had long fled. Although the 9 grand is moot, we acquire a venue worth much more in the process...

We set up for the next party & all goes smooth until the show. Sanchez pops back up with a reformed strategy, having revitalized SYNERGY with Scooby and a handful of his boys – angry black-belts, all of them, swarming our parking lot. I've got a brass knuckle blade I'm fingering, pacing in a rage. Paulie is ready to throw down, Nez is frayed...

Cassum and I deal with Sanchez, who's glassy eyed from meth & spouting off his ties to the District Attorney – threatening to roll over unless he gets half the door!! Sanchez wanders off blabbing threats...

Hours pass as I prepare myself for the eruption of the jigsaw. All the boys are prepared, armed with steel & backed by pistols... *The party goes according to plan, at least 200 heads by 10pm and three dozen cars in the lot...* Paulie & I wander the floors knowing this could be it for us – someone was going to die, we just felt it...

Nez runs up and informs me that Sanchez is in the darkness of the parking lot, all fucked up on crack. He's whipping a handgun around, threatening to shoot anyone that comes close. He's blatantly robbing us by taking every dime of the $5 per car parking lot money...

No more. No one threatens to kill my friends. I knock some brain-dead x-heads astray like bowling pins as I rush to my car. The Horned Dragon is sitting idly on my front seat.

I unsheathe the katana, blade gleaming: "...*we took it, its ours, we took it, its ours...*" I sneak behind him, silently, sword cocked as he is blinded by meth, waving the gun...

Everything is slow motion, heart beating cold and intolerant... His sweaty neck, naked & exposed... It's finally gone too far, and as if in a dream, I ready myself to kill a man... SIRENS WAILING... *Squad cars fly out of nowhere – PIGS EVERYWHERE –* the raid is underway!! *Sanchez runs off, didn't even notice I was lurking behind him with a sword, out of my mind, ready to literally decapitate him...*

Bodies pile out of the venue, party-kids scrambling like rats, frenzied snorts & gobbles of all remaining evidence... Cassum hollers over the walkie-talkie but I'm in my car, encircling the venue to nab our crew...

Cassum jumps out the back window, charging across the rooftop & flinging himself down the side of the building; Ricky & Carl jump into the Escort & we blast off...

Next morning. Cassum is hunched over the steps of Ricky's house, dry heaving blood. The MDMA-burned holes in his absent stomach lining must be infectious... *Death threats from gang bangers overflow MKULTRA's voicemail...* After accumulating nearly $50,000 over 2 years, every last dime is now Houdini ...

The weeks pass, the future grim... *Heroin pertinent, yet no one openly booting...* Uncle Ray drops dead from 3 concurrent strokes... Car transmission buckles, stranded on foot... *The Box is evicted in 1 day...*

The DJ & I try to get jobs and an apartment but it's useless. I take him to get his belongings from his old pad but Sanchez beat us there – and robbed everything he owned by lying to his roommates and just filling up a U-Haul truck!

Like the Grinch Sanchez stole _everything_ – his music, clothes, bed, dresser, socks, dirty underwear, coat hangers, ice cube trays, the nails hanging pictures on his walls...

The DJ's soul was broken. He moved in with his parents, cursing the rave scene to no end and retired...

The last days of The Box were a chaotic, last ditch push at the dream that never materialized. I just wanted to walk from it all.

Word hits us – while Sanchez was squatting in Del Ray and someone chucked Molotov cocktails into the living room of his squat. Sanchez escaped but was finished in Detroit. Legend has it he scuttled off to Las Vegas like the invincible cockroach he was...

Forced by circumstance I invaded my parents' home. During the rocky transition Jade (the XTM "spy") and I secured a little e-bond relationship that lasted a few weeks. It wasn't romantic, but rather an understanding.

I watched her nearly die of a cocaine overdose – after, she told me everything; her substrata lesbianism, subsequent rape, overdoses & military base teen rebellion. She spent the bulk of her teen years in a mental institution and was only recently released.

We both felt an earthshaking change in our gut – not just for us, but the entire world. What lay ahead was a massive gray area undefined in consequence, oncoming with hurricane force...

The Feds brought down the hammer on XTM – raided & allegedly caught with a cache of smuggled guns, 8 pounds of weed, a kilo of coke & 1000's of pills. The coast was clear – August 2001 & MKULTRA was one of the last underground companies left standing...

Jade called on her way to the airport thanking me for everything. As a result of our cathartic dialogues she booked a plane to San Fran, determined to get her life together.

I secured a job as a landscaper, bought a name brand pair of sneakers, received a new car, and finally convinced myself that my paranoia of bin Laden associated WW3 visions were the sum equivalent of all my fears & nothing like that dream of fire in the great city tied to the Islamic Star & the blood red moon would ever come true.

I was bat-shit & rejoicing in the fact – the hills were alive with the sound of music... But still I desired the big score, eyeing this shitty little after party spot in Mexican Town. Shouldn't be hard – no competition, one last party – just bank & get the fuck outta dodge – *Europe was waitin'...*

"You know in High School the principal told me that I received the highest amount of disciplinary write ups he'd ever seen? I'm still so proud of that." Cassum looks like Napoleon statue with his fists bunched up on his hips, that Bruce Dickinson Peter Pan-ism.

"Ever since I was a kid, I've just wanted to do the worse things I possibly could. Like walking the school halls and just randomly punching or kicking someone or stabbing them with my pen. And why? I don't know. I'm just a bad motherfucker."

The scene on Ricky's front porch goes dead silent as we hear a jumbo jet blaze overhead. It's the first plane outside of F-16 attack fighters we've seen all day. 9-11, how surreal it's all been, how quiet and serene. The bluest, crystal clear skies I've ever witnessed.

"Rushing blood transfusions I bet," Ricky communicates.

Cassum takes control again. *"You know what's comin' Ryan? Some dark motherfucking days."* He starts cackling, his body movements like dripping margarine – he shakes like a Parkinson's victim, whether or not that's just something else he's making up...

Cassum declares the *"Big Circle Jerk of Fuck"* campaign in a last ditch attempt towards absolute victory.

The maniac somehow rewires his surrounding environment into a final stronghold located in the middle of a trailer park populated by the last of the line druggies that simply refuse to let the summer of 2000 go. *I want no part of it...*

Cassum continues mooning the authorities at every turn, promoting events like "RAID THIS PARTY" – weekend after weekend a domino effect of continual raids...

Addiction & greed triumph when Maxwell – armed with a pump shotgun – robs Cassum at barrel point. They barged in the trailer with ski-masks – one guy pistol-whipped Cassum & they made off with 2 grand...

1 month later, the State Police show up snooping for Maxwell. He was shipping a pound of weed, sped through a red light & slammed into oncoming traffic – no registration, no insurance & a dozen warrants.

Maxwell couldn't pop the trunk in time – he simply ran away, abandoning the car & weed. He knew he was fucked, and immediately fled the state – *no one ever heard from him again...*

The trailer soon ends with a raid that Cassum, once again, escapes. He throws together this party at a children's water-park with cartoon bear mascots painted on the walls; the park is frozen in sub-zero weather.

1000+ party-kids were in attendance, all having brought packs of Skittles to knock $5 off cover charge (*as per Cassums' demands*).

At 3am, 10 cop cars zip up with sirens blaring in an all out raid. Total chaos ensues. The ticket booth has become a Skittles armory. We're throwing packs to party-kids who rip them openly immediately, pelting cops with all colors of the rainbow.

We shove the money in black trash-bags mixed with red candy-packets. I ditch out through the front, jaunting past the officers while Paulie & Cassum charge out the back door. They rev the engine, slam reverse into a squad car, and launch off for blueberry pancakes at IHOP...

Cassum gets a call from an old promoter – details of a huge party he's offered to orchestrate; instead, they allegedly try to kill him. Cassum kicks the gun away, it blasts the floor & he barrels out, lunging in his car & speeding to a friend's where he blows down 5 vials of Special K...

2 days later he snaps out of it at a diner, no idea how he got there. Cassum then flees to obscurity via hitchhiking, hitting the road on a soul searching odyssey, aiming to outdo Kerouac, Hunter S., Henry Miller...

But, again, that's depending who you ask. And we are talking about Cassum, after all. However, if the past 20 years have taught me anything, it's to never doubt the possibility of a single revelation...

TRANSCENDENCE

Cracks in the wall, slivers of the sun. Somehow the light shines through, jaggedly flowing through the fractures of time, penetrating the introvert core midst a universe cold and impersonal.

"It seems that without exception the experience/behavior that gets labeled 'schizophrenic' is a special strategy that a person invents in order to live in an unlivable situation. In life, the person has come to feel that his is an untenable position. He cannot make a move, or make no move, without being beset by contradictory and paradoxical pressures and demands, pushes and pulls, both internally from himself and externally from those around him. He is as it were in a position of checkmate."

Checkmate – a perfect appraisal. Only the disembodied triggers of association drag the focus into an overwhelming clarity that is ultimately as fleeting as it is powerful.

I cannot recall my life; all visuals summoned remain gray and out of focus. My memories are that of facts, fleeting stills, an endless incomplete paper trail without emotional connotation.

To claw through the barrier is impossible. All methods have failed, all attempts rendered limp. Yet still, without warning, a fraction is occasionally slid beneath the prison door by a mute guard attempting stir from the all-encompassing dream…

Stoned & cruising through East Dearborn I got lunch at a Mexican restaurant Uncle Craig once took me to. The rattle of ice on glass at my empty table emerges a phantom memory...

I'm 13; Mom takes me out to dinner here – just. Yet inside it's a surprise party – my entire family in attendance. No Jesse, Dan or Adrienne

– no teachers, school kids, Cathy or Twins – no Dad, Ed, Toby. Just my aunts & uncles & cousins happy to be with me laughing, loving life.

Uncle Craig puts his hand on my shoulder &shakes me to rouse a smile, Uncle Thomas laughs & nudges Aunt Sylvia to join in. The robot kids are focused to the situation at hand, no GameBoys...

It wasn't my birthday – just a last ditch attempt by a helpless mother completely unequipped to deal with the situation at hand. Family, the only thing that's ever mattered in her life, the last ace up her sleeve to salvage the corrosion between us & pull me – *the only thing that ever mattered to her above all else* – back into the light...

But there was something else that happened here. Something went wrong to make it like this, something I am burying so deep, I'll come unraveled if I remember. I know I'm running from something – I just can't remember what from.

Even with the smiling faces of my family, the mom I knew & loved as part of them grinning back – I know I'm terrified of her, I know I have to get away. I can't remember why – it's not fuzzy, it's a black hole.

She has some kind of tumor, or brain defect – something wrong. But no one sees & no one listens. She's never laid a finger on me, but I know there is an ice-cold streak of violence inherent in her I cannot describe, hitched to a dreamy unraveled self. There is something unnatural & out of her control here. One day it, I know it will go off. No one sees.

One day, something happened. I retreated somewhere dark & distant, so nightmarish that only the demons in my head could touch me again. 8 years later, I directly blame the larger system of misery at play & all the side-effects of a hereditary struggle.

I was simply a product of my environment, cast in iron by the lowest echelons of working poor. My response was forced reaction. Boxed in, shattered, brain chemistry revolting – they took it all from me & I turned my cold heart to Revenge, the only sense of purpose I'd known...

And down came the hammer. I dismantled them all – spit their ugliness back in their faces & left 'em all mangled & locked in misery.

In the end I was victorious but no longer had driving factor – no Great Struggle, no Great War. I was a zealot crusader in a time of all encompassing peace. What else was I to do, but turn it all around & destroy everything good about my life?

I look upon the battlefield of my spirit – friends & enemies slaughtered alike, damaged machinery burning in a fog of black smoke. I try to disassociate the past but feel as if I'm the lone survivor of a horror movie limping into the sunset before the credits roll. Covered in wounds, caked in blood, flesh torn & burnt. *Sequels only bring more violence....*

And still the slivers shine through. Back to the home of my youth. A Saturday in late Spring, sky blue, light wind delicately breezing the drapes in seeming slow motion...

The windows open, fresh air pouring in, the nightmare receded into memory. For once I am just a normal kid. I play my half-tuned piano as mom reads Harlequin romance novels. Jesse drags me outside to play water balloons with Danny & others. I sell lemonade on the street corner. None of it seems so scary...

Other memories return. My mom staying up all night trying to teach my multiplication tables. Her cheering me along alone at a mile run during elementary. The only one ever truly there for me, despite her attacks birthed of monumental frustration...

My mother, a deep well of incalculable sadness. This self-doubting terrified woman. I was her vessel, the only normal thing about her life. Without my fearless child mind for adventure she'd never been able to do the things she did. I was a torch light in a world of darkness, dragging her along my exploits. I became the center of her life...

I look upon my mother, a shadow of what she once was, unable to establish authentic communication outside of gossip papers, depressed celebrities, coworker romances. Just a stranger growing old and tired, long submitted to the inviting glow of the TV screen...

The disparate personal apocalypse in which there is no conclusion. Was I the enemy all along? Nope; I wasn't the hero, villain, anti-hero or beast – *I simply was & simply am...*

I know one day, when this thing finally makes it's way to the world, there will be repercussions. Or will they shrug it off as rantings of a madman? One of those alienated individuals lost in a world of dreams who crawl the outskirts of life where every slip of paper or random occurrence has some distorted message towards an ultimate fate?

Even the remainders of The Family, none of them will ever believe the world that existed inside my head – the illusion they choose to remember will stand in contrast with my "*version of reality.*"

Although some voices may rise against me & claim every sentence is fraud, I swear that every last word is the truth. Who would make up such a story? Furthermore, what would he ever have to gain? There may be differing accounts – but all the facts are essentially straight...

After dropping off my belongings at the new apartment I came back to quickly shower. Midway through lathering my filthy hands Toby flipped in a ridiculous rage, beating on the bathroom door.

He demanded to know why I was still there using "*his*" shower. He started yelling at me for not having the water turned on, that even before I'd signed the lease I should have had the electricity in my name.

I came out wet with the towel around my waist. He was coldly staring out his bedroom window, back turned to me, hands behind and firmly clutched together, as if he was Schwarzkopf.

Pausing here and there for lame effect, biting his contempt: "*You know... I try to teach you... [deep inhalation &] you don't care, about anything ... You don't... like George Bush... Just go, go – leave now...*" It was absurd. I grabbed the rest of what I had; mom told me I was always welcome wherever she lived & she might be joining me soon enough...

At Kluck's we speak of Irish & the good old days which really weren't all that good, burning CD's of *Extreme Metal* – something that has never betrayed me... It is now 5am & my new apartment awaits. I shake Kluck's hand & wander to my car, prepared to flee once & for all...

But in the end there shall be a manuscript. I will expose to the world the story us all. I will force every unsavory deed, every injustice into the blistering light.

Those individuals who were once Gods upon the Earth now so content with letting the past fade into the ancient dust of time will have no choice but to reemerge from the shadows, to claim a mythology theirs...

The endless pinion of Americana; the white picket fence, the 2.5 children, the mini-vans & November turkeys & slow withering that will inevitably convince them to retire to Florida & rot without the slightest hesitation or reluctance – it will be reduced to forlorn ash...

Cassum, Kaitlin Kluck, Simon, Nez, Teeth, Cassie, Robinson, Irish, Brandon, Zoe, Zelda, Kelly Miriam, Linda, Onyx & all of the rest – let them preach their own gospels, pen their own epics.

Christ and all of his apostles have nothing on us, for our bible is far richer. It is an unrelentingly blasphemous scheme that makes every former plan pale in comparison…

I rev the engine & am filled with a surge of triumphant euphoria. Back online, ready to wreak some much needed havoc. I feel like hijacking a 747 & flying it right into the Hollywood sign, parachuting out & dumping aerial vats of thermite over Beverly Hills. I feel like digging up the corpse of Jesus & serving it as bacon bits on salads of a Roman Catholic picnic. I wannaplant marijuana across the mainland like Johnny Ganjaseed, prosecute all lawyers, trample a wild herd of elephants, flood all the snakes of the world back into Ireland. I want to feed *Free Willy* to bloodthirsty Ethiopian children, snuff out god with a comfy pillow, build a time machine & give automatic weaponry to Chief Sitting Bull … *I wanna force feed 1 million schizophrenics the weird, dreaded pink stuff & have 'em erect an Egyptian Pyramid dedicated to the ultra-bodacious awesomeness of my overly inflated, caustic, comic & cosmic ego…*

And as I peel off into the high-rise of I-75 – *middle finger flipping off the haggard skyline of Zug Island* – I jack the stereo to its maximum setting.

Know what comes on?

"Sick City."

Ryan Bartek is a writer & musician from Detroit (MI), now living in Portland (OR). He is author of 6 books: *"Anticlimax Leviathan," "The Big Shiny Prison (Volume One)," "Fortress Europe (The Big Shiny Prison Vol. II)," "Return To Fortress Europe (BSP Vol. III)," "The Silent Burning"* + *"To Live & Die On Zug Island"*

Bartek is a guitarist/vocalist known for Extreme Metal bands SKULLMASTER, VULTURE LOCUST, A.K.A. MABUS, SASQUATCH AGNOSTIC. In addition to Spoken Word Gigs as his plain old self, her performs live solo acoustic as "The Real Man In Black."

LURKING STRANGERS – his brand new, totally rockin', 100% weirdo punk band – will debut 2019.

Known for his journalism in the metal/punk undergrounds due to his travel books & long-time output for zines, Mister R. Bartek is also the shadowy figure behind the Press Relations firm Anomie PR.

All albums & books have been released under Anomie INC / Anomie Press, as FREE digital downloads.

R. Bartek's book collection & music discography 100% FREE @

www.BigShinyPrison.com
– & –
www.AnomiePress.com

...also by Ryan Bartek...

:: Books ::

"Anticlimax Leviathan"
"The Big Shiny Prison (Volume One)"
"Fortress Europe (BSP Vol. II)"
"Return To Fortress Europe (BSP Vol III)"
"To Live & Die On Zug Island"
"The Silent Burning"

:: Records ::

Vulture Locust *"Command Presence"* // (2015)
A.K.A. MABUS *"Lord of The Black Sheep"* // (2006)
Sasquatch Agnostic *"Complete Mammalography"* // (2010)
The REAL Man In Black *"GhostNomad Lives"* // (2016)
SKULLMASTER - *"Self-Titled"* // (2019)

Imagine a world that can scarcely be imagined –
the Old Detroit, at its lowest decline, spanning
the Early 80's – May 2002.

Imagine the life of a strange teen; a young male
indoctrinated with Punk Rock logic & Heavy Metal
obsession – reading comic books in a Misfits
shirt, blasting KMFDM on his stereo &
mosh-pitting at Slayer concerts.

16 in 1997 – when Nine Inch Nails were at peak,
Clinton was still president & Marilyn Manson was
still The Antichrist.

Here, we have perhaps the last of the great
unknown autobiographies concerning a specific
mentality & specimen of American Youth.

Not only does this work uniquely capture such a
mindset, but it expresses a commentary on the
Detroit Underground: from Outlaw Rave Parties to
Extreme Metal gigs, Punk Rock Chaos to The Occult.

It is a tale of anguish as much as hilarity – and
a poignant tract on drug abuse & mental illness.

This work began 9-11-2001 – the author 19, unknown
& unpublished. Completed 2004 & sitting "on the
shelf" 15+ years, it's high time to party.

Here, for the first time available to the public –
sitting quietly "on the shelf" 15+ years –
is Ryan Bartek's "*To Live & Die On Zug Island.*"

* * *

Available Worldwide via Anomie Press
anywhere books are sold October 8th 2019

www.AnomiePress.com

CPSIA information can be obtained
at www.ICGtesting.com
Printed in the USA
FSHW011148100919
61858FS